# Black Entrepreneurs in America

# Black Entrepreneurs in America

## STORIES OF STRUGGLE AND SUCCESS

MICHAEL D. WOODARD, Ph.D.

RUTGERS UNIVERSITY PRESS
NEW BRUNSWICK, NEW JERSEY

**Library of Congress Cataloging-in-Publication Data**

Woodard, Michard D.
    Black entrepreneurs in America : stories of struggle and success /
Michael D. Woodard
        p.   cm
    Includes bibliographical references.
    ISBN 0–8135–2368–0 (cloth : alk. paper)
    1. Afro-American business enterprises—Management—Case studies.
2. Success in business—United States—Case studies.   I. Title.
HD62.7.W66    1997
338'.04'08996073—dc20                                96–16176
                                                      CIP

British Cataloging-in-Publication information available

Manufactured in the United States of America

To my young adult children, Defferen, Nicole, and Aisha.
You are the light of my life.

To my deceased mother and father.

To my mentors, William Julius Wilson and Teresa Sullivan.

To Cherry Virginia Gillis, with whom in high school
I discovered the power of words and the joy of writing.

To future entrepreneurs. May your path be lighted by this book.

# CONTENTS

ACKNOWLEDGMENTS     ix

PART 1 **The Origin of Successful Black Businesses in America**

1   Economic Rights                              3
2   The Impact of Civil Rights                  25
3   An Indigenous Frame of Reference            39

PART 2 **The Life Stories of Enterpreneurs**

4   Starting a Business        THE EAST REGION      51
5   Gaining Access to Capital  THE CENTRAL REGION  101
6   Community Involvement      THE WEST REGION     157

PART 3 **The Outlook for Black Business Development**

7   The Future                                   215

BIBLIOGRAPHY        243
INDEX               247

# ACKNOWLEDGMENTS

This book was written to tell the neglected story of African American entrepreneurs in the post–Civil Rights era. Writing this book has been a journey that would not have been possible without the involvement and support of many, many people. I wish to acknowledge each person.

My children, while still in high school and college, gave me permission to leave the Midwest and go to Los Angeles for my research. They said, "The telephones work and airplanes fly and we'll be out." I could not have contemplated this project without knowing that my children were alright with it. Thanks, Defferen, Nicole, and Aisha. This one is for the sacrifice you made.

The UCLA Center for African American Studies invited me for a sabbatical year beginning fall 1989 that turned into a six-year stay. I wish to thank Claudia Mitchell-Kernan and M. Belinda Tucker for their support and encouraging words along the way. I also maintained close relationships with sociologists at UCLA. I owe a great debt to Walter Allen and Melvin Oliver. They were very supportive throughout my time at UCLA, read my work, and are just great friends. Vilma Ortiz was also very important. For several years I had studied occupational patterns, but Vilma Ortiz said, "Look at entrepreneurship, look at entrepreneurship, that's what we don't know about." It was her rather persistent prodding that opened a new and exciting research area to me. Thanks, Vilma.

This study grew out of a research grant provided by the Ford Foundation. Lynn Huntley, Ellen Brown, and Mark Elliott had the vision and commitment to address the capital gap that exists for African Americans starting and sustaining businesses. Lynn Huntley was my primary contact and handled the many issues as they arose. Thanks, Lynn, for your unswerving support. If this study serves to close the capital gap for only one entrepreneur then it has served well.

Many talented individuals assisted in carrying out this study. Linda Winfield, a consummate researcher and friend, generously shared her wealth of experience and helped with aspects of data gathering. Delois Maxwell, Jennifer Beaumont, Alford Young, Karen Crews, and Defferen Jones traveled across the country to conduct many of the interviews. Kimberly Nettles and Pamela Wright Lytle assisted with the data analysis. La Chandra Wilkerson and Robin Beers provided competent administrative support to the project.

I wrote the first draft of this manuscript while in residence at the Center for Black Studies at the University of California, Santa Barbara. I wish to thank Charles Long, Ina Huggins, and Marty Adams for providing office space and a congenial environment in which to write. I also made many wonderful friends at Friday-night tennis in Santa Barbara. They insisted that I maintain balance between writing and enjoying life, especially during difficult periods. Thank you, my Santa Barbara friends, you are all very special to me.

Macey Prince edited an early draft of the manuscript and helped to clarify some arguments. The following people read parts or an entire manuscript draft and made useful comments: Timothy Bates, Frank Fratoe, Alfred Osborne, and George Russell. I also wish to thank my developmental editor, Bette Kindman-Koffler. She helped to transform somewhat academic prose into language that can be enjoyed by anyone interested in entrepreneurship. Further, I wish to thank the two anonymous readers for their useful commments, which strengthened the arguments of the book.

Special thanks goes to Martha Heller, acquiring editor at Rutgers University Press. She saw the importance of this project and worked diligently with me to bring it to fruition.

The greatest debt is owed to the entrepreneurs who took time away from their businesses to be interviewed for this project. While only twelve cases are included in the book, thirty entrepreneurs were actually interviewed. It is my hope that *Black Entrepreneurs in America: Stories of Struggle and Success* does justice to the tradition that each entrepreneur represents and lights the path for anyone who would consider entrepreneurship in the future.

PART 1

# The Origin of Successful Black Businesses in America

# 1

# Economic
# Rights

Harold Martin was familiar with adversity. Even so, disappointment and humiliation threatened to overwhelm him as he stood in the reception area of the National Bank of Detroit. He tried to recall the events that had led to this day.

After graduating in 1980 from Oakland University with a major in automotive engineering, Harold continued to broaden and fine tune his skills by taking classes in quality control, public speaking, and so on. His first job after college was with General Motors, a dream come true for someone raised in Detroit. He had expected to be employed as an engineer. Instead, he was hired as a mail boy. It was just the GM way.

Shorthanded six months later, GM offered Harold an opportunity in engineering. He worked tentatively at first because he lacked confidence. As his comfort level increased, his engineering skills became obvious. Harold was always the person behind the scenes; throughout his career, he had few opportunities to shine at GM. The procedure ruling Harold's mobility was always the same: as a project neared completion, Harold was somehow carefully moved to another assignment. Although he contributed significantly to many projects, someone else always received the credit.

For instance, Harold worked as part of an engineering group assigned to test drive new-concept cars. In Tampa, Florida, the engineering group grappled with a problem at the biggest Cadillac dealership. The GM "golden boys," all seasoned engineers, had spent three days working on a car owned by a very prominent figure without locating the source of its problem. Harold volunteered his services, but the engineers refused. They wanted only the "right" people working on the car because the president of GM had expressed a keen interest in it. The frustrated engineering group was prepared to leave when Harold said, "Please let me try. You will have to explain the situation when we return to Detroit. At the least, let me drive it around the block." Reluctantly, they agreed. Harold drove the car and quickly identified the problem. The car's fuel-injector stream was blowing up, rather than down, into the cylinders. Although the expert engineers had eliminated that as a possibility, Harold proved it was the problem by using a technique he had developed. He also located a previously undetected problem with the injectors. The expert engineers were impressed, and Harold was pleased with his accomplishment.

Harold continued to excel and eventually had more leadership opportunities at GM. He earned numerous world patents and engineered and managed a number of vehicle programs before leaving GM to start his own business. His patents affected not only GM but also the entire automotive industry. His traction-control patent, which improves car safety on ice, modulates engine power to eliminate spinning tires. He designed a computer algorithms patent that automatically calculates and displays on the dashboard the octane of gas purchased. He developed an oil-pan patent that stabilizes the oil flow and eliminates fluctuations in oil pressure, despite road features such as curves or steep hills. This technological innovation drastically reduced engine stress and allowed GM to offer its one-hundred-thousand-mile warranty.

Although his patents are substantial, Harold's greatest accomplishment was heading the team that designed the most advanced engine and car ever produced by GM: the Northstar thirty-two-valve engine. For that work he received an impressive plaque, an award, and great accolades. But more important, as a result of his work, GM developed new technologies and systems that changed their business practices. Although by 1988 he was viewed as an industry leader, Harold felt that he would never realize his full potential if he stayed at General Motors. The time was right for him to consider building his own business.

Harold had already experienced the business side of companies between 1985 and 1988, when he served as an engineering consultant to automotive and sporting goods companies. By age twenty-two and while working at GM, Harold also designed race-car engines and built and sold engines nationwide while operating his father's business. At first, the race-car clientele was black, but as his engines became successful, he began to draw white customers. Harold and his dad also started competing and winning against the best racing cars. But in 1987, after placing first at the U.S. National Raceway in Indianapolis, they realized they would have to quit. It seemed that burnout and a lack of financial backing would keep them from attaining their goal of becoming world champions. They sold the business for two hundred thousand dollars.

After a year of rest and market research, Harold Martin established MVP Products in 1989. An athletic footwear company, MVP Products specialized in the design, manufacture, and distribution of footwear. His market research revealed that the athletic footwear industry, an $11.6 billion industry, was growing by 35 percent annually. Although it was a saturated market, many companies still made a substantial living. Harold merged the market survey with his personal vision to carve a niche that no one else was pursuing: personalized footwear. He visited many schools in an exhaustive effort to learn how to reach that market. Although he successfully identified what students wanted, his experience with banks and bankers forced him to realize that he would never get financing to introduce the product at the level he envisioned.

Harold first approached the National Bank of Detroit (NBD). He telephoned a branch and explained his concept to the loan officer, who readily embraced the concept as a great idea: "I have seen many concepts and business plans, but I really like this idea!" The loan officer jokingly said more than once, "By the way, I wear a size nine! Bring it in. I really want to talk to you, and I'm going to tell my vice-president." The meeting was set for Friday, three days later. In fact, the loan officer called Harold and said, "Come in on Thursday. I really want to talk this through." Harold was excited by his first effort to get financing. His business plan was thorough and he was more than ready.

Harold arrived at the bank fifteen minutes early for the 9:00 A.M. meeting. At about 8:55, the loan officer ran out of his office and asked his secretary to let him know when Harold Martin arrived. He looked over at Harold and just knew that man wasn't Harold Martin. When the secretary pointed out Harold Martin, the loan officer looked at Harold again, turned beet red, and said, "Wait a minute, I'll be back." About twenty-five minutes later he returned and said to Harold, "How can I help you?"

As they walked into the office, an extremely disappointed Harold reminded the loan officer of their previous conversations concerning the project. Thumbing through the business plan, the loan officer informed Harold that NBD did not finance start-up companies. He further noted that Harold lacked the relevant experience to develop such a venture and that Harold might wish to consider doing something else with his life. Harold's hopes were dashed. His experience with NBD was an indicator of the barriers he would face in his search for capital.

Harold contacted other banks, asking for $750,000, not an unreasonable amount under the circumstances. His personal net worth was approximately $500,000, including his $200,000 home, which he was willing to use to collateralize the loan. His business plan suggested that he could enter four or five states with a 50 percent gross profit margin—and he already had contract commitments totaling more than $1 million.

Manufacturer's Bank was initially more receptive, but they reached the same conclusions as NBD: the company was a start-up venture and the principal had no prior experience in this extremely competitive industry. They just didn't know if Harold belonged there. After visiting forty-nine banks in various cities, including Detroit, Chicago, Cleveland, St. Louis, and Denver, Harold scaled down his business plan and started his business with his own capital. Despite the bankers' gloomy predictions, MVP Products grossed $3 million by 1992. The company has now grown to include a major division, Mavade Footwear.

Harold Martin's experience illustrates the barriers faced by African American entrepreneurs. And it highlights a question: To what extent do African Americans have "economic rights" in the post–Civil Rights era? The simplistic answer is that although black entrepreneurs in the post–Civil Rights era have greater economic rights than in previous historical periods, the level of economic rights remains constricted.

Economic rights are the rights of a group to engage in private enterprise free from institutional barriers erected by race, ethnicity, or gender. The antebellum period, for example, denied African slaves economic rights in the truest sense of the term and excluded them from private enterprise altogether. In contrast, the free black elite enjoyed limited economic rights during the antebellum period and engaged in restricted private enterprise.

In a capitalist society, it is reasonable to expect that a particular group's relative level of economic rights at a given point in history will directly affect both their day-to-day experiences as entrepreneurs and the level of their community's economic development. Although African Americans enjoy a greater relative level of economic rights in the post–Civil Rights era than in previous historical periods, no evidence indicates that blacks and, say, whites enjoy the same level of economic rights.

Despite limited economic rights, an entrepreneurial spirit continues to proliferate among African Americans. Since the Civil Rights movement, increasing numbers of blacks are starting businesses rather than staying in the "traditional good jobs." Between 1987 and 1992, African American ownership of businesses grew by 46 percent to 620,912, and increased over 200 percent from the 1982 totals. During this time period the total increase for *all* U.S. firms was only 26.2 percent. The initiation rate of African American–owned businesses continued to increase and their entrepreneurial spirit continued to strengthen.

What accounts for this flourishing entrepreneurial spirit? How do African Americans make the decision to start a business? What is the source of capital to start businesses? What impact do black businesses have on development within the African American community? This book addresses these and other issues.

Social scientists and policy makers rely almost exclusively on census data to study ethnic minority business development. Unfortunately, census data offers only a snapshot of business at one point in time. Census surveys do provide important data on trends in business initiation, industry concentration, earnings, and discontinuance of black-owned businesses; however, census data provide little insight into the day-to-day experiences of entrepreneurs in general and the African American business person in particular.

This in-depth case-study analysis presents the experiences of African American entrepreneurs as they initiated and expanded businesses. It also captures and portrays the essence of the contemporary African American entrepreneur and provides a rough indication of the level of economic rights enjoyed by African Americans in the post–Civil Rights era.

African American entrepreneurs initiate, expand, and sustain successful businesses against great odds. This is their story. It is a story of how black entrepreneurs achieve goals, breathe life into the entrepreneurial spirit, and demand a bit of the American dream for themselves.

The remainder of chapter 1 provides a historical framework within which to view black entrepreneurship up to the time of the Civil Rights era. Chapter 2 discusses the impact of Civil Rights legislation on black entrepreneurship. In chapter 3, a new conceptual framework is introduced and trends observed in census data are discussed. Chapters 4 to 6 highlight the experiences of eleven African American entrepreneurs as they explain in their own words how they made the decision to go into business, how they gained access to capital and marketed their services and products, and the extent of their involvement within the community. Chapter 7 summarizes and forecasts the future of entrepreneurship among African Americans.

## Perceptions of Black Business

The "perception" of black business in American society appears to be a major obstacle hampering the emerging entrepreneurial spirit. Many Americans think of the black business owner as a man or woman with limited education, training, working capital, and even less organization who runs a small retail shop, restaurant, barber shop or beauty salon, funeral parlor, cleaning establishment, or shoe shop in the ghetto. This vivid image is firmly established within the American psyche, especially among commercial lenders.

The image, in part, reflects the way scholars portray black business. It is true, historically, that black-owned firms were small businesses focusing on the services noted above and that black entrepreneurs of the past had less education and training. However, few scholars have adequately analyzed the breadth of early black business activity in the United States or the hazardous conditions under which these businesses operated.

The Civil Rights movement created opportunities for educational advancement and entrepreneurial diversification that should have dispelled such negative images. Today, the fastest growing and most profitable black-owned businesses are in finance, insurance, and real estate; transportation; communications; business services; and wholesale trade. Furthermore, African American ownership of heavy construction firms has increased substantially. The trends indicate a shift toward more skill- and capital-intensive businesses that are more appropriate for the well-educated and highly trained black entrepreneurs of today (Bates 1985a, 1993). Despite the trends, Americans, black and white, cling to the image of the black-owned business as a small, mom-and-pop operation. The persistence of this image stems in part from a combination of bad history and lingering racial stereotypes.

## A History of Black Entrepreneurship

African Americans have a long and rich history of entrepreneurship in America beginning long before the Civil War. Indeed, they exhibited the same entrepreneurial spirit as did other groups who immigrated to this country. Yet scholars have either ignored or misconstrued the history of black entrepreneurship. The historical overview provided here is based heavily on the incisive work of John Sibley Butler in his *Entrepreneurship and Self-Help among Black Americans* (1991). The intent is to provide just the context within which black business developed over time, not an exhaustive history. How social climate affects black business development mirrors the potential of entrepreneurship to impel individual mobility and community development when the playing field is level.

It is difficult to pinpoint when blacks in America first engaged in private enterprise. Most scholars ignore the fact that commerce and entrepreneurship were central to intergroup coexistence among slaves transported to the Americas from Africa. In fact, African Americans participated in the American economy as business owners even before the American Revolution. Although slavery dominated the African American existence prior to the Civil War, two categories of business owners existed, free persons and slaves (Butler 1991).

Approximately sixty thousand free blacks accumulated capital that they used to initiate and sustain business activities. They developed enterprises in almost every business arena, including merchandising, real estate, manufacturing, construction trades, transportation, and mining industries. Their accomplishments were considerable.

As early as 1736, emancipated slave Emanuel Bernoon established an oyster house in Providence, Rhode Island. Anthony Johnson accumulated substantial property in Jamestown, Virginia. John Baptiste DeSable, a wholesaler and merchant, settled Chicago in 1770. That same year, a free black man was assessed for property taxes on eight acres and a horse in Lancaster, Pennsylvania.

A notable black businessman, Paul Cuffe, born in New Bedford, Massachusetts, in 1759, became a sailor aboard a whaling ship at age sixteen. By 1806, Cuffe was a successful shipbuilder, sailor, and landowner. He established business ties with European and African markets and furnished ships and supplies to blacks who wanted to return to Africa (Marble 1983, 140–150).

Around 1800, Richard Allen established a boot and shoe store in Philadelphia, and William Alexander Leidesdorff owned import-export and ranching operations in California (Marble 1983, 141–145). In Philadelphia, blacks established a beneficial insurance society in 1789 and a life insurance society in 1810 (140). By 1840, African Americans in New York City owned two dry goods stores, two excellent restaurants in the financial district, four pleasure gardens, six boardinghouses, one confectionery, two coal yards, and a cleaning establishment. In Detroit, the tailoring and clothing firm owned by James Garrett and Almer Frances boasted annual gross revenues of sixty thousand dollars (141–145).

In the early 1800s, Cincinnati, Ohio, was the center of black economic activities in the Midwest. In 1835, about half of Cincinnati's black population of approximately twenty-five hundred had once been slaves. Cincinnati was the first point north of slavery where fugitive blacks felt reasonably safe from being apprehended and returned "down South."

Entrepreneurs in Cincinnati were particularly successful. They include Robert Harlan, a horseman; W. A. Thompson, a tailor; J. Presley and Thomas Ball, contractors; Samuel T. Wilcot, a merchant, and Robert Gord, owner of a coal yard (Marble 1983, 141–145). In 1850, J. Wilcox, an Ohio River boat steward, owned a wholesale grocery store in the downtown business district. He quickly became the largest provisions dealer in the city and established trade links with New Orleans and New York. By the mid-1850s, his gross revenues reached an estimated $140,000.

Two African American businessmen, who joined forces in 1851, procured a ten-thousand-dollar contract to plaster all public buildings in Hamilton County, Ohio. Henry Body, a former slave artisan, established a furniture store in Cincinnati in the late 1830s. By 1850, he regularly employed twenty to fifty black and white cabinet makers and was worth approximately twenty-six thousand dollars (Marble 1983, 141–145). This litany of pre–Civil War black entrepreneurs—many of whom catered to white patrons (ibid.)—illustrates that during a time of slavery, free African Americans somehow established and maintained a wide range of businesses and accumulated substantial property and wealth. Entrepreneurship for free people of African descent was difficult, but possible, even in the South.

The second group of black business people in the pre–Civil War era were slaves. Only those slaves with determination and a paternalistic master could engage in business activities. The constraints of slavery were such that even highly skilled slaves were barred from becoming entrepreneurs in the true sense of the word. They did, however, during their limited free time sell their labor and hand-made products to earn money to buy freedom for their relatives and themselves.

Frank McWorter was a classic example. Free Frank, as he was called, was born into slavery in 1777 in the northwestern South Carolina Piedmont. Before the turn of the century, he was taken to the western Kentucky Pennyroyal area, where he labored for fifteen years to develop his owner's farm homestead. By 1810, Free Frank hired out his own time and established a saltpeter manufactory during the War of 1812. After paying his owner for allowing him to work during his own time, Free Frank saved enough to purchase his wife's freedom in 1817 and then his own in 1819.

As a free man, Free Frank expanded his entrepreneurial activities on the Kentucky frontier. He continued to manufacture saltpeter as well as engaging in land speculation and commercial farming. In 1830, he moved to Illinois, where he established a homestead in the sparsely populated Mississippi River Valley area of Pike County. There Free Frank continued land speculation activities and broadened his commercial farming enterprise to include raising stock. During the U.S. expansion period of the 1830s, Free Frank founded the town of New Philadelphia, Illinois, the only documented case of a town founded by a black man during the antebellum period (Walker 1983). In 1837, he legally changed his name to Frank McWorter. Mr. McWorter promoted the development of New Philadelphia until his death in 1854 at the age of seventy-five.

Free Frank's life story reflects the multiple responses of African Americans under slavery. It also bears testimony to an entrepreneurial spirit and the dogged determination of a people for economic development even under the most extreme circumstances.

### THE HAZARDS

It was hazardous for people of African origin to engage in private enterprise, whether free or slave. Codes restricted the economic opportunities available to blacks. Free blacks constantly feared being labeled as a "runaway slave" and being sold into slavery. Even at best, free blacks were not really free.

States also passed laws that restricted the movement of and rights of free blacks. For instance, by 1835, Virginia, Maryland, and North Carolina had passed legislation forbidding free blacks to carry arms without a license. Blacks throughout the South were denied the right of assembly so that benevolent societies and similar organizations were prohibited from convening. These actions hindered the capability of free blacks to earn a living and impeded the development of an African American business class (Yancy 1974). Jacobs noted: "Back in the 1830s, some of the many free Negroes in Washington, D.C., had begun to make solid economic gains. They owned quite a number of business enterprises that served the local economy in many ways. In particular, they were doing well in tavern and restaurant businesses. But the city was controlled by whites, and in 1835, a city ordinance was passed prohibiting shop licenses to be issued to blacks thereafter. The one exception was for carting and hackney work" (1969, 183).

Blacks had very circumscribed economic rights during the antebellum period. Clearly, antebellum law in its intent and design encouraged economic opportunities for whites while simultaneously excluding blacks from the economic arena. Indeed, discretionary law enforcement was much more influential than one's business abilities in determining the success or failure of an African American enterprise. To his credit, Free Frank, first as a slave and then as a free man, shrewdly used the law to promote the profitable expansion of his economic activities and to claim his economic rights (Walker 1983).

The major problem confronting African American entrepreneurs during slavery stemmed from the inability of whites to tolerate the economic success of any single African person. Whites feared that even isolated instances of economic success would undermine the system of racial inequality (Yancy 1974). As a consequence, through the Civil Rights era, the full force of law was imposed and individual whites committed many acts of violence in their efforts to extinguish the entrepreneurial spirit among African Americans. For instance, in 1844, Virginia authorities revoked the license of mulatto innkeeper Jacob Simpson without explanation. In 1852 Maryland prohibited African American membership in building and homestead associations. African Americans who had saved their money to purchase farms discovered that many white homesteaders did not want them in their regions or states. White-owned insurance companies usually refused to do business with African Americans. White bankers refused to cross the color line and make loans to blacks desiring any credit, but most especially credit for business purposes. African American business persons usually could not sue white creditors, even in northern courts. In late 1865 many southern states passed Black Code regulations declaring that any black man who did not have an employer was subject to arrest as a "vagrant," including any black man working independently. Some black artisans working independently were fined, jailed, and even sentenced to work as convict laborers. South Carolina's legislature declared in December 1865 that "no person of color shall pursue or practice art, trade, or businesses of an artisan, mechanic or shopkeeper, or any other trade, employment or business . . . on his own account and for his own benefit until he shall obtained a license which shall be good for one year only." African American peddlers and merchants had to pay one hundred dollars annually to buy the license, while whites paid nothing.

Individual acts of violence were widespread. In Cincinnati, white mobs periodically burned down Henry Boyd's furniture factory. Three times he rebuilt, but the fourth blaze compelled him to cease business because insurance companies refused to underwrite his risk. Mrs. Willie Mae Williams operated a successful grocery store in Starksdale, Mississippi, until a white gunman shot her dead in her store in 1910 (Marble 1983, 141).

In a sociohistorical analysis of black business, John Sibley Butler and Kenneth Wilson (1988) provide a lucid account of how the thriving African American business centers in Tulsa, Oklahoma, and Durham, North Carolina, were completely burned to the ground by angry whites in the 1920s. For white Americans, especially working-class and poor whites, the social prestige they enjoyed was profoundly threatened by the successes of black entrepreneurs. The white reaction was to mobilize institutional resources and use blatant violence with impunity to force African American entrepreneurs to cease business. Although formidable, the institutional and individual forms of economic violence failed to prevent African American entrepreneurs from succeeding.

Laws also had a positive impact on the development of black businesses. Pennsylvania, the first state to emancipate slaves by legislative action, was one of the first to witness the birth of an African American business class. In 1838, the "Register of Trades of Colored People" in the City of Philadelphia listed eight bakers, twenty-five blacksmiths, three brass founders, fifteen cabinetmakers and carpenters, and five confectioners. There were also two caulkers, two chair bottomers, fifteen tailoring enterprises, thirty-one tanners, five weavers, and six wheelwrights. The business register also listed businesses independently operated by African American women: eighty-one dressmakers and tailors, dyers and scourers; two fullers; and two glass and paper makers. Hairdressing, the most lucrative enterprise controlled by African American women, had eighty-nine practitioners.

Another profitable business, sail making, was controlled by African Americans in Philadelphia between 1820 and 1830. The business register recorded nineteen sail makers in 1838. Janee Forster (1766–1841) operated a major sail-manufacturing firm that in 1829 employed forty black and white workers.

Although several individuals succeeded in the manufacturing

trades, catering brought prosperity to the largest number of African Americans in Philadelphia. Robert Boyle, a black waiter, contracted for and prepared formal dinners for people who entertained in their homes. Although catering quickly became popular nationwide, it was most successful in Philadelphia, the city of its birth (Butler 1991, 34–48).

Many of the businesses discussed above required less capital and in no way threatened the larger, white-owned businesses. In addition, before the Civil War many of these black-owned business enterprises operated in a relatively open market, serving both black and white clients. Consequently, their economic health was not tied to providing products and services to only one ethnic group.

Despite risks and difficulties, the relative success of early black entrepreneurs prompted others to view private enterprise as the only path to economic advancement. The entrepreneurial spirit was alive and well among African Americans in the pre–Civil War era. The total real and personal wealth of free blacks at the dawn the Civil War was estimated at $50 million, equally distributed in the South and North. Much of black entrepreneurship after the Civil War would spring from this successful foundation.

### THE OPEN MARKET CLOSES

Among many other accomplishments, Booker T. Washington developed a strategy of upward mobility for blacks based on private enterprise. To be successful, however, this strategy assumed access to an open market. Ironically, access to the open market closed when slavery ended.

When the Civil War ended and the South fell under military rule, people of African origin hoped to enjoy social and political rights equal to those of whites for the first time since the imposition of slavery. However, the promise of freedom and political enfranchisement inspired by the Civil War was short lived. In 1877, Rutherford B. Hayes betrayed African American people. In exchange for support from white southerners during his presidential campaign, Hayes withdrew troops from the South in what became known as the "Great Compromise."

Two Supreme Court rulings also countered the intent of freedom for African Americans. In 1877, the Supreme Court ruled in *Hall v. de Cuvis* that a state could not prohibit segregation on a common carrier.

In the second ruling, *Plessy v. Ferguson* (1896), "separate but equal" became the law of the land. Through these rulings southern whites regained control of a government-instituted system of legal segregation and racism that essentially denied blacks their rights. This pattern of rigid segregation prevailed for the next one hundred years.

Despite disenfranchisement and segregation, Booker T. Washington saw the possibility of African American economic stability through business development. In 1900, Washington spearheaded the development of the National Negro Business League as a way to encourage enterprise. During the first meeting of the league, the delegates concluded that "when an individual produces what the world wants, whether it is a product of the hand, heart, or head, the world does not long stop to inquire what is the color of the skin of the producer. It was easily seen that if every member of the race should strive to make himself the most indispensable man in his community, and to be successful in business, however humble that business might be, he would contribute much toward soothing the pathway of his own and future generations" (Butler 1991, 67–68).

The quote clearly implies that Washington presumed black entrepreneurs would have access to a relatively open marketplace despite his belief that blacks and whites could remain separate in social matters. Washington was mistaken. The southern system of caste segregation applied exclusively to African Americans. Segregation laws restricted blacks from competing against any other entrepreneur in an open market. On the other hand, Chinese, Mexican, Jewish, and Native Americans could operate a business in the open market, drink at public fountains, eat in restaurants, and sleep in hotels.

The intent of the caste system was to deny African Americans social and political rights and privileges, and to strangle their economic rights and opportunities. For the next one hundred years, this virulent caste segregation shaped African American business development. African Americans throughout the country were limited to doing business with the coethnic customer base in their own communities. Their market was further constricted when entrepreneurs from all other ethnic groups were legally permitted to operate within the black community. Although segregation kept black entrepreneurs in their community, it did not exclude entrepreneurs from other ethnic groups (Du Bois 1889).

But African Americans succeeded despite the limitation of a coethnic market. Indeed, the period between 1890 and the 1920s is called the "golden era" of black business growth and development. Black-owned businesses flourished within the context of segregation because the overwhelming majority of blacks lived in the same geographic areas—the South and several northern urban areas. As illustrated in table 1, service businesses remained the cornerstone of the black business community.

Madame C. J. Walker, the grande dame of personal hair-care service, stands out as an example of success despite the odds. Because black hair care was largely ignored by white businesses, Madame Walker took advantage of this opportunity to develop an entire line of hair care and cosmetic products. In 1905, she developed a hair-care system that transformed dry, kinky hair into soft, natural-looking hair. In the process she transformed herself from Sarah Breedlove, a poor laundry worker, daughter of slaves and orphaned at age six, into Madame Walker, the hair-care tycoon.

Madame Walker's products delighted millions of mostly black women throughout the country. She also understood the importance of community development to the future of her people. Before her death

TABLE 1
## Independent Black Businesses, 1890

| Type of Business | Number |
| --- | --- |
| Draymen, hackmen, and teamsters | 43,963 |
| Bankers | 17,480 |
| Merchants | 7,181 |
| Hucksters and peddlers | 2,516 |
| Restaurant keepers | 2,157 |
| Salesmen and -women | 1,166 |
| Packers and shippers | 567 |
| Hotel keepers | 420 |
| Livery stable keepers | 390 |
| Undertakers | 231 |

*Source:* U.S. Bureau of the Census 1890–1915.

in 1919 at the age of fifty-one, Madame Walker built a school for girls in West Africa and endowed it with a grant for one hundred thousand dollars. She also established a school to train the more than two thousand agents who marketed her products. Madame Walker became America's first self-made black female millionaire.

The number of black-owned businesses continued to grow to an estimated 103,872 by 1932. With few exceptions, these businesses depended solely on black clientele. Unfortunately, during the Great Depression many blacks lost their jobs and income, which, in turn, caused many black-owned businesses to fail. By 1940, the number of black-owned business had declined by 16 percent to 87,475.

Another factor, the immigration of various ethnic groups from Europe into urban America, also contributed to the decline of black-owned businesses. European immigrants with limited skills and training settled in mostly northern urban areas, as did most African Americans emigrating from the rural South. Although both groups competed for the same lower paying jobs, European immigrants usually fared better because they were more likely to share the same ethnic background as the powerful whites who controlled the jobs. As a consequence, European immigrants benefited from often overt legal and political maneuvers as well as through more subtle economic and social tactics by getting many of the jobs in industries that previously had been held by blacks. Blacks were pushed from many occupations and enterprises that had once been their ticket to upward mobility and status. W.E.B. Du Bois described the situation in Philadelphia:

> The new industries attracted Irish, Germans, and other immigrants; Americans too were fleeing the city and soon natural race antipathies were added to a determined effort to displace Negro labor—an effort which had aroused prejudice of many of the better classes; and the poor quality of the new Black emigrant to give it aid and comfort. . . . The tide had set against the Negro strongly. . . . A mass of poverty-stricken, ignorant fugitives and ill trained freedmen had rushed to the city, swarmed in the vile slums which the rapidly growing city furnished, and met in social and economic competition equally ignorant but more vigorous foreigners. These foreigners outbid them for work, beat them on the streets, and were able to do this by the prejudice which Negro crime and anti-slavery sentiments had aroused in the city. (quoted in Butler 1991, 70)

## DURHAM, NORTH CAROLINA: A SPECIAL CASE

John Sibley Butler identified turn-of-the-century Durham, North Carolina, as a case study of black enterprise and economic resilience. By the late 1940s, more than 150 African American–owned businesses flourished in Durham. These businesses included the traditional service industries, but Durham was also the home of large, successful businesses, including one of the largest and most successful black businesses in the nation, the North Carolina Mutual Life Insurance Company. Butler (1991) notes: "Forming a circle around the North Carolina Mutual Life Insurance Company was the Banker's Fire Insurance Company, the Mutual Building and Loan Association, the Union Insurance and Realty Company, the Durham Realty and Insurance Company, the People's Building and Loan Association, the Royal Knights Savings and Loan Association, T. P. Parham and Associates (a brokerage corporation), and the Mortgage Company of Durham."

The residents of Durham took considerable pride in and put considerable effort into developing a "City of Enterprise" for African Americans. Community spirit notwithstanding, outside economic pressure and racial hostility in Durham made it impossible for blacks, on a large scale, to compete in the open economy. Jim Crow laws and segregation-by-custom forced most black-owned businesses to trade within their own group in Durham as well as across the country. Nevertheless, the climate of racial tolerance in Durham during this time tended to generate white clientele for the most successful black-owned retail and service businesses.

For instance, in 1940, Smith's Fish Market, established by former postal clerk Freeman M. Smith, supplied Durham's largest white-operated hotel, the Washington Duke, as well as smaller white- and black-owned businesses. In 1940, Smith grossed more than ninety thousand dollars and opened four other outlets throughout the city.

Rowland and Mitchell established a tailor shop in 1930. They worked for "exclusive Whites and department stores." Approximately 80 percent of their customers were white.

Another successful business, Thomas Baily and Sons, a meat and grocery market, opened in 1919 and grossed eighty thousand dollars annually by 1940. The Home Modernization and Supply Company, founded in 1938 by brothers U. M. and R. S. George, grossed more than one hundred thousand dollars, constructed five hundred homes in the Durham area, and employed thirty-five people by 1948.

The Durham textile mill was the only hosiery mill in the world owned and operated by African Americans. The mill operated eighteen knitting machines and did business in the open market. However, their salesmen, who traveled mostly in North Carolina, Indiana, Georgia, South Carolina, and Alabama, were white.

In 1924, because African American businesses in Durham were so stable with such solid prospects for the future, the city was chosen as the home of the National Negro Finance Corporation (NNFC), which was capitalized at $1 million. The NNFC was to provide working capital to firms, individuals, and corporations nationwide. Because Durham hosted the NNFC and other large businesses between 1900 and 1950, the city became known as the "Wall Street of Negro America" and "Black Business Capital of America" (Butler 1991, 180–196).

## A SNAPSHOT OF BLACK-OWNED BUSINESSES

Joseph Pierce (1947) conducted the first major empirical study of urban black-owned businesses during segregation. Pierce surveyed twelve cities across the country, eight in the South, two in the East, and two in the Midwest, to find and document black-owned businesses. Of the 3,866 black-owned businesses he identified and observed, 70 percent clustered into six industry categories: beauty and barber shops, 1,004; eating establishments, 624; groceries, 491; cleaning and pressing shops, 288; shoe shine and shoe repair shops, 130; and funeral parlors, 126. As a result of his work, Pierce is credited with coining the now-famous phrase "traditional black businesses."

Pierce constructed a subsample of data collected from the nine cities. From this data, he sought to identify patterns of initial capitalization, years of operation, and problems identified by owners as barriers to their business success. His findings were startling. The median value of initial capitalization was merely $549, which most people (86.3 percent) took from their personal savings. The second most frequent source of start-up capital came from family members (4.8 percent). Although black-owned banks operated in five of the nine cities, only 3.3 percent of the firms sought loans, and the median amount borrowed was only $500.

At the time of the survey, the median age of retail firms was 5.3 years, 7.1 years for service firms. Of the six major categories of black businesses, funeral parlors had been in business the longest (median age 22.6 years), shoe shine and shoe repair shops the shortest (median age 3.2 years). Blacks identified lack of financial capital as the greatest obstacle to progressive business operation, personnel problems ranked second, and lack of black patronage third.

Pierce's findings endured for many years as the benchmark for understanding black entrepreneurship (Pierce 1947). Twenty-two years later, based on a survey conducted by the Drexel Institute, Eugene Foley (1966) analyzed black-owned firms in Philadelphia. The Drexel Institute survey identified 4,242 black-owned firms, approximately 9 percent of the total number of businesses in the city at that time. Of this group, some were quite successful: 13 manufacturing businesses, 14 wholesale businesses, and 10 businesses in either insurance, publishing, catering, or contracting. However, most of the 4,242 businesses were very small and marginal in their profitability, stability, and physical condition. Corroborating Pierce's findings, the highest concentration of businesses focused on personal services—most commonly beauty parlors and barber shops (35 percent) and retailing and restaurants (11 percent) (Foley 1966, 107–144).

These black-owned businesses, although segregated and located within Philadelphia's black community, still competed with entrepreneurs from other ethnic groups for a share of the coethnic customer base, as was true in other areas. Foley comments: "Almost all Negro businesses are located in predominately Negro neighborhoods, but at least half of the business in these neighborhoods are white-owned. While the white businessman is free to pass through the walls on either side, the Negro businessman cannot look beyond his neighborhood" (Foley 1966, 113).

## How Black Entrepreneurs Succeeded

In the pre–Civil Rights era, African Americans enjoyed very limited and circumscribed economic rights. The greatest force limiting the potential of pre–Civil Rights era black business persons was racism and its resulting segregation. Segregation and racism not only precluded access to an open market but also restricted black business people to an almost exclusively black clientele. In addition to these institutional and environmental restrictions, entrepreneurs from all other ethnic groups had full access to compete for black clientele. But even under the onerous conditions that shaped their environment, black entrepreneurs competed, some quite successfully, and crafted economic security for themselves while contributing to community development.

How did black entrepreneurs succeed in the face in strong institutional barriers? What theories explain the historical and contemporary experience of the African American entrepreneur? Economic detour theory, developed by M. S. Stuart (1940) and expanded by John Sibley Butler (1991, 71–78), explains how African Americans, from the post–Civil War period until the Civil Rights era, were restricted by law from operating their businesses in an open market. The first element of the theory discusses the imposition of segregation laws as an explicit governmental program. As such, the government purposefully interfered with the operation of the marketplace by establishing policies that had a deleterious effect on the development and operation of African American businesses. De facto segregation in the North produced the same effect as did existing laws in the South. Segregation, as a government-sanctioned barrier, was inconsistent with the concept of "free" enterprise because it prohibited unrestricted commerce among its people. This policy was even more devastating in light of the tremendous business accomplishments of both free and enslaved African American entrepreneurs prior to the Civil War.

The second element of economic detour theory is that African Americans were the only group subjected to the policy of segregation. Other ethnic groups were free to develop business niches and operate in the open market. By restricting African American businesses to coethnic patronage, many black businesses were virtually doomed to limited growth and development and all but destined for failure. When restricted to a relatively small coethnic market, other ethnic groups, too, have failed (Bonacich and Model 1980.) It is quite possible that without the one-hundred-year policy of rigid segregation in the South and de facto segregation in the North, some black-owned businesses might have grown to the size of white-controlled corporations, that is, a North Carolina Mutual Life Insurance Company might have rivaled Prudential or MetLife. The historical evidence shows that African American businesses are more likely to succeed if they develop clientele outside of their community.

The third element of the theory of economic detour is that foreign groups traveled the world seeking free markets, emigrated to the United States without service to country or accrued rewards to their credit, and, as noted above, had unlimited access to private enterprise. African Americans, on the other hand, have participated in every major national conflict from Crispus Attucks in the American Revolution to the more contemporary conflicts of the Vietnam War, the Persian Gulf War, Somalia, Haiti, and now Bosnia. And in many of these conflicts, African Americans and other soldiers of color died in disproportionately large numbers because they were more likely to serve in the front lines. But despite their unswerving loyalty to country, African Americans were systematically excluded by policy from participating in the economic arena. Thus economic detour made it possible for foreigners, even the newly arrived and former enemies of war, to gain an economic toehold while excluding African American citizens born in the United States.

Stuart comments:

> This [to be excluded from the business market] is not his preference. Yet it seems to be his only recourse. It is an economic detour which no other racial group in this country is required to travel. Any type of foreigner, oriental, or "what not," can usually attract to his business a surviving degree of patronage of the native American. No matter that he may be fresh from foreign shores with no contribution to the national welfare to his credit; no matter that he sends every dollar of his American-earned profit back to his foreign home and uses it to help finance organizations dedicated to the destruction of the government that furnishes him his new golden opportunity; yet he can find a welcome place on the economic broadway to America. But the Negro, despite centuries of unrequited toil to help build and maintain that highway, must turn to a detour that leads he knows not where. Following this doubtful economic trail, he knows that he will have to find most of his customers within his own race in any enterprise he attempts. Yet, within this limited scope, if only he had an even chance at this approximately 9 percent of the population, a not too discouraging field might lay before him. (Butler 1991, 74)

As a result of the economic detour imposed by the system of rigid segregation, African Americans were forced to create a separate economy while combating stiff competition from nonblacks within that economy. As a consequence, African Americans were forced over time to assume the role of consumer. An even more fundamental problem is that, in the minds of many white Americans, black Americans have never been entitled to the basic economic rights enjoyed by European, Asian, and Hispanic ethnic groups that have immigrated to this country.

This discussion raises an interesting question: To what extent has the Civil Rights movement removed economic detour for African American entrepreneurs? Considering the relative success of the movement, to what extent do African Americans enjoy economic rights in the post–Civil Rights era? Chapter 2 addresses these and other issues.

# 2

# The Impact of
# Civil Rights

The Civil Rights movement was the greatest effort at social reform in the history of the United States because it significantly improved opportunities available to African Americans. It was a reformist movement that focused on altering the structure of oppression that denied African Americans the rights guaranteed other citizens by the U.S. Constitution. The major issues of the movement were clear: eliminating segregation and discrimination and thereby eliminating the American racial caste system.

The Civil Rights movement achieved much of its goal because it fundamentally changed the way in which laws were promulgated. Prior to the movement, laws such as those requiring chattel slavery, Black Codes, and Jim Crow segregation were designed to subordinate African Americans. Beginning with Executive Order 8802 in 1942, and later the Civil Rights Act of 1964, the Voting Rights Act of 1965, and Executive Order 11246, laws were designed to protect the rights of African Americans as well as to promote the more equitable distribution of scarce resources. Taken together, these legislative acts and executive orders are indicators of the success of the Civil Rights movement.

## Improved Access to Capital and Procurement

A significant boost to black entrepreneurship came in the form of the 1967 amendment to the Economic Opportunity Act (EOA). The amendment directed the Small Business Administration (SBA) to emphasize small businesses that were owned by low-income persons or located in urban and rural areas suffering from high unemployment. These criteria substantially increased the proportion of minority-owned businesses that qualified for assistance. The SBA developed two basic strategies to implement the 1967 amendment—improving access to financial capital and improving access to government procurement of goods and services.

The SBA improved access to capital by providing direct loans to small and minority businesses through its Economic Opportunity Loan (EOL) program. In concert with the government's "War on Poverty," the EOL program required that entrepreneurs be economically and socially disadvantaged. In this way, the EOL program assisted less-able entrepreneurs who wanted to operate small businesses in traditional areas such as hair care, groceries, restaurants, retailing, shoe repair, and laundry. Because the program targeted the less able entrepreneur, however, loan defaults were common (Bates 1981, 59–63).

Another type of loan assistance, the SBA 7(a) program, guaranteed bank loans made to small, minority, and nonminority entrepreneurs. This program helped African American business persons overcome the banking establishment's longstanding tradition of redline discrimination. For the first time, African American business owners gained access to commercial bank loans. In contrast to the EOL program, the 7(a) program targeted larger and more promising businesses, such as manufacturing, wholesale, and large retail enterprises, which require substantial capital investment and inventory.

SBA loan programs, however, suffered from significant failure rates, estimated at 26.4 and 53.3 percent for 7(a) and EOL recipients, respectively. These estimates are inconclusive, at best, because the SBA did not keep accurate records on multiple loans and repayment. Nevertheless, the loan defaults and business failures indicated that serious problems existed for small and minority businesses as well as for the SBA loan programs (Bates 1981, 65–67).

Another SBA-related loan program, the Minority Enterprise Small Business Investment Company (MESBIC), also assisted black businesses. MESBICs, though related to SBA, are privately owned and managed venture capital corporations. MESBICs were intended to (1) provide venture capital by purchasing an equity position in businesses; (2) provide capital in the form of long-term debt; (3) guarantee loans by third parties, that is, banks; and (4) provide general management and technical assistance to businesses. MESBICs also had congressional authority to leverage their privately invested capital at a four-to-one ratio by selling long-term debentures and/or preferred stock to the SBA.

Over time, however, MESBICs may have functioned in a way that proved counterproductive to the development of black businesses. Most MESBICs were insolvent for several reasons. MESBICs often started undercapitalized, usually with less than $1 million. They also tended to generate a negative cash flow because equity investments require an extended lead time before they yield dividends. Furthermore, they were unable to successfully balance the risk of financing small businesses while still maintaining their own profitability.

In another counterproductive action, MESBICs frequently made loans to minority firms instead of providing equity capital investments. The loans severely strained the cash flow of small firms and sometimes pushed them into default. Loan defaults then adversely affected the MESBICs. With cash flow problems and their own capital base eroding, MESBICs, too, faced insolvency. Perhaps to counteract their own financial problems, MESBICs may have tendered substantial loans and equity investments in majority-owned firms, a direct violation of law (Bates 1981, 67).

The performance of MESBICs raises serious questions about their viability as agencies to facilitate black business development. Because MESBICs tended to withhold risk capital so necessary for the survival and growth of small businesses, they may have contributed to the failure of some small firms. In an effort to overcome the extreme difficulties experienced by the MESBICs, the SBA eventually renamed the program Specialized Small Business Investment Companies (SSBIC).

Because of heavy defaults and administrative problems associated with loan programs, the SBA shifted its emphasis to providing disadvantaged businesses access to government procurement of goods and services through its 8(a) program. The 8(a) program directed that a portion of all federal government contracts be reserved for competition only among disadvantaged business persons. This concept became known as "set-asides."

Similar to the EOL, the SBA 8(a) program focused on disadvantaged businesses. However, by restricting competition to disadvantaged business persons, which also included nonminority small businesses, the program tended to exclude larger African American–owned businesses. Nevertheless, as a result of the volume of procurement contracts awarded under the 8(a) program—from $8.9 million in 1969 to $4.3 billion in 1985—many small and black-owned businesses stabilized and grew.

The 1977 Public Works Employment Act is another important product of the Civil Rights movement. The law required that all large general contractors bidding for public-works projects allocate at least 10 percent of the contracts to ethnic minority subcontractors of color, regardless of whether subcontractors were disadvantaged or not. Both well-established minority businesses and disadvantaged businesses benefited from this strategy.

In addition to the government's actions to increase minority involvement in procurement, many private-sector corporations also established procurement programs for small and minority businesses. Indeed, Fortune 500 corporations, through the National Minority Supplier Development Council headed by Harriet Michel, reportedly purchased $5.3 billion in goods and services from minority-owned businesses during 1982. By 1992, the volume of purchases had grown to $10 billion.

## The Beginning of the End

In the early 1980s, the SBA was criticized on the basis that its 8(a) program was designed to assist only the marginal entrepreneur as opposed to the talented self-employed minority business person. In 1989, the U.S. Supreme Court struck down as unconstitutional under the Fourteenth Amendment a Richmond, Virginia, city ordinance that required 30 percent of each public-works construction contract to be set aside for minority businesses. In the Croson decision, as it became known, the Supreme Court, in a badly divided five-to-four split, distinguished between remedies at the local/state level designed to address past discrimination in business practices and those that are federally enacted. The Supreme Court further clarified that Congress has more authority than the states to formulate remedial legislation and applied the concept of "strict scrutiny" to efforts to address past discrimination. Strict scrutiny is the most stringent level of court review used to determine the constitutionality of laws that seek to redress discrimination based on race classification. The "strict scrutiny" standard has two components. First, the governmental body enacting the law must have a "compelling interest for doing so," defined as clear evidence of specific instances of past discrimination based on race. Second, the law must be "narrowly tailored to achieve the goal" of eliminating that specific discrimination.

In writing the majority opinion, Justice O'Connor pointed out that the strict scrutiny standard was not intended to be "strict" in theory and fatal in "fact." But the implementation of the Croson decision was far more than a technical clarification of law; it had a "fatal" impact on minority businesses. During July 1987, when a lower court first ruled against Richmond's set-aside program, 40 percent of the city's total construction dollars were spent on products and services provided by minority-owned construction firms. Immediately after the court delivered the decision, the share of business awarded to minority enterprises fell to 15 percent and, by the end of 1988, was less than 3 percent.

The impact of Croson was felt in every business community. The dramatic decrease in state and municipal contracts awarded to minority businesses was repeated throughout the nation. The number of contracts awarded in Tampa to African American– and Latino-owned companies decreased 99 percent and 50 percent, respectively. More than thirty-three states and political divisions dismantled their race/ethnic set-aside programs, and more than seventy jurisdictions conducted studies and/or held hearings to review their procurement programs in light of the Croson decision.

The Croson decision, to a large extent, legitimated the idea of reverse discrimination in government procurement just as the Bakke decision did in education and employment (for a thorough discussion of the role of the Bakke decision in legitimating the idea reverse discrimination, see Woodard 1982, 166–175). This issue has surfaced again with the Republican takeover of congressional power and the Adarand decision in June 1995. Adarand Constructors, Inc. filed suit against the Department of Transportation claiming that consideration of social and disadvantaged status, which is assumed to include women and minority groups, in awarding subcontracts violate the equal protection component of the Fifth Amendment's due process clause. The court of appeals rejected the Adarand claim. In June 1995 the Supreme Court, in *Adarand v. Pena,* vacated the court of appeals ruling and remanded the case for further consideration using the same strict scrutiny criteria established in the Croson decision.

The power shift in Congress has rekindled the call of "angry white men" to dismantle affirmative action and set-aside programs. At this time, the polity appears to be in retrenchment; rethinking the extent to which economic opportunities for African Americans and other ethnic minorities should be guarded. Indeed, the government's ambivalence in supporting economic opportunities for African Americans should be viewed as a reflection of this society's ambivalence on the extent to which African Americans are entitled to economic rights.

It was not surprising that support for set-asides as a remedy for past discrimination eroded quickly during the late 1980s and 1990s. Support for minority advancement is least popular during periods of economic decline, such as in the years between the late 1980s and 1990s. Thus many other gains realized by the Civil Rights movement were also rescinded by court challenges. Nevertheless, the Civil Rights movement helped African American entrepreneurs gain greater access to capital and to government and private-sector procurement opportunities for the first time in history. And as a result, many small African American–owned businesses were able to grow and stabilize.

## The Bifurcation of the Black Business Community

The unfortunate reality is that much of the African American population was unaffected economically by the Civil Rights movement. Black workers lacking skills and education remained trapped by urban poverty and were unable to benefit from the new occupational opportunities. The dire circumstances of this segment of the black population, typically referred to as the underclass, was brought to public attention by William Julius Wilson, first in his 1980 book *The Declining Significance of Race,* and further clarified in his 1987 book *The Truly Disadvantaged.*

The growing black middle class realized the greatest benefit from the Civil Rights movement. Their education and skills prepared them to enter newly opened high-wage, high-tech, and high-prestige occupations.

The Civil Rights movement also provided entrepreneurs greater opportunities in the government and private sector. But these new opportunities in procurement and access to capital had little positive effect on small, traditional firms of the black business community. Indeed, eminent economist and Federal Reserve Board member Andrew Brimmer (1966, 1968), argued that desegregation actually caused the demise of traditional black businesses.

According to Brimmer, segregation provided traditional black-owned businesses with a somewhat protected market; many white-owned firms would not provide the services and products desired by African Americans living in segregation. But purchasing options increased with desegregation. African Americans could now shop comfortably at outlying and exclusive areas previously closed to them. At the same time, white-owned firms realized the purchasing power of African Americans and multiplied their efforts to compete for the black consumer dollar. The end result was that African American–owned businesses captured fewer consumer dollars spent in their own community. Furthermore, many owners of traditional firms in the African American community lacked business management and technical skills to compete in a more open market. As a consequence, their sales stagnated or they went out of business altogether.

Brimmer pushed this line of argument further. In an article, "Small Business and Economic Development in the Negro Community," Brimmer (1971) presented 1967 data describing the income, wealth holdings, and levels of installment debt of black households. He concluded that firms that catered solely to African American consumers tended to be economically weak because of the limited purchasing power of African Americans. Brimmer acknowledged, however, that small business ownership does "offer modest opportunities for potential entrepreneurs, particularly if they seek either racially diverse clients or largely non-minority clientele. Opportunities are better in the national economy because the purchasing power that can be tapped allows firms to expand in size and scope."

Brimmer suggested that African American businesses focus on a racially mixed clientele or the national economy. Historically, black-owned businesses that do so are more likely to succeed. But one should not underestimate the considerable purchasing power of the African American community. With an estimated $300 billion, the African American community is the seventh largest purchasing power in the world. To tap this power, national and international corporations have developed massive marketing campaigns that target specific segments of the African American community. For instance, the hair-care product market, once the sole province of African American businesses, has been severely eroded by competition from large, white-controlled national corporations. In addition, there are chic and surrealistic animated advertising campaigns designed specifically to encourage young African Americans to smoke cigarettes and drink highly intoxicating malt liquors. (It should be noted that the number of ads for alcohol and tobacco products is much greater in the African American community than any other urban neighborhood.)

But there is a more fundamental problem with Brimmer's line of reasoning. To suggest that segregation provided protected markets for African American businesses presents a one-sided interpretation of those businesses' historical development (Bates 1973a, 1973b). After all, laws and customs denied black business persons access to the open market and curtailed wealth accumulation in the segregated community. Indeed, Melvin Oliver and Thomas Shapiro in their important 1995 book *Black Wealth/White Wealth* argue persuasively that institutionalized residential segregation cost the current generation of African Americans mightily in wealth accumulation. Oliver and Shapiro show that skewed access to mortgage lending and housing markets and the racial valuing of neighborhoods results in enormous wealth disparity. Banks turn down qualified blacks much more often than similarly qualified whites. Blacks who do qualify pay higher interest rates on home mortgages than whites. Residential segregation persists into the 1990s, and the authors found the rise in housing values to be color coded; that is, white neighborhoods experience considerable increase in values while black neighborhoods experience little increase or even a decline in value. The lower valuation of black-owned homes adversely affects the ability of blacks to use their residences as collateral for obtaining personal or business loans. Oliver and Shapiro estimate that institutional biases in the residential lending arena have cost the current generation of African Americans about $82 billion. In other words, institutional discrimination in housing and lending markets extends into the future the effects of past discrimination in other institutions. To suggest, as Brimmer does, that segregation provides protected markets for small black-owned businesses ignores the larger purpose of segregation, excluding black entrepreneurs from competition in the open market and locking them out of growth and wealth accumulation opportunities.

The Civil Rights movement created many new opportunities for highly trained African American entrepreneurs, but few for those with less training. Firms emerging between 1970 and 1990 were not mere replicas of earlier traditional black-owned businesses. Many businesses, which were created or expanded with the help of SBA loans, focused on nontraditional areas such as computer and business services, wholesaling, manufacturing, contracting services, and large-scale retailing. Civil Rights–era laws, which were designed to create a more level playing field in private enterprise, stimulated the fastest growth in the skill- and capital-intensive lines of business within the black business community.

Indeed, the post–Civil Rights era is characterized by a duality in black business development. Although there remains a concentration of small traditional businesses, a coinciding trend also exists toward establishing highly skill- and capital-intensive firms, referred to as "emerging firms." Thus in the post–Civil Rights era, the African American business development dynamic is best understood by viewing firms as either "traditional" or "emerging."

The Civil Rights movement created opportunities for African Americans in emerging or growing lines of business. But it is only the well-educated and trained entrepreneurs who start and expand such businesses. In contrast, owners of traditional businesses, who tend to be less well educated and less well trained, are trapped in small, marginally profitable, "mom-and-pop" businesses or have ceased business operation. In other words, business development among African Americans in the post–Civil Rights era is bifurcated.

To ignore the bifurcation is to view black business development in the post–Civil Rights era with lenses corroded by the racism and segregation associated with the pre–Civil Rights era. The post–Civil Rights era has provided opportunities for talented African American entrepreneurs to earn education, obtain work experience and training, and accumulate resources to initiate and build substantial business enterprises. Considering the enormity of their accomplishments, it is surprising that African American entrepreneurs in emerging businesses have received so little attention in the contemporary literature.

## Contemporary Research on Black Entrepreneurs

Studies that examine the economic aspects of business development emphasize the financial characteristics of various ethnic groups. They argue that the comparatively limited business formation and growth among African Americans is a result of a lack of equity or debt capital (Bates 1985b; Ando 1988). The business management research, which focuses on issues such as management, planning, and technical capabilities in producing goods and services, comes to a similar conclusion. African Americans tend to have fewer requisite skills to initiate and sustain viable businesses (Bowser 1981; Sexton and Bowman 1984). Other research, such as psychological and sociological studies, discusses individual characteristics, demographic characteristics, and human resources (McCelland 1961; Durand 1975; Gomokla 1977; Sexton and Bowman 1984; Douglass 1976; Shapero and Sokol 1982).

Although these studies provide critical insight into obstacles that ethnic minorities face in business, none analyze the experience of African American entrepreneurs as they initiate and sustain emerging businesses. Comparative studies that describe differences between ethnic groups in business provide only a glimpse of the African American business experience. Invariably, African Americans, when compared to another group, are found to have less of a trait identified as important to business success. Once they identify a difference, researchers (e.g.,

Ivan Light, Thomas Sowell, Edna Bonacich, Alajandro Portes, Kenneth Wilson, and Shelley Green and Paul Pryde) argue that African Americans have less of the requisite cultural tradition, human resources, organization, wealth, and so on necessary to succeed as entrepreneurs.

The contemporary comparative research tends to view entrepreneurs from a single cultural perspective, that is, Euro-American. Over time, this research literature has ignored cultural differences and/or distorted the negative impact of institutional forces on African American business development. Moreover, this literature is theoretically and methodologically flawed because it fails to control for time of entry. For example, in an often cited study of entrepreneurship in Miami, Wilson, Portes, and Martin (1982) observed that more recently migrated Cuban Americans created ethnic enclaves that had higher levels of entrepreneurial activity than African American communities. The Cuban enclave in Miami has served as the prototype of economic development, as can be seen not only in the work of Wilson, Portes, and Martin but also in the work of Wilson (1980) and Portes and Bach (1985). Characteristic of comparative research on ethnic entrepreneurship, Wilson, Portes, and Martin fail to consider the time-of-entry variable. It is an important consideration that cannot be ignored, because recent immigrants are more likely to gravitate toward small entrepreneurial activities in the ethnic enclave, but successive generations then move toward the professions in the larger economy. The proper comparison would have been Cuban Americans in the 1970s and the black American entrepreneurial experience in certain cities of the 1920s—for example, Durham. Comparative studies that do not control for time are theoretically and methodologically troublesome (Butler 1991, 192–193).

Based on the findings of flawed comparative research, policy makers are led to conclude that *if we can just get the traits/participation rates of African Americans up to the traits/participation rates of Caucasians, Asians, or Cubans, everything will be all right.* The question must be asked, Where are the analyses of African Americans that are based upon the participation rates and cultural frame of reference of African Americans? Where in the literature are the concepts or rates that use African Americans as a standard by which to evaluate African American business development activity? Where do we find African Americans as the subject and object of the ethnic entrepreneurship literature? In order to more fully understand contemporary entrepreneurship among African Americans, research must move toward a frame of reference based on African Americans.

The Minority Business Development Agency of the U.S. Department of Commerce is conducting promising sociological research. One research direction contends that minority business ownership and growth depends largely on the resources of the social group rather than on the individual (Fratoe 1986, 1988). According to Frank Fratoe (1986), a series of internal and external social factors exert considerable influence on business development. Fratoe identifies internal factors such as family, friends, and voluntary associations that can provide support, enabling individuals to start and maintain a business. External factors that can influence black business development include (1) prejudice and/or discrimination, (2) employment structure, (3) economic conditions, (4) political conditions, and (5) residential concentration. Fratoe does not attribute cause-and-effect conditions to his model but suggests that the specific combination of internal and external factors over time determines the rise and fall of business development among minority groups.

The Fratoe model is most useful. The econometric, business management, and psychological approaches lead to the same conclusion, that black business development is comparatively limited, and then places the onus for the limited business development at the doorstep of black entrepreneurs or a lack of a business tradition among African Americans. On the other hand, the Fratoe model goes beyond this "blame the victim" thinking to consider how internal and external factors affect the relative level of business development among ethnic groups. The history of business development among African Americans is clear testimony to the viability of the Fratoe model.

My view closely coincides with Fratoe's but differs in some important ways on the relationship between and among the external and internal factors. I contend that the level of economic or business development of a particular ethnic group is, in large part, a function of its cultural and financial capital counterbalanced by the institutional forces that may enhance or totally annihilate the ethnic group's capital as a factor related to economic development. Furthermore, the racial ideology prevalent during a particular time shapes the way in which institutional forces affect business development among African Americans (Wilson 1973; Woodard 1982).

As discussed in chapter 1, the pre–Civil Rights era institutional forces, especially the polity, somewhat eroded the cultural and financial capital of African Americans. White Americans invoked racial ideologies that rejected the humanity and cultural integrity of African Americans while simultaneously justifying economic subordination. Indeed, many Euro-Americans believed that African Americans had no or few economic rights worthy of consideration. As a consequence, African American business development remained restricted to a narrow range of personal-care service enterprises.

The Civil Rights movement fostered laws and social inventions, for example, "set-asides," that guaranteed some economic opportunities for ethnic minorities. Greater access to capital and procurement, and the gradual recognition of African Americans as competent entrepreneurs, encouraged the growth, stabilization, and diversification of the black business community. In the post–Civil Rights era of race relations, African Americans finally experienced greater economic rights. But racial ideology limits economic opportunities accorded to "out groups" in order to maintain the racial status quo. The Croson decision, the Adarand decision, and the recent Republican-led backlash to government and private-sector set-asides serves, once again, to limit economic opportunities afforded African Americans. Thus, even in the post–Civil Rights era, institutional forces, especially the polity, play a pivotal role in the establishment and growth of black-owned businesses.

African Americans are carving out their economic destiny within the context of economic rights denied, won, and retracted again. To the extent that race remains a divisive issue in American life, it is reasonable to expect that the battle over extending economic rights to African Americans will continue, with African Americans enjoying greater levels of economic rights in some eras, lesser levels in others. Since African Americans have only had either restricted or limited economic rights at any time, it is reasonable that their economic destiny should differ from that of other American ethnic groups.

Therefore, it is not useful or appropriate to determine the relative level of business development among African Americans by comparing the rates of black business formation, growth, or failure with those of other

ethnic groups. Rather, a more useful determination of business development is found by assessing changes in measures of business activities
based on the way institutional (government and private-sector) forces
either facilitate or hinder African American business activities in a particular era.

At this juncture, we may not need more census-based comparative
analyses, but more in-depth ethnographic and case-study analyses from
the perspective of the African American business person. This book provides the basis for such an indigenous frame of reference.

3

# An Indigenous Frame of Reference

This chapter presents an empirical overview that provides the context for the personal stories told in succeeding chapters. The overview is based on data drawn from both the "Survey of Minority-Owned Business Enterprises" (SMOBE) and "Characteristics of Business Owners" (CBO) compiled by the U.S. Bureau of the Census.

## Business Formation, Development, and Characteristics

Table 2 indicates that the number of businesses owned by African Americans more than tripled between 1972 and 1992. The 46 percent increase between 1987 and 1992 is almost 20 percent greater than the increase for all U.S. firms during this same time period. The data show that African Americans are starting business enterprises at a greater rate than Americans in general.

From 1977 to 1992, about 94 percent of black-owned firms operated as sole proprietorships. Partnerships and subchapter S corporations comprised 2 and 4 percent, respectively, of black-owned firms in 1992.

Gross receipts of African American businesses have increased substantially. From 1982 to 1992, receipts increased 342 percent to $32.2

TABLE 2
**Black-owned Businesses, 1972–1992**

| Year | Number of Businesses | Percentage of Increase |
|------|---------------------|------------------------|
| 1992 | 620,912 | 331.0 |
| 1987 | 424,165 | 227.7 |
| 1982 | 308,260 | 84.8 |
| 1977 | 231,203 | 23.2 |
| 1972 | 187,602 | — |

*Source:* U.S. Bureau of the Census 1974, 1979, 1984, 1990, 1995.

billion, although this increase was not evenly distributed among black-owned firms by 1992. A tiny percentage, only .5 percent of black-owned firms, grossed $1 million or more, earning about 40 percent of the gross revenues. In contrast, 56 percent of the firms grossed less than $10,000. The average annual gross receipts for a black-owned business in 1992 was approximately $52,000.

A direct relationship exists between the legal organization of a black business and its gross receipts. Sole proprietorships enjoy significantly less earnings and their share of gross receipts appears to be declining: 49.7 percent in 1992, 50.9 percent in 1987, 68.4 percent in 1982, and 55.7 percent in 1977. Partnerships accounted for 12.4 percent of the gross receipts in 1992, 10 percent in 1987, and 13.7 percent in 1982. In contrast, although subchapter S corporations accounted for only 4 percent of the total number of firms, they earned 37.8 percent of the gross receipts in 1992, up from 1.7 percent of the firms and 17.2 percent of the gross receipts in 1982. The real increase in gross receipts among black-owned businesses occurred among subchapter S corporations.

Overall, black-owned firms provide limited opportunities for employment. In 1972, only 13.1 percent of 187,602 black-owned firms had paid employees and accounted for 62.3 percent of gross receipts. Paid employment has increased slightly over time in absolute terms. By 1992, 10 percent of the 620,912 firms had paid employees and accounted for 70 percent of the gross receipts, with 342 firms having one hundred or more paid employees. However, these 342 firms earned $6 billion in gross receipts, or 26.6 percent of the total receipts of employer firms.

Table 3 summarizes the growth in the ten major industry groups that account for the greatest dollar volume of receipts for African American–owned firms from 1977 to 1992. Historically, a majority of black-owned businesses were service-related. Although these businesses remain important, the fastest growing enterprises since 1977 are in industries requiring a high level of skill and education. These include business services, which have grown by 420 percent and nearly $2.4 billion in gross receipts; health services, with a growth of 201 percent and nearly $2.9 billion; and specialty trade contractors, which have grown by 136.5 percent and nearly $1.5 billion in gross receipts. By 1992, the greatest increase in black ownership was in the wholesale trade industry, which grew 504 percent and logged the highest total gross receipts, with nearly $2.95 billion.

TABLE 3
**Ten Largest Major Industry Groups for Black-owned Firms, 1977 and 1992**

| Major Industry Group | 1977 | | 1992 | | |
|---|---|---|---|---|---|
| | Number of Firms | Gross Receipts (in millions) | Number of Firms | Gross Receipts (in millions) | Percentage of Change |
| Auto dealers/ service stations | 5,002 | $1,108 | 4,040 | $2,384 | -19.2 |
| Business services | 15,461 | $ 358 | 80,330 | $2,371 | +420.0 |
| Health services | 14,560 | $ 399 | 43,860 | $2,859 | +201.0 |
| Specialty trade contractors | 17,126 | $ 497 | 36,057 | $1,466 | +110.5 |
| Miscellaneous retail | 2,080 | $ 590 | 49,381 | $1,247 | +136.5 |
| Eating/drinking establishments | 13,008 | $ 572 | 13,832 | $1,786 | +6.3 |
| Trucking and warehousing | 1,152 | $ 353 | 25,756 | $1,347 | +123.0 |
| Food stores | 10,679 | $ 786 | 8,466 | $ 980 | -20.7 |
| Personal services | 35,035 | $ 399 | 76,988 | $1,469 | +120.0 |
| Wholesale trade | 1,250 | $ 333 | 7,550 | $2,944 | +504.0 |

*Source:* U.S. Bureau of the Census 1979, 1990, 1995.

Although the auto dealers/service stations category registered the third highest amount of gross receipts, it also experienced a high rate of decline, -19.2 percent, probably due to a reduction in the number of service stations owned by African Americans. Ownership of food stores declined similarly (-20.7), whereas eating and drinking establishments posted a slight gain, 6.3 percent. Competitive pressures during the post–Civil Rights era increased in these business areas, which require much lower skill and educational levels. In many instances African American business owners either discontinued or sold their businesses to immigrant entrepreneurs.

The geographic concentrations of black firms closely reflect population densities of African Americans. Table 4 indicates that in 1992 California had the greatest number of black-owned firms, New York the second. About 50 percent of the black-owned firms and 52.8 percent of the gross receipts were concentrated in California, New York, Texas, Florida, Georgia, and Illinois. The District of Columbia had the greatest concentration (28.6 percent) of firms owned by African Americans; however, they accounted for only 4.1 percent of the gross receipts. African American firms in Wyoming represented both the smallest share of business and the lowest gross receipts (.1 percent).

TABLE 4

**Geographic Concentration of Black-owned Firms, 1992**

| State | Number of Firms | Gross Receipts (in billions) |
|---|---|---|
| California | 68,968 | $5.5 |
| New York | 51,312 | $2.2 |
| Texas | 50,008 | $2.3 |
| Florida | 40,371 | $2.3 |
| Georgia | 38,264 | $1.7 |
| Maryland | 35,758 | $1.2 |
| North Carolina | 29,221 | $ .9 |
| Illinois | 28,433 | $1.8 |
| Virginia | 26,100 | $1.2 |
| Ohio | 22,690 | $1.1 |
| Washington, D.C. | 10,111 | $ .5 |

*Source:* U.S. Bureau of the Census 1995.

## Characteristics of
## Business Owners

The 1987 Characteristics of Business Owners (CBO) identified 424,165 African American–owned firms. Table 5 presents the age, marital status, and education of those owners. In 1987, one-half of them were between thirty-five and fifty-four years old. Approximately two-fifths were either aged twenty-five to thirty-four (22.1 percent) or aged fifty-five to sixty-four (19.1 percent). Although business ownership appears to be mostly a phenomenon of middle age, some owners are younger and some are older. The overwhelming majority of business owners are married (68.6 percent). Only 10 percent have never been married. One-fourth of them are high school graduates, and one-fifth are college graduates.

The literature suggests that having a relative in business predisposes individuals to become entrepreneurs because they are exposed to business and more likely to consider ownership. But the data does not substantiate that claim (U.S. Bureau of the Census 1991). Only 27.8 percent of African American business owners in 1987 had a relative in business; 65.7 percent did not (the figures do not add up to 100 percent due to incomplete responses). Of those with relatives in business, only 10 percent of owners worked with those relatives. Few entrepreneurs (9.1 percent) owned a business prior to the one owned in 1987. Perhaps

TABLE 5

**Black Business Owners, by Age, Marital Status, and Education, 1987**

| Age | (%) | Marital Status | (%) | Education | (%) |
|---|---|---|---|---|---|
| Under 25 | 2.1 | Never married | 10.1 | Elementary school | 7.1 |
| 25–34 | 22.1 | Married | 68.6 | Some high school | 14.1 |
| 35–44 | 28.2 | Divorced/separated | 14.8 | High school graduate/GED | 24.4 |
| 45–54 | 22.6 | | | | |
| 55–64 | 19.2 | Widow/widower | 4.1 | Some college | 19.7 |
| 65+ | .9 | | | College graduate | 10.9 |
| | | Not reported | 2.4 | Graduate school | 9.9 |
| | | | | Not reporting | 8.1 |

*Source:* U.S. Bureau of the Census 1991.
*Note:* Percentages in the age category do not add to 100 due to incomplete responses.

socialization by relatives is not as much a factor in determining business ownership as previously and commonly assumed.

Without socialization by relatives and/or extensive prior business ownership, it is possible that African Americans substitute work and managerial experience to learn about business. The U.S. Census Bureau (1991) indicates that 22.2 percent of business owners had twenty or more years of work experience prior to going into business, 23.8 percent had ten or more years, and 11.4 percent had six to nine years. No prior work experience was claimed by 13.4 percent of business owners, less than two years of experience by 5.8 percent, and two to five years of experience by 12.9 percent. About 25 percent of business owners had some type of supervisory experience, either managerial/executive (10 percent) or white-collar supervisory experience (7 percent) or blue-collar supervisory experience (8.8 percent).

A major barrier to business ownership for many is the ability to acquire sufficient start-up capital. Table 6 presents amounts and sources of start-up capital for business owners in 1987. About one-third of African American business owners report starting their business with

## TABLE 6
### Amounts and Sources of Start-up Capital

| Amount of Start-up Capital | (%) | Percentage of Capital Borrowed | (%) | Source of Borrowed Capital | (%) |
|---|---|---|---|---|---|
| None | 30.5 | None | 39.1 | Spouse | 1.5 |
| <$5,000 | 36.9 | 1–24 | 5.1 | Other family | 3.3 |
| $5,000–24,999 | 20.1 | 25–49 | 2.0 | Friends | 2.0 |
| $25,000–99,999 | 5.9 | 50–74 | 4.1 | Credit card | 2.2 |
| $100,000–1 million | 1.0 | 75–100 | 9.0 | Second mortgage | 1.7 |
|  |  | N/A | 40.8 | Former owner | 0.8 |
|  |  |  |  | Commercial bank | 9.5 |
|  |  |  |  | Other loan | 3.0 |
|  |  |  |  | State, local government | 0.9 |
|  |  |  |  | N/A | 80.0 |

*Source:* U.S. Bureau of the Census 1991.

no capital, and approximately one-third started with less than five thousand dollars. About 20 percent of the business owners started their businesses with amounts from five thousand dollars to less than twenty-five thousand dollars. Very few had a substantial infusion of start-up capital. For those business owners who required capital to start their businesses, nearly 40 percent used their own savings and other sources of personal wealth. Only 20 percent borrowed the money, and less than one-half borrowed 75 to 100 percent of the start-up capital. Borrowing has *not* been an important source of start-up capital for black-owned businesses.

Table 6 further indicates the sources of loans for the 20 percent who borrowed money to start their businesses. Slightly more than 10 percent borrowed from "personal" sources, for example, spouse, other family, friends, credit cards, and second mortgages on homes. Nearly 10 percent reported borrowing from commercial banks. Loans from federal, state, and municipal government sources as well as former business owners are neither widely available nor widely used sources for borrowing start-up capital.

## Characteristics: A Summary

The fastest growing business sectors in 1992 included wholesale trade firms, business services, health services, and specialty trade contractors. Only 4 percent of the firms were incorporated; however, they earned nearly 40 percent of the total $32 billion earned by all firms. Most businesses owned by African Americans in 1992 were sole proprietorships with no employees, and average annual gross earnings were $52,000.

Business owners tend to be middle-aged and married, and about 20 percent have at least one college degree. Most do not have a relative who is in business. For nearly all business owners, the business they owned in 1987 was their first business initiative. Nearly one-half of the business owners had ten or more years of work experience, and about one-fourth had some supervisory experience. Two-thirds started their businesses with less than five thousand dollars or with no funds at all.

The data paint an image of the traditional black-owned business that is similar to the one reflected in the literature and the American mind-set. It is a small mom-and-pop establishment with no employees, little or no start-up money, and with average earnings of fifty-two thousand dollars annually.

However, we know little about the 16 percent of firms that do have employees, or about how these firms earn 71.5 percent of the gross annual revenue. We also know little about the incorporated businesses, 4 percent of all firms, that earn 40 percent of the gross annual revenue, and the incorporated businesses are the emerging cornerstone of post–Civil Rights–era economic development for the African American community. Chapters 4 to 6 contain these owners' stories.

## Goals and Methodology

Chapters 4 to 6 graphically illustrate what it is like to be an African American entrepreneur. These chapters expose the issues that African American entrepreneurs must address in order to be successful, including (1) why they chose to start a business rather than remain in the traditional "good job"; (2) the specific steps they took to initiate their business; (3) their experience in gaining access to commercial sources of capital for start-up, operation, and expansion; (4) their experiences with business development agencies such as the Greater Detroit Business and Industrial Corporation, the Business Consortium Fund, and the Small Business Administration; and (5) the extent of community involvement, including philanthropic activities and the use of coethnic employees, vendors, and mentoring. The illuminating experiences of this group of successful entrepreneurs in emerging business fields can serve as a guide for entrepreneurs of the future.

The entrepreneurs serving as the subjects of this discussion are primarily business owners who had successfully borrowed capital from the Greater Detroit Business and Industrial Corporation (BIDCO) or the Business Consortium Fund, New York City (BCF). The BIDCO and the BCF are innovative approaches to financing minority businesses. Almost all businesses served by BIDCO and BCF are considered to be high-risk loan applicants by commercial banks and, therefore, were rejected by them.

The Detroit BIDCO is somewhat similar to an SBA Specialized Small Business Investment Company. It is privately owned by fourteen African American investors and managed by a highly educated and trained staff headed by Catherine Lockhart. Operations began in 1990 with $6 million in debt capital and $653,000 in investment capital. By June 1992, BIDCO had made seven investment loans to start-up minority businesses. The BIDCO provides

1. equity capital to minority businesses (and to nonminority businesses located in economically depressed areas of Michigan) for acquisition, start-up, operation, expansion, and contract financing;
2. capital in the form of long- and short-term debt;
3. guarantees to loans made by third parties, usually banks;
4. general management and technical assistance to businesses.

The BCF, founded in 1989 and directed by Marcial Robiou, takes a different approach to meeting the capital needs of minority entrepreneurs. BCF provides only contract financing. To qualify for BCF financing, a minority business must have won a contract to provide goods and/or services to a Fortune 500 corporation or other eligible government unit.

Fortune 500 companies, contributing members of BCF, support the collective social goal to establish a solid core of minority suppliers. Toward that end, corporations have invested a total of $18,343,275 in the BCF loan fund at no cost to the BCF. Therefore, BCF started with considerable equity capital, unlike BIDCO, which started with considerable debt capital. BCF's only debt was a Ford Foundation investment loan of $1.5 million at a rate of 3 percent, which was repaid in full in December 1993, and an investment loan from the Michigan Strategic Fund of $500,000 at a rate of 9 percent that is still owed. BCF is in the highly enviable position of having relatively few fund-related expenses and making loans only to ongoing businesses with an existing contract to provide goods and/or services to America's largest corporations. By June 1992, BCF had made 114 contract-financing loans to minority businesses.

I met with the CEOs of BIDCO and BCF to identify the businesses to be studied. The 114 selected businesses received a mail survey. Based on the survey results, and in consultation with the CEOs, a number of the businesses were selected to participate in the in-depth interviews.

Chapters 4, 5, and 6 contain the stories of entrepreneurs in emerging businesses as told by the entrepreneurs during their interviews. As you read these life stories, consider four issues that may affect the experience of African American entrepreneurs: business size, longevity, geographic location, and the owner's gender.

The first issue is the size of the business. Only businesses with a minimum gross annual revenue of approximately $1 million by 1992 are included. Using such a criterion excludes traditional businesses and limits this study to the top .5 percent of black-owned businesses in the United States.

The second issue is businesses longevity. Businesses were selected to determine if and/or how the experiences of entrepreneurs in newly established businesses differed from those in businesses started earlier, when Civil Rights laws were not as well formulated. For the purposes of this discussion, first-generation businesses are those in operation for less than ten years; second-generation businesses have been in operation for ten or more years.

Businesses were also selected by region—East, Central, and West—to identify whether entrepreneurs in one region have greater access to capital, markets, and so forth than those in another region.

The final issue is gender. Do female African American entrepreneurs have a more or less difficult experience than males in initiating and sustaining a business? Keep these issues in mind as you read the interviews.

Thirty in-person interviews with entrepreneurs were conducted between June 1992 and August 1993. Where possible, the gender of the interviewer matched that of the entrepreneur. The average interview lasted about one and a half hours. Some interviews required more time and/or were conducted with two partners, sometimes in more than one location. Some businesses that did not meet the size criteria, and a few incomplete interviews, are not included in the final analysis. Some business owners had similar experiences and were omitted to reduce redundancy. Six of the business owners interviewed had no relationship through BIDCO or BCF at the time of the interviews. Eleven businesses that met the established criteria were selected for inclusion in this book.

From the stories of these African American entrepreneurs, one is able to gain a sense of their individual and collective experiences during the post–Civil Rights era. These success stories, which have been condensed without compromising substance or speaking style, are incredibly informative and compelling and provide a comprehensive view of how African American entrepreneurs become successful.

# PART 2

# The Life Stories of Entrepreneurs

4

# Starting a Business

## THE EAST REGION

The decision to start an incorporated business is likely to be complex and difficult for many African Americans coming of age during the Civil Rights era, because they had fewer business role models in their communities and limited experience in corporate business operations. Consequently, it is important to understand how and why African American entrepreneurs made the decision to start a business.

One example of a community with limited opportunities at the dawn of the Civil Rights era was River Town, Indiana, with a population of 150,000 (7.5 percent African American, 92.5 percent Caucasian). A young adult African American at that time had experienced segregation in schools and public accommodations. Employment opportunities were limited to service jobs and some blue-collar employment. A few professional blacks taught in segregated schools or worked in the post office. Two African American physicians, one dentist, and no attorneys served this community.

The few African American–owned businesses in River Town served a coethnic clientele. The businesses included a shoe shop, gas station, funeral parlor, two pool halls, several small restaurants, beauty parlors, barber shops, and fighting taverns. Characteristic of this era, it is not likely that any of these businesses were incorporated. For black businesses, access to capital from banks was nonexistent. By the 1980s, no River Town bank had made a conventional loan to a black-owned business.

Also characteristic of the time, African American parents encouraged their young to "get a good education, and then get a good job" rather than to start a business. As a feature of the post–Civil Rights era, African Americans now consider entrepreneurship as one among many career alternatives: "First get a good education and then a good job. Then start a good business."

Why do individuals consider entrepreneurship? The literature identifies several "push-pull" factors as major motivators. A significant push factor, job dissatisfaction, predisposes one to consider entrepreneurial activity. An extremely dissatisfied employee may perceive entrepreneurship as the only viable employment alternative. The predominant pull factor is an inflated sense of personal gratification commonly associated with independent entrepreneurship. Employees with substantial experience and marketable skills are more likely to leave a job to start a business because of new opportunities rather than job dissatisfaction. Such individuals leverage their experience and skills to increase their income.

Alfred Osborne Jr. (1975) characterized the entrepreneurship decision as a choice between two income streams. Individuals satisfied by earning a set wage each year stay in the good job. Those who crave larger economic profits start their own business.

Another factor African Americans must consider is discrimination. The history of African people in America highlights the importance of considering the impact of racial discrimination on a business before making the decision to start one. Racial discrimination in the pre–Civil Rights era was so prevalent that business success for African Americans was more a factor of the regional racial climate than of business acumen. Although they have greater economic rights in the post–Civil Rights era, African Americans are still influenced by racial issues in making business decisions, unlike many other ethnic groups who never have to consider race when making business decisions.

This chapter explores how five African American entrepreneurs in the East region—Charles McCampbell (Heritage Paper), Ellen Ann Sanders (Sumanco, Inc.), Albert and Sharon DeMagnus (Computer

Management Services, Inc.), and Hamilton Bowser Sr. (Evanbow Construction)—made the decision to start a business.

CASE 1
## Heritage Paper Company—
## Charles McCampbell

*Heritage Paper Company is located in Newark, New Jersey. Charles McCampbell, age fifty-five, started the company in 1979.*

### THE EARLY YEARS

About his early life and starting Heritage, McCampbell said:

I was born in Columbus, Ohio, and raised by my grandmother. Although I am an only child, I grew up with aunts and uncles who were like brothers and sisters because they were close in age.

Even though I was the product of a broken home, my mother and father were in constant contact. My father owned and managed quite a few properties in the town. He was probably the biggest influence in preparing me to cope with life and exposing me to business problems, such as maintenance, rent collection, and how people care for rental property.

My mother was quite supportive. Since I was raised by her mother, my contact with her was continual. My mother was a professional for the state of Ohio Welfare Division. My father left school in sixth grade but was a very worldly person. He believed in communicating his experiences to me, formally and informally. At least once a month, he scheduled get-togethers with me and my friends just to talk about life.

From my father, I learned money management, the topic he preached most about. Earn a dollar, but save fifty cents. He believed that if you could buy something for a nickel and sell it for a dime, you would be all right. So he was very conscious about expenditures on his property. In effect, he was monitoring a serious cash-flow program, although he didn't call it that.

I worked at an early age in variety of jobs, from caddying to a paper route to setting up my own little business. In my junior year, I washed walls and windows in suburbia and in inner-city restaurants. I employed several of my friends. The business was set up primarily to earn money to buy a yearbook and pay senior fees, but it proved to be profitable, so we expanded.

In 1955, I went to Bowling Green State University in Bowling Green,

Ohio, on an athletic scholarship. I majored in sociology and psychology and participated in ROTC, which required me to go on active duty in the army. I was commissioned as a second lieutenant and went into the army in 1959, where I stayed for twenty years and thirty days. I retired with the rank of major.

The army also sent me to graduate school. I earned a master's degree in procurement and contract administration from the Florida Institute of Technology and another in public administration from a graduate school in New York. In addition to the education opportunities, the military exposed me early on to very responsible leadership positions, not only over money and very expensive equipment, but people.

## DECISION TO START A BUSINESS

Heritage Paper Company is a fine paper distribution business. Fine paper is used for printing, xerography, copying, computers, and fax machines. The company does not carry paper products, which includes toilet tissue and towels, for example. We operate as a direct-mill merchant representing one of the biggest international paper manufacturers in the world. We also distribute for Hammermill Paper Company. Our New Jersey operation covers the New York metropolitan area, the southern part of Connecticut, and into Maryland and eastern Pennsylvania. We have a similar operation in Dallas, Texas, that covers the Dallas–Fort Worth area. But essentially, I refer to the company as a glorified paper route. We order paper by the truckload from the manufacturer who then brings it to our warehouse. We redistribute the paper to our customers as they request it, both under contract and through spot business.

During my eighteenth year in the army, I decided that I wanted to enter business after I retired two years later. Become my own person, so to speak. My biggest problem was deciding what business to start. Once I decided on the wholesale fine paper distribution business, I began investigating that industry about a year before retirement.

When I was about forty, I felt that I had endured a very structured, bureau-cratic, protected kind of life in the military where others make decisions that affect your life, whether or not you agree with the decisions. For example, I received orders to report to Vietnam on Christmas Day. I felt that anybody really concerned about me and my family would have never given me an assign-ment like that on Christmas Day. I knew that I would be happier if I was in a position where I could make the decisions and live with the consequences. They would be my decisions as opposed to someone else's.

### GETTING STARTED

In preparation, I spent the better part of two years prior to retirement looking at business issues, reading case studies, talking to business people.

Since my specialty in the army was procurement and contract administration, I worked with many business people. I recall meeting Charlie Moss, a black entrepreneur in the oil-distribution business. If you combined his two companies, they would probably be on the top of *Black Enterprise* magazine's top one hundred businesses. I talked to him extensively regarding the problems he encountered being in business and maintaining his position.

I wanted to learn all about the SBA 8(a) program and how I could use it once I retired from the army, so I wrote my graduate thesis on it. As a result of conducting my research, I met quite a few minority entrepreneurs. From them, I learned what to expect once I went into business.

I initially applied for incorporation in New Jersey. I remember having to name the business. My wife and I listed six different names. We put the top few on the application. And it came back approved as Heritage Paper Company.

### ACCESS TO CAPITAL

When we started, my total investment in the firm was about $1,200 of personal funds at the time. We had no contracts. The first year our grand total was about $80,000. At the end of the first year, we probably had somewhere around $2,500 in retained earnings and no debt.

I applied for a $25,000 loan for operating capital from Midlantic Bank in Fairfield, New Jersey. Even though I was a customer of the bank, my loan was not approved at that time. They said it was denied because we were a new business and had no track record. Certainly, the bank was obligated to only provide loans to proven companies because they were lending somebody else's money. That's the story I got. I had to use my own money and sell my receivables on a factor's basis, so to speak, thereby giving up some of my profits in exchange for operating capital.

As a result of our membership in the New York–New Jersey Minority Purchasing Council, we became aware of the Business Consortium Fund and its relationship with the National Minority Supplier Development Council.

We decided to apply for a loan with BCF although we were now established enough to have acquired bank financing through Midlantic Bank. We recognized, however, that BCF would give us a better interest rate. My wife and I are personally responsible for the loan. All receivables are collateral. The loan is at prime, 8 percent, with a twelve-month credit line that's reevaluated annually.

The BCF had a positive impact on my business because it reduced the amount of interest I paid on business loans. We went from paying 1.5 percent over prime to prime, a 1.5 percent savings.

We use BCF funds primarily to facilitate doing business with corporate members of the National Minority Supplier Council. That's what it's designed to do. We are under contract with several of the companies that belong to and have put money into BCF, such as AT&T, Southwestern Bell Telephone, and Frito Lay.

I think BCF is a tremendous idea. It provides a business person like myself with access to capital under terms and conditions not usually available through a commercial bank.

I've gotten literature from the SBA. I got a lot of help from them when I was writing my graduate thesis on the 8(a) program. But other than that, I have not needed anything from them. I am considering right now applying for the 8(a) program, but I have not done that.

We don't have any government contracts. We never had a set-aside contract. We have gotten some opportunities to quote offers under the guise of these programs, or offering minorities opportunities. But we have not to date had any set-aside contracts.

### REVENUE, ACCOUNTING, AND INVENTORY

In 1990, the gross annual revenue was $4.2 million, and around $3.6 million in 1991. Our business has decreased during the last few years. In 1992, it was $2.6 million; 1993, it was $1.9 million; and 1994 the gross annual revenue was $2.2 million; but in 1995 we expect to be somewhere around $5 million.

It took about three years to get profitable. To get there, we set up ways to closely monitor and control overhead. We have a good relationship with our landlord in an adequate, but not fancy, warehouse operation. I have specifically and intentionally avoided moving into a modern, fancy facility just for appearances. Our product has a good shelf life. It needs to be maintained in a dry and clean facility, and that's what we've done. We also make sure that our equipment is maintained.

In addition, we constantly monitor manufacturers' price changes. Paper is heavily discounted depending on purchase volume. Customers who buy six hundred tons of paper a year are apt to get a better price from the manufacturer than those who only buy twenty tons. To protect your profitability, you need to have a continuing dialogue with the inside mill person who informs you about paper discounts.

For example, I bid on a one-year fixed-price contract with a large firm in New York; they insisted on no changes. During the term of the contract, the market went soft, so my costs dropped and my profit margin increased from 9 percent to 24 percent. I had no obligation to adjust the price with that company. Had the market gone the other way, I would have been stuck. However, we try not to get into situations where we could lose money or have to walk away from a contract that's not profitable.

Inventory control is computerized. We have reorder points for every product line item. For instance, when our stock of 8½-inch-by-11-inch white copy paper gets to a certain level, it's reordered. We also know how long it takes for reordered paper to come in the door. That does change over a period of time. Keeping track of the lead time is one of my wife's responsibilities as vice-president for administration. When paper comes in, it is logged into the computer. The record indicates the warehouse and location in the warehouse where it's stored, and the acquisition cost and date. So keeping track of inventory is not a problem. However, keeping the right inventory is more of a problem. That's always a guess, but we're getting more professional as the years go by.

One person is responsible for monitoring receivables. We get a weekly printout that reports account aging. On contracts where customers agree to pay us within thirty days but don't, we make phone calls on day thirty-one. We also select our customers carefully. We don't respond to just anybody calling up saying they want a truckload of paper. We investigate references, D&B reports, and we actually call prior suppliers to find out about their payment history.

Our accounting systems are handled by the same firm we've employed for the twelve years we've been in business. Besides getting advice when we need it, they prepare our quarterly and annual reports.

Our competitors are other paper distributors who, like us, are direct representatives of manufacturers. Some small office-supply houses and, of course, the large superstores, such as Staples, are competitors.

To be competitive, we try to be responsive, to deliver product immediately if not sooner. And, we are linked by telefax to the offices of a couple of our larger customers, and we're also implementing an EDI system, where users can order directly from us. And it's our strategy and belief that setting up that kind of operation will endear us to the customer, simply because they've gone through some outside arrangements in order to get this in place. We're hoping that they get very comfortable with the system and continue to use us.

We've done a market analysis. We don't do any advertising on a routine basis. We found that the direct approach has been more beneficial, along with attending various business fairs that these purchasing people might attend. Our manufacturers do national advertising for the product. Most people are familiar with Hammermill paper, for example. But we make direct contact with our customers, by correspondence and appointments.

## COMMUNITY LINKAGES AND INVOLVEMENT

### Customers, Suppliers, and Employees

Our customer target group is the Fortune 1,000 companies. We found our own niche in the paper business, and that is those corporations that have what is referred to as in-plant printing operations. They are large firms that have copy centers within their walls, and we supply them with the paper. We ignore, to some extent, the small paper users, like the storefront copy centers and printers, the one-to-five-carton-order business. We have not pursued it, primarily because it takes a lot of time to monitor that kind of business, and to be responsive to it. You almost have to have a dedicated person.

Less than 2 percent of my business is with minorities, a few Hispanics, Asians, and blacks. No Native Americans. Ninety-eight percent plus of my business is with whites.

We have not used black or other minority suppliers. We have seven employees, four black, one Asian, one white and one Arab. We advertised in the newspaper, and word of mouth from current employees.

### Role Models

I didn't have a role model, but I did have some sort of mentor assistance just getting into the paper business; getting in a position to receive paper from a manufacturer. This particular person was an officer I had worked for when I was in the army, who left the army and took a very senior position with this paper manufacturer that became my first source of supply.

### Succession

I hope to retire in the next three to four years. We plan to put a couple of young people now working for us in the position to manage at some point down the road. It will depend on their maturation and development, and when I'm comfortable with giving up some of my responsibilities.

### BARRIERS

I haven't had any problem getting insurance, but getting bonding was a problem. Fortunately, we haven't had many occasions where it was required. When we did need it, we couldn't get it in time. We were bidding with the City of Philadelphia, and we contacted some bonding companies in New Jersey. They suggested that we use the company that provided our business insurance. We finally issued a certified check as a bonding commitment in order to bid.

Initially, availability of finance and capital was a barrier. And secondly, getting into a particular field on an equitable basis was a barrier. My surprise in trying to enter the paper business after spending twenty years in the army, supposedly defending this free-enterprise system in the United States, was shocking when I attempted to just buy paper directly from the mills. I thought it would be easy to do. I found out that not only was it not easy, it was next to impossible to get into that particular game of distributing fine paper. And to this day, to my knowledge, there are only three or four minorities who are distributing paper in the country, on a direct-mill basis. Even our company, we've only been able to acquire two major mills that will sell directly to us in twelve years. So it's a closed kind of game. For minority people to get an opportunity to buy on a direct basis, so they can compete with the established dealers who've been out there for a hundred years, that's a problem.

### ADVICE TO FUTURE ENTREPRENEURS

For anyone considering going into business, I think business is the key thing that this country understands. I think we should pursue business with vigor, because I think it's the only way to acquire an equitable piece of this pie. As long as we continue to take nine-to-five jobs, we won't make a tremendous difference because we won't have the capital that is recognized as power in this country.

### THE FUTURE OF HERITAGE PAPER

My immediate goal is to deal with this economy, to keep the customers I have, and acquire some more. That's a problem because this business is almost viciously competitive. Even if you have a contract, some competitors are trying to grab those contracts by offering better deals even in the middle of your contract. We've lost some business that way. We've struggled to win a contract on a competitive basis, only to have it terminated —even with major companies—because somebody on the outside gave them a better price.

Another aspect is payment. People and corporations sign contracts committing to you, you do your part, and you may or may not be paid on time. Instead of paying in thirty days as they contracted, they might pay in forty-five. You have to decide whether to complain. If you do, you subject yourself to possible termination at some point for whatever reason by some disgruntled buyer who says that you're being "uppity" for complaining that you haven't been paid on time, as they agreed.

You're always faced with those decisions. Do you rock the boat, or do you stay passive and watch your business fail because somebody who doesn't care about you or the agreement they've signed can make a decision that affects your ability to survive.

Survival, that's what you're talking about in business—surviving. The only way to survive is to make sure that you get yourself into situations that are not detrimental to you. I'm talking about contracts, leases, employment arrangements. Make sure they're not taking advantage of you. And if they are, stay aware, and know when it becomes dangerous. At that point, get away from it or reject it somehow. That's what I try to do. Not to say that I haven't been surprised before, but I certainly try to anticipate what those surprises will be.

### CASE 2
## Sumanco, Inc.—Ellen Ann Saunders

*Sumanco is a commercial furniture business located in Philadelphia, Pennsylvania. Ellen Ann Saunders, forty-nine, CEO and president, started the business in 1984.*

## THE EARLY YEARS

I grew up in Bluefield, West Virginia, a small college town that is the home of Bluefield State College, then a predominantly black college, and Bluefield College, a white college. My mother and father, who both went to Bluefield State College, graduated as teachers with bachelor's degrees. We were middle class. I'm the oldest of seven. We're a close-knit family, even though we live all over the country.

My mother is a pioneer, a woman with vision. She wanted us to do something different, so she moved us in that direction. When I was growing up, I was probably the first papergirl in town. When I was eleven, I made papier-mâché dolls that I sold for Christmas. My mother was a strong force in shaping my destiny.

During my childhood, Bluefield was a segregated community. Blacks lived on one side and whites on the other. My elementary, junior high, and high schools were all black schools. In the local theaters, blacks sat in the balconies and the whites sat down front. Restaurants, too, were segregated, and that became a Civil Rights issue for us. When I was in my first year of high school, we experienced the whole Civil Rights movement, which I think helped shape my ideas.

I went to Bluefield State, majored in music and political science, and earned a B.A. degree in 1968. Then I moved to Philadelphia, became a social worker in the Welfare Department, and became involved in the union and labor movements. And I think that, too, was a big influence in my life.

## DECISION TO START A BUSINESS

At the time I worked for Philadelphia's Welfare Department, I began to position myself to move up. I was fortunate because I advanced through the system quickly. I knew that, eventually, I wanted to be in business, but I didn't know what I wanted to do.

I had become the director of training for the Welfare Department and an assistant to the Philadelphia regional representative. I held management positions for ten of the fifteen years I worked for the Department of Welfare. I really enjoyed my work, but I had some experiences that motivated me to leave. Although I had a boss, I also had a great deal of flexibility. I wasn't as closely supervised as most people, because it wasn't really necessary for what we were doing. I felt as if I were my own boss. So I knew that moving into a corporate situation or moving within the system into something different was going to stifle me.

At that time, we were designing and implementing management-training programs for staff. I represented the department on a number of boards. That moved me in the direction to where I knew that, ultimately, I did want to be in business. I had moved through the system to where there was no place else for me to go. And, I didn't want to start another employer-employee relationship.

### GETTING STARTED

So I went to Antioch University at night and weekends and, in 1981, I earned a master's degree in organizational development with a concentration in business. We learned decision making, problem solving, and leadership skills. I also studied a construction firm, thinking I might go into the construction industry. I knew there were not many of us, especially females, in construction. But after careful research, I knew that my personality and disposition were not a good match for that industry. That's when I started looking at the office-supply industry.

I initially started an office-supply business because I felt there were no females or blacks in the office-supply industry in the Philadelphia region. It was a good idea, but at the time we were in the middle of a recession. Profit margins were decreasing rapidly because of competition from the office-supply superstores and the many purchasing co-ops that were formed by corporations. After three years, I knew that I would have to get out of office supplies or go out of business. So I started to look at the furniture industry. Like office supplies, the furniture industry is a closed industry. In order to sell to major corporations, I knew that I had to become a contract dealer for a major manufacturer. That took time. Most of these dealerships are decided by the corporate headquarters or their regional headquarters. Their decision is based on the geographic marketing conditions of area, just how many dealerships they are going to have. Furthermore, many had no minority businesses at that time in their dealer network. It was an uphill battle to get that in place.

I contacted a number of manufacturers. For about five years, I wrote to Steelcase, for example, the largest manufacturer in the industry, and never got any real results, primarily because they felt they had enough dealerships in this area and did not need another. But I started with them anyway because they were the biggest, had a presence in the city, because a lot of the major corporations were buying Steelcase. It seemed smarter for me to contact the manufacturers that were doing well in Philadelphia.

At that time, about 1985 or 1986, Philadelphia became the hottest area in the country for furniture dealerships. The dealer network was growing rapidly because of commercial development in and around Philadelphia. Many of the manufacturers, such as Steelcase, Hayworth, Westinghouse Knoll, Herman Miller, Verco, Holland, for example, had few blacks in their dealer network. Over the last three years, more minorities have become involved because more municipalities and major corporations now require minority and female-owned participation in the purchasing process. But there were few when I started.

We're Hayworth dealers. We are contract dealers, offer design services, provide modular furniture, which many companies are looking at now. We plan a person's work space and environment, so I have a space planner on staff. If you want to furnish your office in systems furniture, the space planner talks to your staff and gets a sense of what type of modular configuration you need. Normally, it's determined by the task and the function of each person within that office environment. She'll develop a modular schematic, show it to the staff, make modifications, and then we place an order for product. That's how we do space planning.

As contract dealers, we provide services more so than product. The industry has moved away from inventoried product. Most of our customers in municipalities and corporations purchase customized furniture. And because of that, design service is crucial. We also do interior design, reupholstery, and window treatments.

Money was the major factor to consider before going into this business. And also I entered an industry in which I had studied but had never worked—the office-supply industry. That was another major factor. Once I was in the industry, I discovered that there weren't many blacks and the industry itself had some problems with blacks being in it.

As a part of the master's course of study, we wrote a thesis on the particular industry we were looking at. We had to incorporate an actual work setting into the academic portion. The first rule of thumb is to develop a business plan. That sounds good on paper, but in reality, once I developed that business plan, specifically the financing portion of it, that's when the roadblocks jumped up and out at me. What I lacked was the real-life experience of actually being in business. You're confronted with issues that you think you're prepared for, but you're really not. You haven't been there and you don't have a family history of people who will know what you're confronting.

### ACCESS TO CAPITAL

When I started this business, I took my business plan to the Mellon Bank with the hopes of getting capital. They referred me to the Philadelphia Commercial Development Corporation [PCDC], an organization which worked with start-up businesses. PCDC, in turn, referred me to the low-interest loan program of the state of Pennsylvania, designed to fund minority businesses. But I felt that program was not really designed to help small businesses, especially minority-owned. It took a year just to hear that I had been rejected for the loan because of the type of business I was in.

After approaching lots of banks, I realized that Philadelphia was gradually shifting from a manufacturing orientation to a big business orientation. Many of the banks did not work with small business. It was too time-consuming. It was not in what they perceived to be their best interest. As far as minority businesses were concerned, by the time I came into business, the banks had no real desire to do business with blacks.

I'll tell you what I found. I thought I had a good business plan with good cash-flow projections, especially from 1986 to 1987 and on. I went to seminars to learn how to create cash flows and how to read a balance sheet. I was invited by one bank to participate in a seminar designed for women in business. I was the only black female there. I quickly found that my set of issues was different from those of the other women there.

I felt that my loan applications were not considered seriously. The banks were not interested in start-up businesses or businesses less than three years old. If you wanted a credit line of twenty thousand dollars, you had to put up collateral of twenty thousand dollars. This is still going on.

When our present governor was elected, he held a small business conference and invited a number of banks. There were women's groups, large groups of black business people who attended. We asked the governor to tell us how he was going to ensure that women and blacks receive their fair share of the business loans, and how do we go about it? The comments we heard were that banks are set up for large businesses, not for small businesses.

I saw instances where banks loaned just enough for a company to fail, and people did not know how to walk away from that. If you know you need a $120,000 loan and you only get $60,000, you are doomed for failure. Many people did not know nor understand that they were in trouble. I think, too, that we're more intimidated when we approach the bank. They are supposed to provide us with a service, but by our thinking, we're there to provide them with a service.

I used about $20,000 from my personal savings to start the office-supply business. You learn that you don't have to eat and that you can live by credit cards. I knew that $20,000 wasn't enough to do it right. I needed about $100,000. But I encountered other obstacles with the office-supply business. One was establishing the lines of credit with the suppliers. In a way, it might have worked out for the best, because with $100,000, I would have ended up sending out supplies on COD, which they would have stretched out forever.

As a black company in a white industry, they immediately thought that I was going to be selling to the federal government or to the city. They don't want to sell to you if you're selling to the government or to the city. Basically what they were saying is, we don't want to sell to you, period. I think that selling to the federal government and the city wasn't really the issue. They didn't see too many of us interacting with the major corporations, and that's where I wanted to go.

That turned out to be an effective method of blocking. I talked to people in New York and in different parts of the country. To really establish an office-supply business, you had to have catalogues. Without catalogues, you couldn't sell to corporations. The only place to get the catalogues was from a handful of major wholesalers. They had criteria for being able to buy their products, which might have been fifteen thousand dollars' worth of inventory. But they define the criteria for inventory and what it means. The definition might change, the closer you got to establishing that inventory. These ways were effective in blocking attempts to get established in a particular industry. What I finally did was have a law firm write letters to suppliers and ask for their criteria for inventory.

One thing in my favor was my labor experience and knowing how to deal with the Establishment. Since I saw them as the Establishment, I thought, we'd battle this one out.

I started off in a business incubator. While I was there we had group meetings with several banks. One bank's [Continental] representative happened to be an AME [African Methodist Episcopalian]. One thing you learn in business is to develop a support system; people have to look out for each other. When I met with this particular bank officer, I told her what I was going through. So after I was in business for about a year, she gave me a $10,000 loan at about 11 percent interest to use for cash flow and inventory. It was still not enough, but it was better than what I was getting. My personal net worth was about $100,000. I owned my home, and in 1984, the equity was about $55,000.

Shortly after going through Continental, I was awarded a contract with the state of Pennsylvania for $1.2 million. I needed approximately $150,000 to finance the contract, and I wanted to use that contract for collateral. Fidelity Bank agreed to a loan, but would only lend $60,000.

At the time I had the loan with Fidelity Bank, the Business Consortium Fund had just started but had no relationships with any Philadelphia banks. I went from bank to bank but found that they were not interested in doing business with minority companies. So I introduced the Business Consortium Fund to Fidelity. I told the bank that the BCF program will provide 75 percent of the funds and the bank the other 25 percent. This greatly reduced the bank's risk, if that was their major concern. I got a contract for duplication supplies from University of Penn, a participating BCF member. I asked Fidelity for a loan against the contract as collateral. I don't know what Fidelity did with the application, but after months they still had not decided.

Other banks I approached were not interested in the BCF program. I also discussed the BCF with representatives of Meridian Bank at the Pennsylvania Chamber of Commerce dinner. Meridian was moving into Philadelphia. Real pioneers, they were very proactive in working with minority businesses and wanted to be visible in Philadelphia. Meridian became the BCF bank! In less than four weeks, they had the BCF funds in place. I became the first recipient of BCF dollars in Philadelphia. The loan was only $70,000, at about 11 percent. With Meridian, I was able to establish a credit line in addition to the BCF. It was a $200,000 line at about 11 percent. I put up my house, my life, everything I owned as collateral. The loan is now paid off, and I'm considering going back to BCF.

The BCF loan helped us get beyond a difficult point in the business. Now profitability has gone the other way because of the slim profit margins—people are giving away products. But BCF helped a lot.

## REVENUE, ACCOUNTING, AND INVENTORY

Our gross annual revenue in 1990 was $1.1 million; $900,000 in 1991; and about $1.7 million in 1992. We also just got a contract for $1 million per year for five years.

We're still in a deep discounting mode, which has not been helpful. Since we are only eight years old with only five years in furniture, we are the new kids on the block. Although our volume is high, our margins are low. That's not going to give us the profitability we need. So I've got to be very creative.

Many of my competitors are going out of business. This is a very competitive industry, and Philadelphia was a very competitive market that's now turning down. It went down very quickly in 1989.

I operated differently from my industry peers basically because of my academic background. I never stocked a warehouse full of furniture that was difficult to get rid of, because people's desires change. Because I didn't, my administrative cost was much lower. For large projects, I could subcontract the installation to another company and not carry the overhead, which made a world of difference.

I also have people doing multiple tasks. The manufacturer requires dealers to specialize; however, to provide one-stop shopping, you would need a staff large enough to provide all specific services. That's an astronomical expense that I resisted carrying. They didn't force me to do it the way the others do it, but I don't think they quite understood what I was doing. Now, it's become the wave of the future.

The new buzz words are "lean" and "mean." All along, I felt you could do it without all that inventory. A lot of companies spend off inventory. All you do is sit on it. So I think that's helped a great deal.

Our accounting process is computerized, but Connors Associates, an external CPA, does the bookkeeping. ADP [Automated Data Processing] does our payroll. The bill paying is still internal, but Connors supports that. I keep that internal because of the economy. We get a biweekly ADP report because our payroll's biweekly. Connors gives us biweekly information, but they do reports on a monthly basis.

I worked with the West Philadelphia Project, an extension of the Wharton School. They've done marketing studies for us. Each year we review the marketplace and try to do new cash-flow projections based on what is and what is not coming annually. Then we look at where we are. What we've achieved, what we didn't achieve, and why. So I usually have a good picture of what the next year will bring, because we try to project based on real work as opposed to what might be out there.

We advertise in the business journal a couple times a year. We also advertise in publications that look for female-owned minority businesses, and we're in the yellow pages. We used to have a big advertisement in the yellow pages, but it turned out to be a waste of money.

Media advertising is not always the way to go. When people are looking for certain products, they don't look where you think they're going to look. They'll either look to their network or a directory. Rarely do they go to the media.

We try to target markets that have money and are not difficult to market to in terms of advertising strategy. We have started to emerge because some dealers are downsizing and others are disappearing. We're using our existing support system and network to get our name out there as well as some of the visible projects we have done. People want to see furniture, especially systems furniture, before they buy. When it comes to systems, the key to a successful project is the design and installation.

We try to sell to people at the top. I'm not sure it's that way in other cities, but especially in Philadelphia, if you want to do a major project, the influence comes from the top down. You will never do it through purchasing departments. I shouldn't say never, but it is more difficult.

## COMMUNITY LINKAGES AND INVOLVEMENT

Our planning includes being involved in the community. Our printing services and computer services are done by black companies. In fact, our large computer system was put together by a black company. Our insurance agent is black. We buy almost everything from black companies. My copier, that is half a century old, I bought from a black company, too. A group of us really tries to support each other. We identify a project and then we try to bring others into it.

### Customers and Employee Profile

Our customer base is the major corporations, municipalities, the state of Pennsylvania, and the universities. About 5 percent are minorities, if that much. There are seven employees—two men, four women. Of the four women, one is white and everyone else is African American.

### Community Activities

I've been involved in numerous community organizations, such as New PENDEL, which is the Regional Purchasing Council for BCF. I'm also involved in Philadelphia Citizens, the AME church organization, the Urban League. I've mentored a number of high school students. I'm now involved with a committee of the school board looking at the lack of minority female-owned business participation in the bid process and what they can do to ensure participation.

I have financially supported Mother Bethel AME Church and the United Negro College Fund. I also contribute to Mother Bethel's scholarship fund and the Lamplighters' fund for students going to college.

### BARRIERS

One of the reasons that I'm involved in black community activities is because we don't interact with the white community as often as we could. Our barriers are really not knowing how business is done from their perspective. Not that their perspective is correct, but really it's knowing how business is done.

We are often excluded from opportunities. I'll give you an example. At the school board, we're looking at why minorities aren't involved in the bid process. What we've found is that minority businesses are primarily forced to purchase products from wholesalers or wherever they can, so their prices are not competitive. It's not because minority businesses don't reach out, but they're not competitive because they've been excluded from the distributor network. And the companies who exclude offer a thousand reasons why minorities can't be a part of their network, such as financial strength and other factors they manage to get around with our white counterparts. The biggest obstacle is that we don't know how it's done and we've never seen it done, since we're not even in the loop. There are too many industries that exclude us that we don't even look at—food service, sports equipment. Consequently, we're not in those industries.

I overcame the barriers just by not going away or giving up, by being tenacious, learning their systems, and trying to understand how it's done. I feel blocked when I don't understand, so I try to get beyond it to understand how it works. They may tell me it works one way, even when I know it works another. I've tried to get beyond the information barrier.

Information is kept from us. That's a major, major barrier in doing business successfully. If you don't have the information, you can't do business.

### ADVICE TO FUTURE ENTREPRENEURS

I would say that the barriers I experience as a black female are the same for black males—lack of information and not being accepted as part of the business system. I felt that much of it was because I was black. I see white females work around a lot of things. If the newcomer is a black person, they'll see color before they see anything else. It just raises a red flag, but it shouldn't deter us. I think we can turn that around and make that a positive, too. There are so few of us out there, and we're becoming fewer in number.

Know yourself. Being an entrepreneur is stressful. You have to know your breaking point. If you know that, it helps you get beyond the barriers you have to overcome. Second, I always tell students that no doesn't always mean no. Often, we're turned away from a project only because the purchasing people question whether we're really serious. So I've learned that no sometimes means maybe.

### CASE 3

## Computer Management Services, Inc.— Albert and Sharon DeMagnus

*Albert and Sharon DeMagnus, husband and wife, own Computer Management Services, located in Burtonsville, Maryland. Albert, who started CMS in 1987, discusses his business experiences. Sharon's comments are included as well.*

### THE EARLY YEARS

*Albert:* I was born in Philadelphia, Pennsylvania, but I call Glassboro, New Jersey, home. My father, Albert A. DeMagnus, was a minister and a doctor, a renaissance person—he did a lot of things. My mother, Emily, was a practical nurse. She also helped him in his office. I was four years old when they divorced. I am the youngest of four children. I have three sisters. One lives in Philadelphia and one in Glassboro. The youngest is deceased.

I went into the military service at the age of seventeen. After completing three years, seven months, twenty-six days, and thirteen hours in the service, I worked for a short while with the electric company and then went into data processing. When I went to school for data processing, my lowest mark was a ninety. They asked me to stay on as a teacher, and I did.

When I pursued increasing my salary, I was told that I needed a college education. I went to Rutgers University because I was recruited by Dr. Jesse Paul Clay. Rutgers had a data-processing problem that I solved for them. When they couldn't pay me, they gave me an education instead. Dr. Clay later went to Howard University and has since retired. He lives down the street and is still a good friend.

After getting my degree from Rutgers University, I worked for a short time for the state of New Jersey, and then the U.S. Department of Labor in 1978, where I met my wife, Sharon. I had a marvelous time at the Department of Labor and achieved a number of major accomplishments. I guess the best was stopping riots in Puerto Rico by getting unemployment checks out on time. We did this by moving the governor to another building while making sure his computer stayed up and running. We also organized the Department of Labor's data processing procurement program as it related to all their other programs in Washington.

After leaving the Department of Labor, I worked for one vendor in the procurement program for about eighteen months. During the first year, I earned them $14 million gross. During the next six months, we were up to $18 million, and I realized it was time for me to leave. I went back to Howard University, where Dr. Clay was. For a time I worked from the president's office in data processing. But most of that time, I was thinking about how we could get into business.

*Sharon:* I never thought of being an entrepreneur growing up in Washington, D.C. My father owned several mom-and-pop stores, but they weren't successful because he took from the till. When I was in the eighth grade, I remember I had to write an autobiography. My uncle had already done a lot of research on our family and even had it published. My father told me it was in the Library of Congress. I read the little pamphlet about our family. So when I read that pamphlet, all the men on that side of the family wanted to have their own businesses. They did not want to work for anyone.

After I got my B.S. degree in business, I went for an M.B.A. because I wanted to help small businesses succeed. I knew that to succeed they had to invest all the money back into the business for at least five years. You can't take anything from the business; you've got to build it up.

I was working at a corporation at that time, where I stayed for thirteen years. I drove thirty-three miles one way to work. Although people told me I was doing a great job, they were not promoting me.

One day in 1990 I came home and was really fussing about the job. My husband said, "Resign on Monday and work with me." I agreed. We had talked about it before, but I didn't think I could work with him. I knew I could not stay where I was. If it did not work out with my husband, I would do something else. With an M.B.A., I should go to a large corporation. But after working for a small corporation, I think this is where a person should start because you get to use all of your skills. I really enjoy working here, but I never thought of being an entrepreneur.

### DECISION TO START A BUSINESS

*Albert:* When I was at the Department of Labor, I realized that I just wanted to work for myself. If I could do so much for other firms, I could do it for myself.

I was a project manager when I worked for the state of New Jersey. At the Department of Labor, I was at the GS-14 level, and at the Fortune 500 company, I was the management level. After I left Howard, I was a salesman at a company like CMS, and then I was at an executive level at an 8(a) firm.

An SBA seminar called "Success Seminar" helped me a lot. I had questions that needed answers—about business plans and financial plans concerning the corporation. I knew how to sell and how to run a business, but I did not know how to develop a business plan. At the seminar, I learned everything I needed to formalize Computer Management Services. I bought the tapes, took them home, and began one step at a time. Everything the narrator mentioned, I did. What you see presently is the result of the plans put together from that seminar.

We started Computer Management Services in 1987 as an S corporation. CMS provides systems integration services to Fortune 500 companies and the federal government. For Fortune 500 companies, we provide contract programmers and analysts. For government contracts, we provide the total project team. All of our work is in data processing—everything from large mainframe computers to PCs.

*Sharon:* A series of things caused Al to go into business. He probably doesn't remember them, but I do. A personality conflict pushed Al to leave the Fortune 500 company and go to Howard. Later he went to another company, similar to this business, where they kept dangling carrots. We always felt that it was racial. His supervisor could not see a black man making seventy-five thousand dollars a year. It was always, "Well, you've got to wait ninety more days."

From there he went to the 8(a) corporation. By now, Al had perfected his marketing expertise. He is a natural. But his performance review said he was too aggressive, that he always wanted to close the deal. That was so nonsensical. Isn't that what you're suppose to do? We talked about it, and I told him he should go out on his own. He said it could be tough. But with his background he could get back into data processing anywhere. Why not give it a year? He started in August 1987, and in October he had his first contract.

I had done much for the corporation I worked for. So much revolved around me, and I had so much authority. I was comfortable there. I had great benefits, "the good job"; however, they always gave me excuses instead of the title. Since I could not advance, I started promoting my nonexempt employees. One-third were working on their master's degrees. As they graduated and transferred to other facilities, they too were given excuses as to why they weren't promoted. They were black.

The straw that broke the camel's back was a young lady who had applied for a promotion three times. The second time they turned her down they told her that she had not read the *Fog,* which is comparable to saying "you have not read the *Encyclopedia Britannica.*" The next time she did not get promoted was because of cost accounting. However, they promoted a secretary who had just gotten her A.A. She was white. My nonexempt tried to overcome those things, but she said, "I can't take this. It's ruining my self-esteem." She quit without having another job. In her heart she knew she was doing the right thing. I felt helpless. Two months later, I just decided that nothing could be as bad as this. When I left, they asked me if there was anything that they could do to make me stay. But I had seen too much. It was time to go.

GETTING STARTED

*Albert:* First, we incorporated. Then we formalized the business plan, which included a financial plan and a marketing plan. Once the plans were written, we began marketing. The focus was very narrow in terms of what we were trying to accomplish. The financial plan indicated our dollar goals, what I call the "get out of bed" number. To make it worthwhile to get out of bed every morning, I needed to at least do this much work in this amount of time. There is also a "win" number—if we get this much, then heck, we're well on our way. I started the company on October 1, and by October 19, I believe, we placed our first person in a Fortune 500 company. We were very fortunate.

I did the business plan so I would know where I was headed. I had a lot of thoughts, but they weren't targeted or organized. I needed to stop going over things more than once. Basically, the plan let me know that I was headed in the right direction.

### ACCESS TO CAPITAL

We started this business by borrowing on my credit card. I think it was a total of about ten thousand dollars. Now, I am a very optimistic person. Realistically, that was not enough. We needed to have much more capital to sustain us than that. The bottom line is, we never missed any of our payments on any credit card or mortgage during that particular period, by the grace of God. That was only because we were fortunate enough to leave the jobs one week and the next week place somebody into an account. I should mention the fact that I did not take a salary until . . . I don't know how long when I started.

Then, I was just trying to get fifty thousand dollars at the bank. I had a guy on a contract for me and we started talking about money. I told him that the bank turned me down for a fifty-thousand-dollar line of credit because we weren't in business long enough. That guy officially started his business that day he was in my basement. One week later, he got fifty thousand dollars from a bank.

So how did he do that? Tell me. We had receivables, and we were willing to use our house as collateral. My net worth was maybe a half million, including property and savings. We were almost debt free. He had nothing; he lived in an apartment. All he had was his status as a majority person and a few small contracts that weren't worth nearly as much as mine. The bank figured he needed at least fifty thousand dollars and gave it to him. So, this is what we've run into. That is a fact of life.

*Sharon:* By 1991, I had already gone to three banks. Two indicated a real interest. One looked at our financial records and said we could get a $300,000 line of credit. I wanted a real line of credit based on receivables.

He said no problem. Then he called back. The loan committee only wanted to give us $75,000. Our receivables were already at $300,000. Not only did they not accept our receivables, we also had to put up our $300,000 house as collateral. "Is it because I am a minority?" I asked. He said no.

That same day I got a letter from Bell Atlantic about the Business Consortium Fund. If we had contracts with any member of the Minority Purchasing Council, we could get funding up to the amount of the contracts. The certified lender was the bank that had just turned us down.

I asked the banker why he didn't tell us about BCF. He knew that most of our clients were members of the Purchasing Council. We finally got the $300,000 line of credit based on our contracts. He even brought a photographer to the signing because we were their first loan under this program. True, they invested in us because their risk was 25 percent—the original $75,000 they wanted to extend to us. However, we were making their Community Reinvestment Program look good.

I don't think it occurred to them that they were not helping. If we were a white-owned company, I think their first inclination would be to investigate other options. Not so with a black-owned company. I am not saying they consciously wanted us to fail, but I think it is deep-rooted enough for them not to try all avenues to help us succeed.

We signed the papers in June. By August, I saw that we were getting more federal contracts. We needed additional financing. I called the bank and asked whether they were interested in being our banker beyond the BCF. When he said no, I told him we would be looking for another bank. By the end of August, he called back and wanted to take us to lunch.

The banker told us that in January they would probably be working more closely with SBA. I told him that wouldn't help us now. So he volunteered to turn over our file to the government unit. We met the new representative, a woman, in September. Now, I want to remind you that earlier in that year, the same bank said they would only give us $75,000. The woman banker said she did not have to go through a committee, she had signature authority, and she could give me a $1 million line of credit. I asked her what had happened between February and now to change the bank's position. She said they had to get to know us. I said, "Well, I don't need $1 million." So they could lend the money, but it had to do with us being a minority. You're never going to tell me that it didn't.

I see that attitude even on the federal side. During negotiations they said, for example, "We're taking a chance on you. The last time we worked with a minority firm." I said, "You mean you've never had a bad experience working with a white majority firm. Do you stop doing business with them?" You've got to look at us as individual firms.

Our BCF experience was basically very positive. Once we found out about BCF, I put the banker and Mr. Robiou [the head of BCF] into contact with one another. Shortly thereafter we had the picture taking session where we signed the papers and got financing.

*Albert:* We are an 8(a) firm. The experience of becoming an 8(a) was more than interesting. Some people helped us get our 8(a) classification. After getting it, I can agree with Mr. John Smith who said they don't appear to be helpful and the marketplace has a tremendously negative impression of 8(a)s. That needs to be changed. I don't know everything that goes on. At present, we are working as best we can with the SBA. There are always people willing to help and give their best, and then there are those who, instead of being proactive, find reasons why something should not happen.

There's no question that SBA must be changed. Let me give you an example. We had just given a bid to a company, and we knew our price was right. We had fourteen people already working there. We did not win. Let me take that back. They told us that we did not lose the bid; we just weren't selected. That meant we did win, but they gave it to someone else. That's the way this game is played in the real world. If they would have judged us by the quality of our work, services, and prices, we would have gotten the contract. They told us there was nothing wrong with our cost or our technical qualifications. We could not have done anything better. Nothing was lacking from our presentation. We just were not selected.

This incident lets you know that the programs out there are necessary. It is a shame that they are necessary, and, yes, we have gotten business from them. Unfortunately, the programs need more "teeth."

We provide quality service; we aim to satisfy our clients each and every time. If they would just judge us by our track record and if the playing field was level, I don't think we would have a problem getting business. If they would just consider us as a business.

REVENUE, ACCOUNTING, AND INVENTORY

Our gross annual revenue in 1991 was $2.5 million, and probably about $1.5 million in 1990. Our expectation for 1992 is between $5 and

$6 million. We are still making money. During the first five years, new businesses are supposed to have losses, but I had none. In 1991, we had a loss of about $18,000 or less, because we were gearing up for federal business. We hired contract people with experience working on federal contracts. Otherwise, we would not have had that loss last year.

So far we haven't taken any money out of the corporation. We are leaving it there to make the business more attractive to the banker. When it gets ridiculous, we will take it out and do something else with it. But for now, we feel it should remain in the corporation.

Every time I negotiate a contract, I negotiate profit. I don't go after loss leaders. I don't do something just to get in the door. Maybe that has worked for others, but I am here to make money. If there is no money to be made in a contract, then I don't want to do it. If I don't make money on something, then there's a mistake someplace.

My competitors are Compu-Staff, CGA, Compu-Ware, and other companies, small or otherwise, that do exactly what we do, i.e., supply people. How do we increase our competitiveness? By making sure our client is satisfied each time and every time and that our rates are competitive. Our bottom line and reputation are based on providing good quality people to these clients.

We have a TQM process in place, and it is well used. Basically, we make sure that we provide total quality management for everything we do, whether it's a proposal, recruiting people, or monitoring our employees at client sites. It is quality process all the way. We want to know how we are doing.

Quality begins with me; I am the corporate quality control person. I have a manager who makes sure that the procedures are written down and followed. But my job is to make sure that everyone in this organization knows that we stand for quality, integrity, honesty, and forthrightness.

## COMMUNITY LINKAGES AND INVOLVEMENT

### Suppliers and Vendors

Whenever we can, we use African American suppliers and vendors. Every time we spend dollars, we first look to see if an African American firm can do it. Our printer, our suppliers of software and hardware, we are always looking for minority vendors and suppliers. Our objective is to make the dollar turn over more than once.

### Employee Profile

We employ around fifty-six people. The staff is about 50 percent black, 40 percent white, and 10 percent others. One-half are women. We advertise for employees. Each of our offices has a full-time recruiter who monitors the corporations where these people are working. We have a total pipeline to these people. We also subscribe to résumé houses, but we rely on our recruiters, who make sure they know where the talent is at all times.

### Role Models

Dr. Clay made sure I got an education and has been with me since that day. In terms of companies, Emmett McHenry and Joshua Smith, who are graduates of 8(a), are role models. Their two firms tried to establish a mentorship program.

### Line of Succession

I don't think about retiring. I don't see that day. We are still in the process of developing a vision that goes beyond what CMS is presently doing. The vision focuses on putting African Americans to work. Although I hear about enterprise zones, for example, I'm not confident that majority groups care enough about building a factory that can employ our uneducated as well as educated people in the inner cities.

The answer is that people such as myself will accumulate capital and invest money in those inner cities to build factories. To that end, we have forged relationships with companies such as IBM and Harris Corporation. We want them to have enough confidence in us that, once we accumulate this capital, that the digit that sparks their new widget will be produced in the inner cities, where some of our people have never left. Some of our people have never seen the downtown of our cities. We need to put the factories where they are. That's my vision. There is no retirement in sight for me.

We have two little ones, and I have an older daughter who worked here for awhile. She has since gone back to Philadelphia. But we hope to involve our kids. One is almost nine, and she is dying to come in and help us. She is almost to the point where she can do the xeroxing! We're not going to force them, but we want them to have the same work ethics that we have.

### Community Activities

I am a member of the chamber of commerce and similar groups in Maryland and Washington, D.C. I have plaques and a certificate for helping youth in the Entrepreneurial Academy. One is happening tomorrow, an excellent program given by the Galilee Baptist Church called "Young Men under Construction." These programs basically try to instill correct values in young men as they grow up. They asked me to chat with the young men about career alternatives, so that they can see that people can be other than what they normally see at a job.

### BARRIERS

Bonding is a major issue, although in our business it is unnecessary. But when it is required, it is generally used as a barrier to stop black entrepreneurs because it's difficult to obtain. Insurance is a little bit easier.

Financing is the biggest barrier to going into business today. You are redlined because you are an African American. Second to that would be the perception of your company. Remember, people buy from people. That is important.

Another barrier is that many black people refuse to do business with themselves. The perception is negative. If we learn how to deal with one another, we will open up a new market for ourselves.

There are barriers wherever you look. Business is not for the faint of heart. One employee told me that if everyone could do what I do, there would be more businesses around here. Certainly, we need more black businessmen and -women. To me, the objective is to be in a position where we can employ our own. If we do that, I think we would be dealing with a whole different world. Economics is at the forefront of this battle.

### ADVICE TO FUTURE ENTREPRENEURS

I am very realistic with young people who might be thinking of going into business. A lot of people who go into business have not thought things out. Make sure this is what you really want to do. It is almost like being in love. Would you die for this love? When you get into this business it's not something you are doing for just a moment or two. When you go into business, it's hell or high water. If you don't know how to swim, you had better learn over the weekend. No one is going to turn you around. So you need to make sure that this is what you want to do.

The second story I tell at seminars goes like this: There once was a multibillionaire who started with a small business in the basement, just as I did. He invited a group of small businessmen like me to his place. He had a fabulous spread, to say the least. He had many swimming pools. He was rather eccentric in that alligators lived in some of the swimming pools. As he passed one of the alligator pools he said, "You know, if anyone can jump in this pool and swim to the other side I would know they were really serious about wanting to be an entrepreneur." We all laughed and walked on.

He said, "As a matter of fact, if anyone can do that I will give whatever he or she asks for." As we walked on laughing, we heard a splash. There in the pool was a brother swimming for all he was worth.

The alligators were right behind him. Just as he was getting to the end, we ran over to the pool and pulled him out before the alligators could eat him. He was breathing hard. The billionaire said, "Gee, you must really want to be an entrepreneur. Well, I told you that I would give you anything you wanted. So tell me what you want." Still out of breath, the black man looked at him and said, "I want the name of the person who pushed me into the pool."

Understand that entrepreneurship is a deep and difficult pool. Once you jump in, the alligators are at your heels. That's what it's all about. It is not always going to be a rosy or pretty picture. Whether you work for someone or for yourself, you'll have good days and bad days, ups and downs. But if you work for yourself, the rewards can be great.

## CASE 4
### Evanbow Construction—Hamilton Bowser Sr.

*Evanbow Construction, located in East Orange, New Jersey, is owned by Hamilton Bowser Sr. Bowser, who has one son and two daughters, has operated this business for twenty-four years.*

### THE EARLY YEARS

We are fourth or fifth generation living near East Orange, New Jersey. My brothers and I all attended school in East Orange and graduated from East Orange High School.

My mother, who came from Louisiana, went to school until sixth or seventh grade. My father studied architecture in night school but could not get a job working as an architect. He earned an architecture certificate from what is now the Newark College of Engineering, the school from which I graduated.

After serving as an apprentice, he applied to the state to become a licensed architect. But he couldn't get a job working as an architect until the early 1950s, almost fifteen years after he graduated. Since there were no jobs for black architects, my father drove a truck. He watched his pennies, worked very hard, and had part-time jobs that produced income as a real estate salesman and collector for a savings and loan association in the black part of Newark, where white folks feared to tread. We were never hungry. We never had a great deal, but we had a good life.

My father and mother encouraged us to graduate from college. My oldest brother, Ed, graduated from college as an architect and had his own practice. My second older brother, Lucius, is a licensed pharmacist with a master's degree in public health. My younger brother, Robert, is a civil engineer, licensed land surveyor, and licensed planner. My background is in civil engineering and, now, construction.

### DECISION TO START A BUSINESS

A few years after I graduated from college, I earned a master's degree in structural engineering. I was an engineer in private consulting engineering firms for almost eighteen years. I changed jobs regularly so that I would have a broad background in the different aspects of engineering—industrial buildings, waterfront construction, highways, and chemical plants.

My final job was vice-president of engineering at a consulting engineering firm. I supervised about one hundred architects and engineers who primarily designed industrial buildings and chemical plants. It was a go-go company in that we turned out very good work, very quickly, and made money. During the last three or four years I was with that firm, we started a construction division. Although it was not under my supervision, we provided a great deal of input. I got the feeling that construction was a very interesting business.

I found it is also easier to get contracts for construction than for engineering. The selection process for engineering contracts is based on personal relationships. And, based on what was happening, I had the feeling it would be difficult to get engineering contracts if I were in my own business. I figured that construction was better because it's in the public arena. If your price is low and you're bonded, you get the job. At that time, my friend, whom I had gone fishing with for years, had a construction business. We decided to form Evanbow. Evanbow is Evan from Levi Evans, and Bow from Bowser. He would run the field operations and I would run the office.

We started Evanbow in December 1968 and won our first contact in early 1969. Levi Evans was experienced in residential construction, and in the early years, we did mostly residential. After he retired in 1978, I moved away from residential. Now the company primarily does industrial and commercial buildings. We no longer do any residential work.

I've always worked and been around business. I was an entrepreneur at eleven, when I ran a very active newspaper delivery business. One summer, I even had two employees helping me distribute papers, and I was making twenty dollars a week. After the newspapers and before I joined the Marine Corps, I ran a supermarket meat department when I was seventeen to eighteen years old. I was experienced in handling money.

By the time I was old enough to consider starting a business, my brother sold his drugstore. My oldest brother, Ed, had his own architectural practice. And my younger brother, Robert, now had his land surveyor's license so that he could practice on his own. I was always around people who were trying to do something on their own. It was time for me to try. A fellow I worked with at my last job told me that if it didn't work out, I could always come back to work with him. So I had a fall-back position.

In 1967, I joined the Interracial Council for Business Opportunity, an organization assisting minority persons start businesses. As a board member, I had worked to improve the number and quality of minority people in business. There seemed to be a lot of opportunities. But I believe much of it was talk and public relations. It wasn't really happening. We started not only in the construction business but with my brother Bob's engineering practice. And, as I thought, it was difficult to negotiate contracts with white folks who really don't want you there anyhow. And it was difficult getting enough contracts to keep an engineering business going. So we finally closed that.

### GETTING STARTED

To learn more about the construction industry, I took courses, seminars on taxes, workmen's compensation, bookkeeping. I didn't do bookkeeping when I was an engineer. And, I took more courses related to construction: construction scheduling, cash flow in construction. I broadened my education in bits and pieces. Not being bashful, I also joined trade associations, attended dinners. You can learn many things by talking across the table. Most of the trade associations are predominantly white. You hardly ever see any of our folks there. That's a shame. We talk about getting ahead. You can't sit home at night and get ahead. You got to go spend the hours and get some experience.

We didn't develop a detailed business plan until SBA asked us to do it as an 8(a) contractor. We built the business plan into something we could use. At the end of every year now, we look at where we're going next year. Every fifth year we ask a professional company to take a look at us and write a report.

### ACCESS TO CAPITAL

You need access to capital at different stages. When we started, I put in about thirty thousand dollars that first year. My partner, Evans, primarily contributed his time and the equipment he had accumulated from his construction business. I think we valued his equipment at about the same value as the cash I put in. We had no debt.

As our projects got larger, we needed operating capital. We got a loan, not from a commercial bank, but from the Presbyterian Economic Development Corporation in New York. The Presbyterian church sponsored an equity fund to encourage minority businesses. I heard about the fund through a black fellow who had a pharmaceutical manufacturing business in this area. He was a corporation board member and told me that they were unable to lend to anyone. At his suggestion, I borrowed some money. I went through the same procedure as with a bank, e.g., presenting financial statements, et cetera. We repaid it, borrowed more a few years later, and repaid that, too. We developed a good repayment history.

Overall, they did not lose money, although they made a few bad loans. One I remember clearly was for a catfish farm in Mississippi. It was a good catfish farm but, apparently, the fish developed a virus and died instead of growing and getting chubby.

About four or five years after we started, we developed a line of credit with a commercial bank, but this was an SBA-guaranteed loan because the banks were still not lending. We did not establish a regular line of commercial credit until almost ten years after we were in business. The money just wasn't there in the early 1970s because the banks weren't lending.

Since we're general building contractors, our business is not equipment intensive. We don't need much up-front money to buy a piece of equipment to do a job. What we do need is operating cash to cover payroll and to buy materials if we don't have credit. In construction, you bill once a month for work completed that month. The client pays for up to 90 percent of the value of the completed work. So if you bill properly, you start turning over money sixty days after you start. By doing that and working carefully, you don't need a lot of money to operate.

But you do need to generate cash flow to get past that sixty-day period. Also remember that they're retaining 10 percent of your money. You can't let this retainage build up on ten jobs at the same time. Then it's really big money that you don't have because the owners are sitting on it. So the need for cash isn't in the same proportion to the dollar value of the contracts you have.

If your cash equals about 8 to 10 percent of the total dollar value of your annual contracts, you should get through the year okay. We don't need a big chunk of cash. During the first year neither Evans nor I took a salary. I was still working for the consulting firm. Evans took a minimal salary until we had enough volume for a reasonable salary. That first year wasn't easy for Evans. And the cash that I put in sort of offset the fact that he wasn't getting paid what he should have been. We always kept the value of our participation the same. My cash offset his whatever. After the first year we had enough work so that we could pay both of our salaries. Again, neither one was great. In fact, I probably took a 50 to 60 percent cut in salary to come into the business. For the first two to three years, we scratched.

Our net worth when we started was probably about fifteen thousand dollars.

The BCF is an excellent program for getting financing. I hope it can be expanded to make more dollars available and more people understand how to utilize it. The BCF loan process is easier than it is with a commercial bank. The loans actually come from a commercial bank, but the BCF contributes to the loan and guarantees part of it. The commercial bank feels more comfortable about making the loan if they're partially protected. That's a big help when trying to convince these white folks at the bank to loan us money. The minority firms that I know that have used it are satisfied with the treatment they received from the commercial banks and the BCF staff. I think it's a wonderful program.

Oh, you sign your life away like you do with everything else. Your house, your kid, your dog, and anything else. On that loan, I offered the building. But as I recall, the interest was 1 percent over prime, while most loans are still 2 to 2.5 percent over prime.

I could have obtained a loan through our commercial bank, but not at a better rate. I'd probably have to pay 1 percent more. It's also easier getting a loan through BCF than a commercial loan at a commercial bank.

I'm a preacher for the BCF. We have been conducting seminars for small minority businesses one Saturday a month for the past fifteen years at Essex County College. We have speakers who talk about financing, bonding, contract opportunities, accounting, and changes in the laws. At least once a year, we have a representative of the BCF talk about the availability of financing through them. So yes, we preach for them.

I've also dealt with the SBA. For a long time, about twelve years ago, I was an 8(a) contractor. But we did very little work through the program. Over the twelve years, we probably averaged about $250,000 a year. Much of the work we did was when another minority firm was thrown off a job for incompetence. We fixed the work and tried to keep the program looking good. So my guys were running all over—upstate New York, the southern end of New Jersey—cleaning up after people who were blowing it.

We also tried to encourage the SBA to get better job assignments into the 8(a) program. Government agencies would try to stick SBA with the dirty jobs. We figured if we showed SBA we can do these jobs, they'd ask us to do them. What happened was that about a half a dozen of us around the country began to get dirty jobs, like fixing the airplane hangar doors at Lakehurst. The doors were forty feet high, immense, and heavy. It was a tough job. Not many people would tackle them. We just did these dirty jobs and SBA was happy. We didn't get enough work, but what we did was interesting.

I think the program was reasonably successful, because in the early stages firms like ours got experience and some technical knowledge. Agencies saw that we had capabilities and they were getting upset when they couldn't prove SBA wasn't doing a good job. So they, again, started complaining about the SBA people, who had to be advocates. Advocates always have somebody mad at them, and crazy indictments were coming against some of these people because they were doing a good job.

In the late 1970s and early 1980s, a lot of us quietly put up a big effort to save these people. They were only doing their job. And, it got very quietly dirty, until we were able to convince the U.S. attorney general to get off their backs. You gave them jobs to do, and they're doing them. It doesn't always follow all the rules. But they're getting the job done. What the hell else do you want us to do? That was another interesting fight. So in that sense, the SBA did a reasonable job with the 8(a) program.

SBA's biggest problem is their people aren't always top-notch. And some are only looking to get to their pension; therefore, they can't always be advocates. And yet this is an advocacy program. They're caught between wanting to advance in government and not wanting to antagonize somebody who could ruin their record. So we don't always get the best people or even the really good people for these jobs.

SBA had a large amount of money allocated each year for direct loans. It also had a U.S. Treasury collateral program for loan guarantees. It didn't actually handle the money, it just issued the collateral. I understand, and I haven't kept up with it, that the amount of money available for direct loans has decreased substantially over the years. Between 1975 and now, funds available for direct loans is probably one-tenth of what it was then.

SBA has another very interesting program, 7(j), which isn't used very often. If I needed four backhoes, I can tell the SBA banker that I want to get four backhoes from the government, which has surplus backhoes. Companies in the 8(a) program can go to the government agency that has these backhoes and buy them at a very reduced price. For example, I could get a million-dollar piece of equipment for about ten dollars. 8(a) contractors who know about this program can get this stuff for practically nothing. It's there. And, now with government downsizing, a tremendous amount of equipment will be available.

Also as part of the SBA 8(a) program, funds under the 7(j) component can be used to assign technical people to you who are knowledgeable in your business. They sit down and talk with you, make suggestions, write a report, and come back and visit. We were fortunate to get a very helpful fellow named McMoon, who came to visit. So yes, they have some good men who are outside consultants, not staff.

We haven't done work for government agencies since 1984, except for Port Authority, which is not really a government agency because it is exempt from many of the public bidding laws. We have been relatively successful working with private clients, such as Jersey Central Power and Light, Pathmark Stores, Anheuser-Busch, Exxon, and Bell Laboratories.

We don't bid government work because we were unable to get sufficient bonding. Everything was in place. We had all the good things required by bonding companies. We had cash, experience, people, liquid assets, and, in twenty-four years, we have never defaulted on a job. Their chances of losing money on us were practically zero.

It would seem that with our business volume and the amount of cash on hand, we should have qualified for three times the amount of bonding that we could get. In other words, if we were limited to $2 million, we should have been able to get a $6 million bond. We couldn't get a bond out of these doggone bonding companies! Now, we don't bid government work because, some people say, I'm too principled about certain things.

I am an active member of the National Association of Minority Contractors. All of our studies pointed to bonding as one of our biggest problems. I've spoken before Congress and a number of other places about the white-owned bonding industry. In fact, I just wrote a negative report on the status of bonding in this country. Our association should and will do more to correct this problem.

We have a small black-owned bonding company in Washington. It needs money because the size of the bond it can loan is based on the amount of cash it has. We're trying to get foundations and insurance companies to invest in this company. Not as a loan, but an equity investment. This is our biggest thrust right now. If I'm going to be an advocate for bonding and against the surety industry, I can't be a hypocrite and take out bonds. Right now, the only place I could get a bond is from a white bondsman. So for the last eight years, I sought no bonds. Without a bond, we can't bid on government contracts.

Next year, however, we probably will seek bonding because it limits what we can do. We should be bidding on more public work, because right now there is more public work available than private. This has hurt us. So you see, sometimes I put principle ahead of business.

REVENUE, ACCOUNTING, AND INVENTORY

We normally gross annual revenue between $4 and $8 million—a real yo-yo. For 1995, we'll do about $8.7 million. We've made money every year except for two or three disastrous years.

You never stop taking steps to be profitable. Every day you look at what you're doing. I talk to the warehouse fellows every morning at 7:15 before they start work. I talk to all superintendents almost every day just to keep in touch. A good part of our expenses are field labor costs, so staying in touch helps me stay on top of situations. Otherwise resources dribble away. It's like a bean sack with a hole in the bottom. If you don't watch out . . .

We don't have a lot of inventory. We order by job. The superintendent assigned to the job keeps track of leftovers we've collected in the warehouse and tries to use that up first. Once we buy it for a job we don't inventory it. Unused materials just go back to the warehouse. We don't plan that it's available for future jobs. When we get small jobs, we look at what we have and try to use it first. But we don't price based on the fact that we have stuff in the warehouse.

Since about 1983 or 1984, we've done our accounting on an in-house computer. Our microprocessing unit is a little old and a little slow. But it does all of our financial accounting for payroll, cost reporting, and taxes. Since our financial accounting is integrated, we can do job cost accounting from the data generated from payroll. It works reasonably well. We have a controller who does that and keeps things up-to-date.

We run reports only when somebody needs them. If I'm project manager on a job and once a month I want to see where my job is going, I ask for and get a report.

We've had the same black CPA auditor since we started. Our audited annual statement is based on a report form we've developed which is appropriate for use in our industry. If we have to go for bonding or financing, these people like to read statements in a certain order so they can evaluate what we're doing. The CPAs prepare and print a year-end statement that compares current-year figures with the past two years. Again, the banks want to see if we're progressing.

We reinvest money into upgrading existing equipment and in people. As general contractors, we're primarily managers, and as such, we need people. So we've invested in training a couple of good, young engineers over a period of time. To me, it's an investment, since we won't get the same return that we get from hiring a more experienced person.

We are not now putting as much back into the business as we would like, primarily because we've had a few disastrous years recently. We did a series of dumb things. We bid a job too low. We finished it but lost money. Another was our "favorite." We built ten or twelve stores for McDonald's, two on the Garden State Parkway. They asked us to do two on the New York State Thruway. We spent probably $80,000 to $100,000 in preparation— bidding, assigning people, saving superintendents—instead of putting them on other jobs. We were ready to do this job, but they dragged it on and then canceled both. There was no way to recoup the money we had already spent. And, then, we also lost money on that beautiful conference center we built for Allied Signal. So we had a period of two or three years where we had some "good ones." That's why when you ask me about business and I shake my head, I'm saying, what the hell am I doing here?

Our principal competitors are white- or black-owned companies who bid in our size range. We try to run our business better so that we are more competitive. Improving our estimating skills helps us cost out a job and then bid a price as tight as possible so that we can do it and still make some money.

We're trying to upgrade the skills of our people so we can be more competitive. Superintendents and project managers participate in an ongoing training program. Last year they and a few younger fellows who want to be superintendents took classes in either New York or New Jersey. The classes were on different things—scheduling, planning, estimating. The senior people took financing and bidding strategies. This year our project managers took at least two courses, and our field people took either one or two.

We're trying to improve our bookkeeping in job accounting so that if a job goes for a period of time we can predict early enough if we're controlling it well enough to meet our target.

As principal salesman I'm doing more selling this year. I'm also getting my fellows out more. Some could do more contract work and others can take more responsibility for corporate relations. Ram handles in-plant work at Anheuser-Busch. I sell to Anheuser-Busch at the corporate level. George Knowles handles Port Authority work. To get a broader base, we're trying to get the fellows to take on more of the selling aspects of keeping good relations.

We're also trying to save more money so that we have more cash in the bank for other things. That's hard—keeping up with the cash.

## COMMUNITY LINKAGES AND INVOLVEMENT

### Location

We've always been in East Orange, within two blocks of where we are now. Both Evans and I come from East Orange. It seemed reasonable to have our business here, since we knew the community well and the community knew our families well.

East Orange is now probably 85 to 90 percent black, with a few Hispanics, and a large Haitian population. When I grew up, there were probably six thousand blacks and seventy-five thousand whites in town.

We've been in business for twenty-four years. Our basic field crew is very stable. We employ ten full-time people who have been with us for an average of seventeen years. They know that we will look out for them, pay them regularly, and offer benefits and pension. In exchange they work. We don't have to sit on them. That's very important.

We make a determined effort to use black employees. In fact, last year when we did a job for Exxon, they accused us—"Don't you hire any white folks?" In fact, I understand our company is the only company ever cited by the Federal Equal Employment Opportunities Commission because they claimed we didn't employ enough white folks.

Well, I think this got to be a joke with them. They never did anything about it. We've only been investigated once, about seven or eight years ago. They asked to see a list of the people we had hired and in what jobs. They said that we don't hire any white folks, which wasn't quite true. We've hired a number of white folks, but percentagewise we're so much better.

Right now, including office staff, I have twenty-four employees. As general contractors, we could have only two people managing a $9 million people-mover system. At any one time, we may be responsible for forty to fifty people on a job site through subcontracts. Except for one Asian, I'd be hard pressed to find anybody working for us right now who's not black. We have one female assistant project manager, but she's more of a paper pusher for the job manager. But overall, in staff of twenty-four I think we've only got three.

We keep our eyes open for new employees or advertise in the newspaper. My nephew has been our controller for fourteen years. He's now thinking about going full-time into insurance. So we've advertised for a controller. We don't have any white folks. Maybe I ought to hire a white controller. Right away, other black folks will say, "Hey, don't you trust your folks with the money?"

Our best years of control were with a white controller. Jack was with us for ten years and retired. He died two years later. He wasn't too young. A good man. All three of his sons worked with us, and we trained them. Two are now in their own contracting business. The third got a law degree. He's the only one making money!

### Suppliers and Vendors

We don't use many black material vendors. But we use a fair number of black subcontractors. Without bragging, we probably have a better record for subcontracting to minority firms than any other minority business in New Jersey. Not all are black, some are other minorities. We try.

We also try to give business to members of our association, our New Jersey chapter of the National Association of Minority Contractors. Two-thirds of those firms are black, one-third Hispanic, and a few Asian. I'm probably the only person in New Jersey who knows at least one minority firm in every trade that we need to build a building. I know them, they know us.

We did a $2 million job for Pathmark in Paterson, where we built an addition and completely renovated the existing store. And I think, except for the structural steel contractor and the sprinkler contractor, everybody was black. The company was pleased because the building was in a black neighborhood and the neighbors could see black folks working. Because of that, we got invited to two churches up there. Some of the subcontractors don't work too well. But, then, some of the white folks don't either.

### Customers
Most of our clients are white-owned corporations: AT&T, Anheuser-Busch, Jersey Central Power and Light. Most of the work we do for black folks is churches. This morning, I met with a committee to discuss an addition to a church in Newark. Not a big addition, $250,000. We've bid to a number of black-owned businesses. In New Jersey, we have probably forty black-owned businesses who are really considered in business.

### Advertising and Marketing
We advertise. We send out calendars once a year to our regular clients, people that we've done business with before that we think we can do business with again. It's something handy that they can keep on their desks. We advertise in the National Minority Supplier Development Councils booklets. Their readers are corporations, and we find that they do private business. If a trade journal comes out that might reach a market we're interested in, we might take out an advertisement. For instance, I take out a business card advertisement in the American Society of Civil Engineers, because I'm a member of the New Jersey chapter. I think I've gotten two calls over the last fifteen years.

We are members of the association of buyers from large corporation called the National Association of Contract Agents or something like that. Anybody can join, so we did just to let them know we're in business.

We have been active in the Minority Suppliers Development Council. The New York–New Jersey chapter of the Minority Purchasing Council has minority board members from the Vendor Input Committee. The committee is made up of ten minorities who advise the board of the local chapter. We've been active in that.

Last year at the National Minority Suppliers Development Council's annual conference in New York City, twenty of us each kicked in two thousand dollars. We ran a breakfast where we played a video about our firms and gave out literature just to keep our names before the buyers.

The National Association of Minority Contractors, of which I am president of the board, has a Major Corporation Participation Program. Membership includes about twenty major corporations, such as United Airlines, American Airlines, Frito Lay, and a few manufacturers. We also have ten or twelve general contractors and construction managers who gross $3 billion a year. We keep these relationships because some of them can ask Evanbow to do some work. That's what it's really about—a relationship between the buyers, the large, white, private or public major corporate participants and the general contractors and construction managers. But we encourage everybody to use our subcontractors and vendors.

We do not do a lot of newspaper advertising because it doesn't bring any business. It's readers are usually not the people we do business with.

### Community Activities

Right now, I do little in the community. Over the years, I've been on the boards of the Urban League, United Fund, and, for over twenty years, the YMCA. I'm still active in my church. I belong to a club called the Men of Essex, started thirty-five years ago. It's a club of ex-athletes interested in high school scholarship. So we have a scholarship program that we call a grant program. We give kids money if they have a particular need, not a scholarship. A lot of scholarship money is around, so we have a system of referring kids to particular scholarships. We can tell kids interested in engineering which schools have scholarships for black young people. It's even easier for a woman, because there are programs for bringing women into engineering.

We try to encourage junior high kids through mentoring. We try to help them keep up their grades so they have an easier time in high school. The club has a good cross-section of membership, so we can counsel kids about a variety of vocations, before and after college. The club has been around so long, we're getting the second generation of kids into the organization. We now have three father-son combinations.

Every year we give awards to the best scholar-athletes in the county. Not athletes, scholar-athletes. Sometimes this gets to be a problem in the black community. Quite often the best scholar-athlete is white. Probably, over the years half of our top awardees have been white. We've created other programs that award not just the top scholar. We make sure that every year we give awards to black kids. We also give plaques to all the black Merit Scholars and finalists in Essex County to recognize scholarship.

I give about $200 a year to the Legal Defense Fund. We have a corporate membership in the Urban League, which is $150 a year. We give $100 a year to the NAACP, NAACP Economic Development Corporation, and Jesse Jackson's Operation PUSH. More of my money goes to the National Association of Minority Contractors. NAMC, because I think it has a greater economic impact.

Operation PUSH is an interesting organization in that it has probably gotten thirty or forty corporations to agree to work with them to improve employment opportunities. PUSH has been effective by pointing out to companies like McDonald's or the Kroeger supermarket chain that they don't employ enough black folks in management or other positions, and they don't buy from black businesses. PUSH tells them that we're going to boycott their stores until they change their ways. The threat's valid, but I don't think they ever picketed anybody.

The NAACP Economic Development Corporation did the same thing. I guess we've been kicking in about five hundred dollars a year for their operation. I've never seen a report on how much they think they've accomplished, which is another weakness of black organizations. They don't communicate their accomplishments, and their office is right around the corner from us!

To see what we could do to work together, I organized a meeting in Orlando, Florida, about five or six years ago and invited the counsels of Operation PUSH, NAACP Economic Development Corporation, National Minority Suppliers Development Corporation, National Minority Business Enterprise Legal Defense Fund, National Association of Minority Contractors. This was the first time these folks ever sat down together. We agreed to some direction and a division of work. It helped eliminate some of the overlapping things we do. It also gave everybody a chance to describe what they were doing, so that we could find out where we had gaps and how we could support each other.

The moderator was Gus Heningburg, a radio show host who also heads the Urban Coalition in this area. We reached several agreements at that meeting. Whoever sponsors a conference would invite the other organizations to exhibit in a free booth. Now that isn't much, you might say, but it takes some of the financial pressure off of showing up. It saved us five hundred or a thousand dollars. We also agreed that it's time to teach black folks something about economics to help them get off welfare. So if the NAACP had a conference, it would invite the other organizations to run a seminar about doing business. And to sell to groups like the National Baptist Convention. We would talk to them about building churches. If they build with black folks' money, then black businesses should be building the churches. Of the original organizations, NAMC has probably been more active than the others, but we work together in different ways at different times.

These relationships were very helpful in 1989, when the Supreme Court ruling known as the Croson decision began shooting down set-aside programs. Because we knew each other, we met in Washington to plan what to do, how it would get done, and who would do it. We put together a joint traveling road show with a lot of help from Parren Mitchell, and we were on the road within thirty days. We went around the country to the best of our limited resources to tell people how to do better disparity studies, and to get ready for new legislation which would be acceptable to the Supreme Court.

Our association was on television twenty-four hours later. In fourteen days we distributed a policy paper on the issues. We were out before the white folks and before the white lawyers' association, because white boys knew they could make a bundle telling white folks what to do about this. So we hit TV and the papers first. Not enough coverage, but we had a national audience through CBS and NBC.

On the road we split up the United States, and our executive director and one of our other people went. MBELDEF sent two of their people. Because of the way they're funded, National Minority Suppliers Development Council thought they ought not be too active. So we got our message out and we developed good training manuals on what to do. I went on six of those road shows.

### Role Models

I've always admired my friend, Levi Evans, who started the business with me. He ran a reasonably successful small business doing residential and commercial work. My father was a good, hardworking guy. He tried very hard during a very difficult period of time to work in a field in which there were no other blacks. In fact, my brother was the second black licensed architect in the state of New Jersey, my father was the fourth. My friend Henry Henderson was in the manufacturing business. We've been very close. So if you call those role models, yes. And the businesses I worked for, I could see how these white guys worked hard and went out and took a shot. They didn't all make it the first time.

I know a lot of white folks mainly because they had the businesses I worked for. I had this interplay with them, so even though I went into business, I still know them. When I have to hire folks to compete against a big firm, I can call one of these guys and ask, for example, about the salary range for project managers.

I have a lot of friends and acquaintances who do what we do, and I'm not bashful. I ask for advice. We recently built a bridge over railroad tracks. One part has to stay open to keep the trains running. The part where we're working is closed in the middle of the night, for safety reasons. When we had a question, I called one of the steel fabricators and asked him about the best way to do certain things. People will talk to you, particularly a vendor who might get some business out of it. So don't be bashful.

I can also talk to my own friendly banker, if I think he can be straightforward. We have a black accountant who's been with us ever since we started. I call him about tax stuff and how to improve our accounting system. Lawyers too.

When you have a business legal problem, you need somebody who knows business law and knows how the court system deals with business problems. Most of our firms don't. One of my cousins is a lawyer, but I think we've lost two court cases because he is black. It was pathetic how he was treated in court. And there isn't much you can do about it. So I now follow the path taken by my friend Henry Henderson, who manufactures control panels and motor control centers. When he started his business he made his own sales calls, but he wasn't getting much business. Then he hired a white salesman, and told him not to tell the customers about the owner. For the first fifteen or twenty years, probably nobody knew that Henry Henderson was black. His engineers or salesmen were white. He stayed at home and made sure the product got built.

Henry did this because that's the way the world was and, to some extent, still is. I've told some black business people who drive up in their Mercedes or big Cadillacs that white folks don't want to see you drive that. You deal with purchasing people who make forty to fifty thousand dollars a year. They don't want to see a black man making that kind of money. If you drive up in a fifty-thousand-dollar car, they think you don't need the work. I lectured some of my friends to take the old Volkswagen. Better yet, a small Ford. Not a foreign car. We joke about this a lot, but there is still this bias among white buyers not to want to do business with people of color, particularly black folks.

### Succession

When I retire, we're considering a senior project manager, who's reasonably good, to take over. My brother, who's seven years younger and not now on our payroll, has been helpful. Right now he's doing some work for us with the board of education. They couldn't hire a consultant, so he's on staff. They're happy, and he's getting their work done. He's also establishing good relationships, so maybe we can do some future business with them. Bob is administratively good. He ran Bowser Engineers and Associates when we had about twenty engineers and architects doing design work.

About three or four months ago, my thirty-year-old son, for the first time, expressed an interest in working for the company. He has a degree in history, a master's in business administration, and has been doing contract preparation and monitoring for General Dynamics Corporation in Michigan. He's getting good administrative and pricing experience, and he's developing business relations because he helps to negotiate contracts for General Dynamics. Although their business is different, the principles of doing business are similar enough that with a good field staff and a good operations person, he can do the rest of it. He's also worked here during the summers, so pushing a broom and digging a hole is not foreign to him.

God has blessed this home; all three of my children received good educations. They also were good students. Two are actively employed, the other is just out of college and taking some time off. My older daughter worked for of the city of New York and one of the agencies in public relations. My other daughter is still in the Washington, D.C., area. Neither will come into the business. My son might; it would be nice if he did.

Of all the questions you asked me, our weakest position is a good line of succession. We've got to do something. I'm not twenty-seven anymore.

### ADVICE TO FUTURE ENTREPRENEURS

The best advice I could give a young African American person regarding entrepreneurship is get a good education. Learn to speak and write the

English language. That's probably the most important. Why can't we get this idea through to most of our kids? This damn street language stuff is for the birds. The world doesn't communicate that way. They communicate in the English language. Listen closely to the rappers. Many of them enunciate extremely well and are very clear. If they aren't, you won't get their message. The structure of their English sentences is so poor. They distort everything to make things rhyme, or whatever it is that they do. But they speak very clearly. Even after they stop singing and they're being interviewed, many of them speak clearly. But their structure is terrible. They haven't learned, for example, that some words have an "s" on the end. Somebody said, "We be here." Somebody ought to write a book on how black folks use the verb "to be."

### THE FUTURE OF EVANBOW

In the near future, I'm going to withdraw from many of the organizations I have spent considerable time working with. It's time to take care of number one, which is our company. And by spending more time with our company, I look to double our sales in no more than two years and to bring in some young people who can take over and continue the company. I want all the black contractors to become a stronger force in construction in our area. White contractors know we're here. They also know we're small. So they know we're not going to challenge them in a lot of projects to get the work. I'd like to see us grow so that we can compete against them.

We also have to develop additional staff. We want to be good at what we do so we can feel proud of it. We have never left a job where they could complain about what we did.

Between the early 1970s and the early 1980s, we built for RCA. Then only American companies put satellites in the air to use for TV broadcasts. RCA contracted with NASA in Florida to shoot the satellite into space. It would be circling and, at some point, NASA scientists would stop it from turning and it would stay there. It turns with the globe, so it's always right where the globe is. They call the procedure "parking." We bid on a job to design and build an addition to an RCA satellite control center in New Jersey.

We got the job. We designed it and we were working there when RCA told us they were going to launch another satellite in six weeks. They were bringing in extra control trailers. They asked us what we were doing so that they could coordinate everything. I'm listening to their story about this

$35 million satellite up in the air, and I'm thinking, if something goes wrong, who the hell are they going to blame? So one week before the launch, I gave them notice that we were leaving the site. We finished what they wanted us to, and we left. NASA launched the satellite, it started circling, and the NASA scientist in Florida transferred control to RCA in New Jersey. But the satellite wasn't turning quite right. The RCA scientist tried to adjust it but he lost it. He lost this $35 million satellite in space. It was gone. I was really glad we had left!

When we went back the following week, the guy was so dejected. The facility manager said they had insurance for about $28 million of that $35 million and most of it was with Lloyd's of London. When they lost it and couldn't find it for a few days, they put in an insurance claim. Lloyd's told them they had to prove it was lost!

We did another job up there last year. The manager told me that Lloyd's paid the claim, but they also told them that they had to find some other way to prove where the satellite is. He told me they never found it. That was almost six, seven years ago. That satellite is still floating around up there!

## Summary

Although their business interests vary, the four successful entrepreneurs profiled in this chapter share common characteristics or experiences that eventually inspired or provoked them to start their own businesses. Each identified, to some extent, the importance of their childhood, formal and informal education, early work/job experiences, and the incident that made each realize, in DeMagnus's words, "it was time to go."

Family and childhood provided pivotal experiences that set these entrepreneurs on the path that eventually led to their own corporate doors. Although only McCampbell had a parent involved in business, Saunders, DeMagnus, and Bowser had at least one parent with a college degree and/or a profession. All mentioned their parents as either influencing and inspiring them or setting by personal example the standards to which they aspired as adults.

Several acknowledged that their entrepreneurial spirit existed even in childhood. McCampbell "worked at an early age" as a caddie and a newspaper carrier. As a teenager, he started a successful wall and window washing business to pay for the high school yearbook and senior fees. Saunders, at her mother's encouragement, became the area's first female newspaper carrier. At age eleven, she made and sold little papier-mâché dolls for Christmas. Bowser, too, began a newspaper carrier business, which at the age of eleven, he expanded by adding two employees.

Different reasons prompted each to decide on going into business, but all made their decision after years of work experience. For Charles McCampbell, the motivation to start a business appears to be a combination of "push-pull" factors. Unsatisfied with the consideration given to him by the military, he wanted to succeed or fail by his own decisions as opposed to someone else's.

Ellen Ann Saunders's journey to entrepreneurship was fueled by a desire for personal challenge and an altruistic ambition to create opportunities for other African American women. She wanted greater challenges than either her job or an employer-employee relationship could provide. As part of a master's degree program, Saunders investigated the construction industry. She relished the prospect of opening a field that employed few African Americans, but her personality was not suited for the construction industry. She eventually decided on the office-supply industry. After three years and too much competition from "superstores and corporate co-ops," she carved a niche in the office furniture business.

The "glass ceiling" and racial discrimination pushed Albert DeMagnus to start Computer Management Services. Armed with a strong self-esteem and confidence in his data processing abilities, he decided the time had come for him to do for himself what he had done for others—make money. Sharon DeMagnus joined him a short time later. After thirteen years of driving sixty-six miles each day to her corporate job, she quit in frustration. By then she had heard once too often that she was doing a great job but would not be promoted "this time."

By comparison, Hamilton Bowser's experience seems almost serendipitous. As vice-president of engineering of a large corporation, Bowser successfully supervised the work of one hundred architects and engineers. At that same time, he sat on several community boards, including the Interracial Council for Business Opportunity. Through his council experience, Bowser began to consider business opportunities:

"I was around people who were trying to do something on their own. It was time to try." Bowser smoothly moved from employee to employer as his longtime fishing partner became his business partner.

Why these four entrepreneurs decided to start their own businesses is best expressed by Albert DeMagnus: "If I could do so much for other firms, why couldn't I do it for me?"

# 5

# Gaining Access
# to Capital

## THE CENTRAL REGION

Fair lending is good for business. Access to credit, regardless of race, gender, religion, or national origin is essential to the economic health of lenders, borrowers, and society in general. However, the saliency of race in America seems to influence lending in the commercial arenas of the past and the present.

The history of black entrepreneurship "has been shaped by *limited access to credit,* limitations in education and training opportunities, and prevailing attitudes about what roles minorities should assume in society" (Fusfield and Bates 1984). For the post–Civil Rights era, however, the census data on business initiation, diversification, and the educational level of entrepreneurs indicates a reversal in some of these historical limitations. The African American business community is now characterized by emerging businesses that are diversified, provide more jobs, are larger, more profitable, and better integrated into the broader marketplace. Yet these improvements appear to have little impact on the availability of financing.

A 1988 study analyzed the business performance of thirteen hundred established firms and the ability of their owners to obtain commercial bank financing (Ando 1988). The study reported that when factors such as education, hours worked, size and nature of firm, debt ratio, and geographical location are equal, firms owned by African Americans and Latinos performed as well as those owned by Asians and non-minorities. However, while Asian, Latino, and nonminority business owners appeared to obtain loans easily in the commercial bank market, African American business owners did not.

To compensate for their lack of access to capital in the commercial bank market, the SBA and other business development agencies such as the Greater Detroit Business and Industrial Development Company and the Business Consortium Fund offered loans to African American and other minority owners of established firms. Even with the existence of these organizations, attracting capital is still a crucial problem for today's African American entrepreneurs.

According to a 1992 Roper Organization Poll, lack of access to credit and capital remains the major barrier to business start-ups and explains why so few American businesses (3 percent) are black-owned (*Wall Street Journal* 1992). Although commercial lending agencies may not be expected to cure America's persistent racial dilemma, lenders do have a fiduciary responsibility to ensure that stereotypes, negative attitudes, and prejudices do not systematically interfere with the equitable distribution of credit. Fair lending must be an integral part of America's financial community's mission and each financial institution's business plan. Consequently, any policy concerned with economic development of the African American community must focus on strategies designed to gain access to capital. Greater access to sources of start-up and expansion capital will surely result in increased business formation and growth among African American–owned businesses.

This chapter investigates the availability of commercial credit and how it shaped the businesses of three successful African American entrepreneurs in the Central Region: Bill Mays (Mays Chemical Company, Inc.); Bettye Daly (MayDay Chemical, Inc.); and Anthony Snoddy (Exemplar Manufacturing, Inc.).

CASE 5
## Mays Chemical Company—Bill Mays

*Mays Chemical Company is located in Indianapolis, Indiana. Bill Mays, age fifty, is president. He is married to Rose M. (Cole) Mays, and the couple has two children, Heather, twenty-four, and Kristin, twenty.*

## THE EARLY YEARS

I grew up in the Bayard Park area of Evansville, Indiana. We lived only three blocks from Lincoln Avenue, the drag, the hip spot. As I look back now, I would call us middle class.

I went to elementary school at Chestnut Walnut with 90 percent of all the African Americans in Evansville. We went to Lincoln High for grades six through twelve. Lincoln had no zones, at least none for us. You could come from anywhere. The building wasn't very large. Integration started, Lincoln closed, and we were shipped to the predominantly white Central High School for my senior year.

I noticed some differences in going from Lincoln to Central High School. The teachers at Lincoln, who were all African American, took a much more personal interest in the students. I actually got very solid foundations in high school and in elementary school. I had no real problems adjusting to or competing with students when I got to Central. As a matter of fact, I graduated tenth out of 316 and was the number one male graduate of the class of 1963. Martharee, my sister-in-law, graduated eighth in that class.

Even with that high ranking I never got a single scholarship offer—a 3.65 out of 4.0 average and fourteen credits over graduation requirements. Had I been at Lincoln, I would have gotten offers because there would have been a lot more interest from counselors and others.

Fortunately, I didn't need a scholarship. To some extent, Dad was secretive with his own finances. He may not have wanted to divulge the financial aspects of our existence and wouldn't fill out financial-aid forms because he didn't feel we needed financial aid. But, there's a difference between financial aid and scholarship aid.

I went to Indiana University and graduated with a bachelor's in chemistry, and went to work as a test chemist for Linkbelt, a division of FMC [Food Machinery Chemical]. From there I went into sales at Procter and Gamble. Since I had no business training, I went back to graduate school on a fellowship and completed a master's in business administration from Indiana University.

Dad taught science and math at Lincoln High School. His first teaching experience was at Shorter College in Arkansas. He got a master's degree from Indiana University in chemistry, a master's in education, and finally a master's in art in teaching from Colorado College. He told me that going to Indiana University in the early 1940s was an experience. And, while his goal was to get a doctorate, it wasn't cost effective. He felt that being African American had held him back. A couple of people he started out with at Indiana

University subsequently got their doctorates, but it was an excruciating experience. He said it wasn't worth it.

Mom was also a teacher. She had a master's in special education from Indiana University. She taught special education part-time, also at Lincoln. After my dad passed, she taught full time until she retired.

I have two older brothers, no sisters. Ted, who turned fifty-four, works for Mays Chemical. He handles personnel and manages the company properties and vehicles. His twin, Bob, stayed in Evansville and is director of student teaching at the University of Southern Indiana. I guess all three of us ended up staying in Indiana, just good old Hoosiers.

Bob married Martharee, his high school sweetheart from Evansville. Ted married Bruceil, whom he met when he was at Tennessee State. We've all been married for longer than twenty-five years to the same people.

My family was influential in my life, especially my dad. I really admired his education, experience, and willingness to do menial tasks to support the family. Since teachers don't work in the summer, he worked at the ice house making minimum wage so that we could have some extras. So I think he really instilled the drive for hard work. He died when I was nineteen and a sophomore at Indiana University. I know he was the real push that made me excel.

None of my close relatives were in business. The closest was my dad's brother, who managed nightclubs, but I really didn't have any relatives as business role models. There was nothing in the school curriculum either in high school or college that helped or encouraged me to become an entrepreneur, or even mentioned entrepreneurship. It was a new word that I had to learn. Looking back now, I think that my business drive was developed serendipitously.

## DECISION TO START A BUSINESS

I started Mays Chemical in March 1980 as a subchapter S corporation. The company is a chemical distribution business that supplies chemicals to industry. We specialize in products going to the food and pharmaceutical industries. We also diversified into automotive, photochemicals, and a variety of other industries. We are the middleman between the chemical manufacturer and the chemical user. Manufacturers can do very well by producing only a few products, but we handle literally hundreds of different products.

I seriously thought about being an entrepreneur when I left graduate school and went to work at Cummins Engine Company. The realization hit me that to be successful in business you have to move up the ladder. As I look back over my experience at Linkbelt, Procter and Gamble, and Eli Lilly, I realize that there were very few blacks in top management.

Cummins Engine Company was the exception. In the early 1970s, they had three black vice-presidents. Probably no other Fortune 500 company had blacks that highly placed in operations, marketing, or accounting. I asked myself how was I going to get to the top of this or any other major corporation. At that point, I began to see the barriers to moving up the ladder. Today, we call it the "glass ceiling." So, when I got a chance to run a small chemical distributorship in 1977, I jumped at the opportunity.

The opportunity happened when a friend of mine, Bill Norman, executive vice-president of Amtrack, joined Cummins to work on affirmative action issues. He had been in the navy on Admiral Zumwalt's staff and currently was on the board of directors of Chemical Investors, a new company in Indianapolis started by former Lilly, Inc., employees.

They wanted to do manufacturing. They thought that a faster way to generate the revenue they needed for manufacturing was to set up a minority-controlled distribution operation. They could move into distribution quickly, because the barriers are relatively minimal compared to manufacturing. As a minority-controlled business they could get access to governmental "giveaways" and "set-asides."

Their first president, a Hispanic named Maria Hester, was totally incompetent and could not run the company. Ms. Hester was basically a puppet of the parent organization, but since she knew nothing about chemicals or business, the customers saw through that very quickly. Furthermore, she was a minority only because she happened to come from Puerto Rico. She was very wealthy and her husband contributed a substantial amount of money to form the company.

After nine months, the company recruited me from Cummins. I was a natural for the job with an undergraduate degree in chemistry and business experience. The offer got me out of Columbus, where Cummins was located, and back to Indianapolis. My wife had been commuting from Columbus to Indianapolis because she was teaching at the IU Medical Center in Indianapolis. This was an ideal opportunity for both of us. I left Cummins in 1977 to run Specialty Chemicals, as it was then called.

Chemical Investors, the parent company, owned 49 percent of Specialty Chemicals, and 51 percent was owned by thirteen minorities. These thirteen individuals lost control of the company when they couldn't show a united front to Chemical Investors. When I came in, the company moved from a few hundred thousand dollars in sales to close to $5 million by 1979. At that point, it was generating $100,000 in after-tax profits.

Specialty Chemical was growing faster than Chemical Investors and controls were lacking. As the president of Specialty Chemicals, I was a "belligerent" African American who did not want a "front" operation. So, they changed the board of directors of Specialty Chemicals in such a way as to make it majority control; votes would always be three to two. In January 1980, Specialty was no longer minority-controlled. I resigned on January 28 and set up Mays Chemical on March 4. So I really started Mays Chemical because I was out of a job!

### GETTING STARTED

I started Mays Chemical at age thirty-four. I had been president of Specialty for three years, spent four years at Cummins acquiring a solid foundation in planning, marketing, and finance, and three years at Procter and Gamble managing myself as opposed to managing other people, but I managed some major accounts. I had the management experience and was comfortable with my ability to run an organization of the size and complexity that Mays would ultimately become. I also have an M.B.A. from a major institution which teaches you how to run companies the size of General Motors.

At first, I was not going to set up a separate business, but instead try to buy Specialty. I already owned 10 percent of the company, so it seemed a logical decision. And, I wanted to gradually buy the company. But the real impetus for starting my own company happened when I was faced with the cold reality that Specialty was going to be operated as a sham.

I had some good friends in the industry. An older white gentleman, Byron Bettis, who ran Superior Chemical, was one of the most successful independent chemical distributors in Indiana. I was telling him my tales of woe because we were very close. And he said, "Well, why don't you go out and start your own business." I said, "I don't have the money to do that." He said, "You've taken Specialty up to where it is, you know the industry, you built the company. Chemical Investors had nothing to do with it, why don't you go out on your own?" He says, "I can certainly help, what are you talking about when you say you need money?" I said, "I don't know—it takes thousands and thousands of dollars." And then he says, "Well what does it take?" I said, "I don't know, I suppose $100,000." He says, "Well what if I told you that I'd loan you the money?" At that point, the one excuse that I had evaporated.

I set up an office next door to Byron Bettis and actually engaged his secretary to answer my phone while I was on the road. I paid, I think, $150 a month. Judy typed what little correspondence I had and answered my phone. I also got access to the coffee machine and Xerox. On the Friday that I left Specialty, I had a big blow-down party that night. On Saturday morning I met with the accountant to make sure that I had all my little ducks in a row and picked up my business cards. On Monday morning the attorneys said I was incorporated, and I was on the road to Chicago by ten o'clock that morning.

I learned a lot from that gentleman. Byron ran one of the most successful independent chemical distributorships in the country. We remain friends today. I did take him up and borrowed $50,000. I did not need the $100,000. Mays Chemical became profitable almost immediately because I knew where to go and what to do. I paid him back the $50,000 plus interest in two years and never looked back. I did the classical kinds of things. I put a second mortgage on my home. I cashed in all my savings bonds. I had some Procter and Gamble stock. But that's how Mays Chemical got started. And that's probably why today I am so interested in entrepreneurship for others and why I put so much time and energy and money back into the community and back into business to try to help others to get started.

A trusted attorney from Branes and Thornberg, one of the largest in the state, walked me through the process of setting up the business structure. At that point Mays Chemical was an S corporation because the lawyer said that we would probably incur losses in the beginning. We incurred losses for only two months. It really wasn't a big factor, but the idea was good. Then he introduced me to accountants at Price Waterhouse. Today, we still deal with this same law firm.

The business plan was probably in my head. It has never been committed to writing. The strategy is pretty straightforward, and people ask me all the time how I ever put Mays Chemical together without formally writing something. That's because I was living it and dying it as I was doing it. I didn't need a road map, and I also didn't need to justify what I was doing, because Byron was the only one who had a financial stake in the business. Byron already knew the business and had faith in me.

Today, phases of the company have a business plan. We drive that through the financial model; we're more interested in a sales plan that projects revenues and bottom-line profits. Today, we can give you a budget, tell you the customers we are pursuing, the products we expect to sell to them, and the sales we expect to get. So, we're more sophisticated today.

Rose, my high school and college sweetheart and wife, provided much-needed support more than anything else. When I left Specialty, Rose asked, "What took you so long?" At that point we had two young kids. She said, "I'll continue to work. The kids will be able to eat. There's no problem. If you decide this is what you want to do, I think you ought to do it." That has been her attitude through the entire process. She continues to work today even though from a financial perspective, she doesn't need to. She enjoys doing her research, and she now has the security of knowing that she does what she wants to do. Providing encouragement was the biggest role Rose played.

### ACCESS TO CAPITAL

I put in $10,000 dollars as equity into the business, and obviously in the first few months did not take any "salary" as such out of the business. It was at the end of that year, December 1980, that I sat down and looked at everything and said I can finally see daylight and I wrote myself a check for $25,000 dollars, which was a lot of money from my perspective. But $10,000 dollars was the only equity capital that went into the business.

Obviously, I was not bankable at that point. The other sources of start-up capital really came from trade suppliers as far as just getting credit. In the chemical business, as in many businesses, if you can get credit from your suppliers, then you can fund a great deal of the business. The technique that I used was to get trade suppliers to extend me credit and also extend terms a little beyond the normal thirty days. And then I asked customers to pay faster than thirty days. And so I set Mays Chemical terms up as net fifteen days. And while most customers did not pay in fifteen days, they paid in less than thirty. And suppliers did not formally change their terms to extend beyond thirty, but they did not get upset if I didn't pay them until forty days. So with that slow buildup of working capital and cash flow I was able to get the business pretty well grounded.

My net worth wasn't very much when I started. I never even filled out a net-worth statement. Probably at that point, if you look at the house and whatever, it was less than $50,000. The reason that I know it was somewhere in that $50,000 range, when I went to one trade supplier and asked for credit, they said, "We're willing to give you $100,000 credit, but we want you to sign over your home and personally guarantee this." I said I'm not sure that I'm worth that much, and they said, "Well, we'll give you $100,000 in credit if you in fact sign over your house and give us a personal guarantee. The rationale is that if you know you stand to lose everything if you screw this up, then we think you'll operate the business more prudently and you'll lose sleep before we even know there's a problem." And I did that and so I have never been concerned about putting everything on the line. [With] that supplier today, Occidental Chemical, then it was named Diamond Shamrock, we have credit certainly in excess of $5 million.

We got our first bank loan in November 1980 from the Indiana National Bank [INB]. My friend Andy Payne was then executive vice-president of INB. I served with him on the board of the IU School of Business. He's now president and chief operating officer at NBD [National Bank of Detroit]–First Chicago. So it never hurts to have friends in the right places.

I approached INB with the idea of a working capital line of credit secured against receivables. We had excellent receivables at that point, because we sold only to twenty customers, all large Fortune 500 companies: Upjohn, Abbott, Lilly, Inc. The receivables were bankable. People were telling me about debt-to-equity ratios and other necessary requirements. When I got the first loan from INB, Mays Chemical had a seventeen-to-one debt-to-equity ratio. So when we talk about what can and cannot be done, it's a matter of who wants to do it. I got a $200,000 line of credit secured against receivables, personally guaranteed from INB in November 1980. Today, Mays Chemical has a $12 million credit line with NBD–First Chicago. The total concentration of the Mays's entities is well in excess of $35 million. At the present time, we have zero long-term debt. INB's gamble paid off handsomely for them.

The $50,000 loan and the $10,000 I put in were sufficient to sustain the business during the first year. Because I had been in business and understood where to go and how to go about it, I didn't waste time digging up customers. I knew the customers and the products they used. Mays Chemical turned profitable in sixty days. The first year's sales ($2.2 million) were substantial enough to generate cash flow and profits so that I didn't need the second $50,000.

All of these events happened in 1980. The industry relationships I had developed and my reputation for integrity within the industry allowed me to get trade credit. Today, if you talk to competitors, customers, or suppliers about

Mays Chemical, they all agree about the company's integrity and its willingness and ability to pay its bills on time. To me, this is much more important than my net worth when I started.

My experiences with BCF are positive. I was involved from the beginning and worked hard to help the National Minority Supplier Development Council set up the fund in Indianapolis. The Treasurer of the National Purchasing Council, Wilbert Little, was a former vice-president at INB.

When the BCF started, we held a kick-off celebration in Indianapolis. The president of the fund attended and INB formally became one of the first banks in the country to participate in the fund. To get the fund started, Mays Chemical borrowed $250,000 with the idea of repaying it in a year. Even though I did not need it, I borrowed the money because I wanted to document the process of getting a BCF loan.

At that time, few guidelines existed. INB complained because of the paperwork and their low profit margin. INB made the loan to Mays Chemical for $250,000 at prime plus one when I explained that I wanted to document the process. So we kept it for a year and repaid it.

I tried to get a commitment from the heads of each of the major banks in Indianapolis to participate in BCF. To my knowledge, no business has requested a BCF loan from any of these banks. I know the bank presidents personally and the commitment was there. And, of course, if you don't use it, who knows?

I also spoke to representatives of several banks in Cincinnati about BCF at the request of Marlana Raime, the minority coordinator at Procter and Gamble. Three or four banks participated, but they made no loans, even though businesses applied. Their situation was the reverse of ours. In Indiana, participating banks were willing to make loans, but no requests came from entrepreneurs. Cincinnati banks had requests but made no loans.

I first went to the SBA in 1982 to qualify for an 8(a) loan, sometimes called "the panacea of minority set-asides." An attorney friend and I filled out tons of paper. But, we got to the point where the requirements to qualify for SBA 8(a) participation were so onerous it wasn't worth the trouble.

For example, I set up a partnership that would own the cars we lease to the company. It was perfectly logical to apply the resulting investment tax credits to me personally as opposed to the corporation. SBA had problems with that, and they also had problems understanding why I owned 50 percent of another chemical distributorship in Kalamazoo, Michigan. My partner at MayDay, a black female, owned the other 50 percent and ran the company. SBA wanted me to divest my interest in MayDay because SBA regulations precluded an 8(a) company from owning part of another company in the same area of business. I finally decided that the SBA loan was not worth the time, effort, and energy required.

I'm proud to say, I built Mays Chemical into the country's largest minority-controlled chemical company without assistance from SBA. I would encourage anyone going into business not to look to SBA for help but, instead, apply for commercial sector capital. As you can see, I'm not overly enthused about SBA, even though I have awards from SBA on my wall. Excellence is not related to participation in the SBA.

We do business with the government, but our focus remains on the commercial sector and prime contractors like Allison. We supply quasi-government entities like Crane Naval Avionics in Newport News, Virginia. But the government, whether it's federal, state or city, has virtually no impact on our business.

I suppose we benefit from government set-asides, because government prime contractors are obligated to include minority businesses as subcontractors. I think Lilly Pharmaceuticals, Inc., would say that they deal with small and disadvantaged businesses because it's a requirement. But I think Lilly would also indicate that they do $5 million in business with Mays Chemical because we have become an integral part of their purchasing patterns, not because we're a minority-owned business.

Mays Chemical cash flows itself. At this point, we don't need debt capital. In 1985, we bought Specialty Chemical, the company that I left in 1980 to form Mays Chemical. I fired everybody. We didn't borrow for that acquisition because the company had deteriorated badly. We simply made payments over a period of years.

The second acquisition was for United Chemical at $1 million in 1987. Again, we didn't need acquisition capital because we paid the owners over time. We made the last payment last year. United Chemical, an Indianapolis-based company, sold antifreeze to the automotive industry. The way the automotive industry was set up, the only way we could gain access to the industry was by purchasing an existing company. While everybody said we paid too much, we were really buying the opportunity to get into the industry. That acquisition is now interwoven into Mays but remains a separate division. It probably generates $1 million a year in pretax profits.

We looked at other acquisitions, including Superior, the company that had loaned us the money in the beginning. When we were right down to the wire, had we been a little more venturesome in 1986, we would have bought it. At that time, Superior was twice the size of Mays. But they had environmental problems that I was uncomfortable taking on.

So that's why I can say we're in a different situation today because access to capital is not a problem. When I see the BCF folks at meetings, they ask when I'm coming in for another half million. But our credit line at INB is $12 million. We have $10 million in a working capital line that we borrow at prime unsecured and $2 million in letters of credit as we need them. From time to time, we do. But we have established trade credit of such magnitude that virtually every supplier we deal with represents six-figure credit. Except for discounts—and we take all discounts—we rarely pay up-front for anything. We have adequate capital for anything that I can envision.

### REVENUE, ACCOUNTING, AND INVENTORY

The gross annual revenue for 1990 was $50 million; $56 million in 1991; and for 1992, $60.9 million.

In 1992, we were ranked thirteenth in *Black Enterprise*'s Top 100. I had chosen not to be in *Black Enterprise* for some years because I didn't want the publicity. I felt that the companies listed in *Black Enterprise* did not necessarily represent excellence. Instead, they represented the company's ability to generate gross revenue without regard to profit.

I agreed to be included that year because it was their twentieth anniversary. If you analyze that 1992 list or any year's list, you will find twenty or twenty-one companies not included in the previous year. To some extent, I think the list chronicles the vast majority of minority businesses, but by no means all.

We never had an unprofitable year and rarely have an unprofitable month. If we do, it's probably because we paid bonuses that month or it's December when year-end adjustments are taken. But we pride ourselves in trying to operate the company at the high end of the industry. We're one of the twenty-five largest chemical distributors in North America.

We've experienced steady growth over the years. In 1993, our gross annual revenue was $65.1 million; 1994, it was $88.9 million; and for 1995, it was $106.7 million.

We are profitable because we deal with customers who can pay. We also deal with customers willing to pay a little more for quality. So we can sell products with higher profit margins.

We pride ourselves in making about $1 million in sales per employee, on the average. We keep expenses at a reasonable level and try to operate a fairly cost-effective organization. Average profit margins of chemical distributors are probably between 2 percent and 5 percent pretax. We are at the top of that range. A chemical distributor turns inventory an average of six to seven times; we turn seven to eight times per year. From a capital investment standpoint, our equipment is top-notch, both because we can afford it and because it keeps breakdowns and maintenance to a minimum.

We hire extremely talented, highly educated, young, motivated people who are very skilled in their disciplines, and we pay them well. Probably one-half of the employees have college degrees. About 10 percent have a master's degree or better. I think our investment and reinvestment into plant, equipment, and people make the difference in our operation. It makes our customers want to do more business with us.

We know the products that are turning, and are very conscious of inventory. An inventory person gives me a monthly report. We probably turn inventory twice as fast as our competitors do. Obsolescence is minimal for us, and we rarely speculate on product. We only bring in product because we have an order or a contract that covers the product.

We warehouse product based on a specific customer. We may have eight customers that use a specific product. Although we can't tell how much Customer One will want of this product tomorrow, we can be sure that over the course of the next thirty days, one-half will want the product. So we're able to move the product in that way.

We try to take in money as fast as we can and pay it out as slowly as we can. We probably have excellent controls at this point in the development of the business. We track everything electronically, and we generally invoice within twenty-four hours of shipment. Our collection policies and procedures are well documented. I guess the best testament to our procedures and practices is that our bad debt write-off amounts to less than one-tenth of 1 percent of sales. To be honest, I would say over the years, the biggest hit on bad debts has come from other black-owned businesses. They probably constitute less than 1 percent of our sales, but about 50 percent of our bad debt.

Price Waterhouse performs annual as well as monthly audits. Our internally generated statements are quite accurate. Because we have worked with Price Waterhouse for so long, our systems are in place and well documented.

Even though sales have increased over the years, distribution businesses are not all that complex. The biggest problem area to manage is usually inventory, then receivables, and obviously you hope you have some cash to manage. We basically farm out cash management to the Investment Division of INB, with some guidelines from us. Only recently have we had a significant amount of cash.

Our advertising is more community-service related. Because of the nature of our business and the fact that we are a minority vendor, most of our advertising is done through trade shows. We are strong supporters of the Purchasing Council and participate in ten to twelve council-sponsored trade shows across the country. We also participate in the national trade show.

We've started doing more trade publication advertising. For example, once a year we advertise in the *OPD,* a specialized chemical publication, and in the trade show magazines. As a company, Mays Chemical gets a wide range of publicity in Indiana and neighboring states. We're well known and, with a sales force of sixteen, we make a lot of face-to-face calls.

We consider no minority chemical distributor in our area to be strong competition. We do have competition in other cities: Cincinnati (Orchem, $15 million–plus), Houston (Cole Chemical, $20 million–plus), and Charlotte (Continental, $40 million–plus, which happens to be Native American–controlled).

Beyond the minority companies, we consider local independents in our markets as the most fierce competitors. Ulrich, a fifty-year-old family-owned business in Indianapolis, is about the same size as Mays. Ulrich probably has $50 million in sales. Superior has about $70 million. Tab Chemical, a regional family-owned business based in Chicago, is a closely held and well-run distributorship.

Several national distributors compete for the same business here. In this particular area, the nationals are not as strong in the product groupings that we handle. We're not overly threatened by them.

I foresee a shakeup coming to the chemical distribution business. Every year, more distributors are selling out. Companies with less than $10 million in sales will become obsolete. They can't compete because they are unable to support necessary systems, quality programs, and the environmental and regulatory staffing. In addition, they are unable to generate the sheer volume needed to qualify for buying discounts.

## COMMUNITY LINKAGES AND INVOLVEMENT

### Location

Mays Chemical is not located in the African American community. When we moved to the northeast side of Indianapolis, it was undeveloped land. You know, people don't like to be neighbors to a chemical operation. Our only neighbors were another chemical operation north of us, Boehringer Mannheim, one of the leading diagnostic companies. We moved here because of the easy access to the expressway.

The location and the building were suitable, so we bought them. The building covers 32,000 square feet, with 24,000 square feet of warehouse and 8,000 square feet of office space. We also own 120,000 square feet in the Fairfield Business Park, four blocks away. Mays Chemical leases about 20,000 square feet, and independent businesses lease the rest. But we wanted to buy land nearby so that we could expand as we needed to. We also own six additional acres as a buffer.

We have another warehouse facility on the west side of Indianapolis, with 300,000 gallons of storage, 15,000 square feet of warehouse, and a laboratory. We lease 20,000 square feet in Chicago, and we have public warehousing in Rochester, New York; Cincinnati, Ohio; and Detroit, Michigan.

### Suppliers and Customers

We don't buy chemicals from African Americans because I know of none who manufacture chemicals. We try to buy from black-owned businesses when we can, even if we have to pay slightly more for the product, whether it's office supplies, cars, entertainment, et cetera. We also try to be decent corporate citizens and make contributions to the Urban League, the NAACP, and other entities.

Since our major customers are Fortune 500 companies, we basically don't sell to minority companies. The only exception is the ethnic hair-care market. In the past, we've sold product to companies like Soft Sheen or World of Curls. We quit dealing with them when they didn't pay their bills. It took six months to get paid. I assume that's because of poor business management. World of Curls is probably in the $30 million range. They are eligible to go into *Black Enterprise* if they choose to. So there's no excuse for their payment pattern.

I had a similar experience with Soft Sheen when they did not pay within a reasonable time. I finally stopped doing business with them rather than lose the friendship of Ed Gardner, who may not even know what his organization is doing. I'd be willing to resume a business relationship in the future if Soft Sheen is in a position or has a mind to pay reasonable terms.

In contrast, several companies in the ethnic hair-care market are good customers and pay promptly. Dudley in North Carolina, Luster in Chicago, and Proline are all good customers. However, the number of black-owned businesses that we can either buy from or sell to is very, very small.

### Community Activities

Both I and the company are extremely active in community activities. Each of the vice-presidents serves on at least one community board. Mays Chemical is a member of the Two Percent/Five Percent Club, which means that the company donates between 2 and 5 percent of its pretax profit to charitable organizations. We've been a member ever since the group was chartered in Indianapolis.

The number, amount, and variety of contributions we make and the community service activities we participate in indicates our commitment both inside and outside of the minority community. For an example, I headed up the United Way campaign for central Indiana and we raised more than our goal of $31,565,419.

On the average, the company probably donates between $100,000 and $150,000 a year in cash to various charitable pursuits. I personally add about another $25,000. My alma mater, Indiana University, is a strong beneficiary. We contribute to the Graduate Fellowship Program consortium, and Indiana University probably gets at least $10,000 in various forms from Mays Chemical annually.

We support the brothers in the Alpha Chapter of Kappa Alpha Psi at IU in many ways, including scholarships. We donate to the United Negro College Fund, NAACP, Center for Leadership Development, National Association of Black Accountants, Indianapolis Professional Association, Black Expo, church groups and black arts (theater- or music-related), and many more. I co-chair the Circle City Classic, which is the largest predominantly black sporting event next to the Bayou Classic.

### Trade Association Activities

For years we've belonged to the National Association of Chemical Distributors located in Washington, D.C. We also belong to Cincinnati Drug and Chemical. Some people belong to and participate in the National Organization of Black Chemists and Chemical Engineers. We are an associate member of the only real trade association in the black arena, the American Institute of Health and Beauty Aids, which includes black manufacturers of ethnic hair-care products.

### Role Models

Johnny Johnson, the head of *Ebony,* is a good role model. As I observed him and read about him, I admired him even more, because he started with very little and developed in some extremely difficult areas. [Arthur] Gatson, from Birmingham, took the concept of an insurance company, expanded and developed it at a time when it was very difficult to do so. I consider Percy Sutton [in the radio industry] and Bruce Llewellyn [owner of a Coca-Cola distributorship] as examples of opportunistic entrepreneurs who moved aggressively in the last few years.

Athletes turned business people are good examples of a probably positive trend. In the past, athletes earned money but for whatever reason ended up with nothing once they were beyond their playing days. Megastars, like Jordan or Doctor J, who have invested money in various businesses and teamed up with black entrepreneurs, will do well in the future.

When I have a business problem or a concern, I generally talk to other entrepreneurs. Being an entrepreneur is a fairly lonely life, because few people can relate to the magnitude of your problems—making payroll, struggles with the bank, turned-down purchase orders. Sometimes I talk with Vernon Stansbury, one of my best friends, who operates businesses in the Washington, D.C., area. We worked together at Cummins Engine Company. He was president of the President's Black Roundtable, a distinguished group of black business owners in Washington.

### Employee Profile

Excluding college and high school summer help, we employ about 110 people, including a sales force of 25. About 60 percent are African American, a Native American, a Hispanic, and the rest are obviously Caucasian. About 40 percent are women. We look so positive on our EEO1 form that, in the past, companies have returned the form saying they didn't believe it.

Several family members work for Mays Chemical. My brother Ted runs personnel. Then from time to time as my daughter, Kristin, has a need for additional income, she will come in from college to work in the company. She loves numbers and works in the accounting area. And then my niece, Ted's daughter, Carolene, most recently has joined the company after five years with Occidental Chemical.

Heather, my oldest, does not choose to work in the company. She's interested in children, and so she teaches. She graduated from Hampton University and is working in Indianapolis. So you see there are some folks that are not motivated by money.

### Succession

I have no plan to groom someone to take my place when I retire. Our vice-presidents are prepared to continue the business should anything happen to me. Kristin might have an interest and perhaps might be a candidate for successor. Although the business is my love, I'm not necessarily committed to passing ownership to my family. It may be more logical to sell the business or convert it from direct ownership of the Mays family. Then the family has time to decide what they want to do. I don't think that I'm hung up on building the Mays Chemical dynasty, as such.

I suppose that my goals for my children are that they develop the quality of life consistent with the expectations of the upper middle class. I want them to finish college and be successful in their chosen field. Beyond that, the ball's in their court. They will have access to significant financial resources so that their decisions will not be hampered by a lack of access to capital.

### OUTSIDE INVESTMENTS

I do not have a perfectly organized plan of how to identify promising entrepreneurs and nurture businesses. However, my philosophy is based on the recognition that Indianapolis needs more successful black-owned businesses. I look at unique ideas with a chance of being successful; that's probably the most important criterion. The investment is in the person rather than the idea. I'm willing to invest in the person, even though I might have doubts about the idea. This way, even if the idea fails, the person gains the experience and the confidence necessary to bounce back and do better with the next idea.

I have invested money in between thirty and forty different businesses over the last five or six years. I think the question becomes how to narrow the choices. A good idea may be importing raw labor from Mexico or discovering oil in Nigeria that can be exported to America. Or invest in actual businesses with a product or service. I've been approached by a film company and several acting troupes. We support a gospel music group in

Indianapolis that one day we hope will have a successful label. After spending $500,000, we're still hoping it will be successful.

I've invested in a construction company, a filter company, a boat company. I have certainly invested a lot of money and time in other businesses that didn't make it—a computer business, a trucking business, a different construction company. I've probably invested in, either for controlling interest or substantial input, a dozen businesses in and around Indianapolis, including the *Indianapolis Recorder* newspaper, which I own.

Newspapers, the *Indianapolis Recorder,* basically, don't make much money. I mean major newspapers don't set the world on fire, and ethnic papers probably do even worse for a variety of reasons. The *Recorder* is one hundred years old. I have been working to try to modernize the paper, to get away from the blood-and-guts format. And when the people who owned it decided that they were tired of scrimping from hand to mouth and wanted to sell it, I stepped forward to buy it. I bought it in August of 1990 and while I still haven't been able to turn much profit yet, it is a much more credible product today, and people are much more willing to have it sitting on their coffee tables from a subscription standpoint and businesses are more willing to advertise in it today. In the not-too-distant future, we will turn a reasonable profit.

I go back a long way with the *Indianapolis Recorder.* I carried it when I was seven years old. I was Chairman of the Board when the Stewart family originally sold part of its interest to Eunice Trotter, who was then an assistant editor at the *Indianapolis Star* newspaper, who came over to run the paper. She asked me to serve on the board and I agreed to do that and ended up as chairman of the board in 1987. So that was my first involvement. I served in that capacity for a couple of years. As the opportunity presented itself, I bought 15 percent and then finally 85 percent of the paper, August 31, 1990. Probably outside of the purchase price, $300,00, I've invested another $500,000.

It was never going to reach its one-hundredth anniversary the way it was going, not because the people weren't sincere and dedicated and hard-working and trying, but it takes resources and it takes updating of equipment. The facility that it was in was falling apart. I'm not sure they really understood what a computer was. They had no desktop computers. There was no real photographic equipment. There was no delivery equipment and on and on and on. The printer had not been paid current for at least thirty years. So the printer ultimately went bankrupt into Chapter 11. I stepped in to pay the printer two and a half months of printing bills in cash at one time, more than forty thousand dollars. To give the printer that much cash and he still goes into Chapter 11 indicates to me he was operating on very tenuous circumstances. So there were many reasons why it makes sense for somebody to step in to save this institution. This is not a money maker; very few weekly papers make money, particularly serving the minority. It has to be a bigger vision than money. So when the Indianapolis black clergy threatened a boycott, I told them very nicely and calmly that I really wasn't too concerned about their boycotting the *Recorder,* because all they do is save me ten thousand dollars a month, because that's what I subsidize the *Recorder* with, so you can pull support and all you've done is put a black institution out of business but you haven't touched Bill Mays or Mays Chemical. So I'm glad they gained some insight into why they weren't going to accomplish their goal, whatever it was.

The circulation is probably about ten thousand now, but those ten thousand today are probably 50 percent different that the nine thousand or ten thousand even five or six years ago. Probably 25 to 30 percent of the *Recorder* subscriptions are nonminority. I think that the paper is read by a much younger audience. The older readership has either passed on or decided not to renew. So as we look at the statistics, we think that the readership is getting younger and probably more middle class and certainly more focused toward economics and business, because we do not feature the blood and guts as the *Recorder* once did.

I think the community at large, both black and white, recognizes the change in the paper in terms of how it looks. The real challenge is how to take that change and make economic benefit out of it. For example, we have written proposals to get grant money to allow young African Americans exposure to print media, and the result of that exposure periodically produces something that we call "Jaws." "Jaws" is an insert into the newspaper that is written solely by high school students that are predominantly African American. So we can address the whole aspect of saying we don't have a lot of blacks who are trained in journalism who understand reporting and the newspaper business. One of the advantages of the *Recorder* is that we train fifteen to twenty students each year so that over time we will be able to send a cadre of young blacks off to college that have five, six, or seven years of hands-on experience in writing, editing, and producing a newspaper. That's got to give them a leg up as they get to college or go to journalism school. So we have a very excellent relationship with the Creighton School of Journalism, Franklin College School of Journalism, and Indiana University–Purdue University at Indianapolis. We have these kids working on computers. They have access to the latest equipment and we think that alone is an incredible kind of contribution to the community. Now the community at large may not recognize it at this point 'cause we don't talk about that, but the fact that Lilly Endowment and the Indianapolis Foundation have seen fit to fork up fairly sizable six-figure grants says a lot—that one, there was a need, two, that they respect the fact that we're better able to provide training than the majority papers, who obviously should have been doing something but choose not to fill that void, and I guess three, wanted to encourage us that we were doing something along the right track.

My short-term goal for the *Recorder* is to become profitable or at least break even. The long-term goal is to make the *Recorder* a viable, respected voice and a credible institution in both the African American and the majority community.

I want to sponsor other businesses. I think, after you lose a lot of money, you conclude that there's got to be a better way start or expand minority-controlled businesses. I recognize that Mays Chemical has neither the financial nor technical resources to do the kind of minority economic development needed by this or any community.

In 1989, I set out on a mission to raise substantial capital from the majority community to set up a MESBIC, a Minority Enterprise Small Business Investment Corporation. In September 1991 we formed LYNX in Indianapolis, Indiana's first MESBIC. Twenty corporations, including most of the major banks, contributed to a pool of $2.5 million. When we get our license from SBA, these funds can be leveraged four to one, which means that our $2.5 million will bring up to $10 million in venture support.

We have a capital pool in Indianapolis, in addition to the BCF. Maybe eighteen to twenty folks have completed the first phase of filling out preliminary paperwork. I'm sure there are more inquiries. But we have a minimum loan requirement of $75,000. Some minimum is necessary; otherwise the cost of administration is too high. At $75,000, ours is probably too steep, because we're finding that many of the businesses are not equipped to handle that amount.

Now that we are one of the best capitalized MESBICs in the country, I am focussing my attention entirely on investing in start-up businesses. We're involved in diverse enterprises. We get at least one proposal a week from entrepreneurs interested in MESBIC. I occasionally invest in one. I recently invested about fifty thousand dollars in a Fort Wayne company that would be very viable if it had access to capital and an opportunity. That's probably the only sizable investment made in 1992.

That company, Alpha Rae, a personnel training employment operation, competes for the business of the state of Indiana. It did take a call to the appropriate people to get them to see the light. But again, that's an advantage. I can make a phone call that might cause someone to take another look at a particular situation. The call resulted in a contract that was the difference between life or death for this company. I think it has a bright future.

I also invested about $35,000 in a company making a film in Indianapolis. Any other investments this year have been related to past investments, business where we're already involved.

I've been involved in two construction companies. J. Chris Construction started in 1983 and went belly-up in 1987 at a cost of about a half million, mainly because it outgrew the ability of the people who were running it. They had too much access to capital and too much work. In 1986 or 1987 they grossed up to $5 million doing general construction, finish work, and woodworking. The company worked on the Walker Theater, built the fire station as a joint venture with another majority contractor, and on Union Station. It did some very significant projects in the community.

The company was headed by Jimmy Beard, a skilled roofer and nice guy. However, Jimmy knew little about running a company, managing people, or about building trades other than roofing. He was unable to manage the five or six projects that were usually going simultaneously. I don't know all the reasons why the company just couldn't weather the storm, but I got tired of putting money into projects that ended up losing money.

My next involvement with construction was different. In 1989, I bought into Harmon Construction, a family-owned business where the principals had solid educational, business, and management experience. They understood both the day-to-day operations of the construction company and business in general. What they lacked I was able to provide—access to capital and the credibility of marketing. Since I became involved in the company, it grew from doing a couple of million dollars to between $8 or $9 million this year.

Our end-of-year goal for Harmon Construction is to be the largest black-owned construction company in this part of the state. The only larger companies will be those that have been in business longer, for example,

Powers (Gary, Indiana), Battes (South Bend, Indiana), or an outside construction company, like Oscar Robinson. Harmon does more work in Indianapolis now than any other minority-controlled construction company.

The machine shop, AMG Engineering and Machines, Inc., is just an investment without a controlling interest. I'm doing this with Ted Gary, who owned the company when I bought in, in 1985. He wanted to continue to be an entrepreneur even though he was unfamiliar with the area, but he's learned a lot by buying a machine shop that makes precision parts for Detroit Allison and others manufacturers. At this point, AMG is the largest black-owned machine shop in the city. They even made a modest profit last year of a few thousand dollars, as compared to the substantial $100,000 loss of a previous year.

I think the future's very bright, because we've reached a turning point on the learning curve. We got Allison to institute a retroactive price increase for nine months to cover the money we were losing because of our ignorance. They knew realistically what it costs to produce the parts and that we couldn't have produced them for what we charged. Unless we adjusted the costs, we would be out of business. If that happened, our customers would no longer have a supplier. We encouraged our customers to treat us fairly so that we'd be around to work with them in the future. They issued the nine-month retroactive price increase.

The boat company [Boat Sales, Inc.], which is a majority company, has no minority employees. I own 49 percent and my partner, Mike Hoffman, owns 51 percent. The company was written up in *Inc.* magazine as one of the fastest growing companies in America. In fact, it grew so fast that it outgrew its capital base as well as the features that change with growth.

In 1989, I plunked down several hundred thousand dollars to become a partner. At that time, I told the management that we needed a trust level to allow us to communicate, and he could lean on my business experience. It's got nothing to do with race—black or white. A cheap boat costs around $25,000, and we deal with boats in the $100,000 range. My investment in this company is more a matter of my personal interest in the individual and not as much in the industry.

Most black folks have never been exposed to the lifestyle of a boater. The boats we handle are expensive—not some rowboat. The gross annual revenue in 1991 was roughly $8 million and about $.5 million in profit. But, we've lost $1 million over the last couple of years. We're just getting to the break-even point. Nineteen ninety-two will be a great year if we do the same business we did in 1991. It's a gamble, but I think that Mike can do it, especially with the stability and the communication we have.

As a matter of fact, I'm going to Bloomington tomorrow so we can talk. I decided that was the only excuse I could give myself for spending the day on the lake. Those luxury cruisers—$200,000 crafts—have a bar, a refrigerator, and two bedrooms. They are better than most people's homes. It's easy to get hung up on the lifestyle. But boats don't mean any more to me than do widgets. So I'm not passionate about the business. For me, it's strictly business, and that's what Mike needs to talk to me about—business. Once he's focused on that he does a very creditable job.

Folks like to play golf, although I don't. However, the golf training facility [Gray Eagle Golf Course] is supposed to be one of the finest in Indiana, and it's located in the right area near the right people, Carmel, Indiana. I'm working on a deal to get experts to run and further develop the facility. We've already invested about $700,000, and we'll probably approach one of the major banks for an additional $1 million. The only holdup is that they want me to personally guarantee all of the money, and I'm not willing to do that. I own one-third and will guarantee my part; however, the partners have to carry their part.

### THE MAYDAY-MAYS CONNECTION

MayDay Chemical was formed by Bettye Daly and me in 1981. MayDay Chemical is one year younger than Mays Chemical. Bettye Daly had a solid background in chemicals at Upjohn when she went to work for a competing chemical distributorship. The new relationship was not working out, so she approached me with the idea that we would create a company to access the Michigan market while I expanded into Illinois and Ohio. We each put up five hundred dollars as the capital investment in the MayDay, and Mays Chemical funded everything else for the next six years.

Bettye ran MayDay, and I ran Mays Chemical. I turned over all my accounts in Michigan to MayDay when we formed our partnership. When I bought Specialty Chemical in 1985, I also transferred their Michigan business to MayDay. When MayDay was just starting, we allowed them to use us as a supply base until they could develop their own suppliers.

During the early years, MayDay bought virtually everything from Mays at our cost plus 2 or 3 percent and then resold it. This arrangement helped us increase our volume, our penetration of suppliers, and share discounts available through volume purchasing.

I sold my interest in MayDay (50 percent) back to Bettye in 1987 and signed a noncompete agreement for all industries except automotive, because I already owned United Chemical. The idea was for MayDay not to compete directly with Mays. I sold my interest in MayDay because we had different philosophies about how to grow and operate the business. Today, Bettye owns all of MayDay, and we still have very friendly relations because MayDay is housed in a building owned by a partnership in which I am involved.

We arranged for $1 million in loan guarantees through Indiana National Bank. Mays Chemical loaned MayDay as much as $100,000 at any one time. The chemical business requires a lot of money to function, but loan guarantees will do a lot of the work. At one point, we were so heavily connected to May-Day that our auditors questioned whether to qualify our financial statements.

MayDay eventually repaid every dime owed to Mays. I sold my interest in MayDay when it was clear that Bettye and I wanted to operate the company in ways that were incompatible. So I decided to sell my share over time and give her full control to structure the company without concern about competition from Mays or any other company.

According to the terms of the 1987 buyout, the price was $150,000 over a period of three years. During that time, Mays would not compete for business in Michigan other than what we already had through United Chemicals, which wasn't MayDay's competitor anyway. MayDay would have exclusive rights to Michigan and anywhere else it chose to go, including Indiana. We lived up to our agreement.

The agreement terminated about May 1991. In 1992, Mays entered Michigan and tried successfully not to disrupt MayDay. Now major companies like Upjohn, Parke-Davis, Dow Chemicals, or General Motors have two minority companies to compare for pricing, service, and quality of personnel.

In 1992, although it probably made little economic sense to my management people, I offered to buy MayDay for $1 million. At that time, MayDay was not profitable, had negative retained earnings, and had not invested in plant or equipment during the three-year noncompete period. Bettye's response was that she needed a million dollars after taxes. There was no economic justification for such a proposal. For $1 million we could have established a substantial operation in several parts of Michigan, not just in Kalamazoo.

We currently do more business in Michigan than does MayDay,

particularly in products not sold by MayDay. However, as we try to establish ourselves as a viable distributor in Michigan, we will have to compete directly against MayDay, since some of their customers already buy Mays products. When we approach Parke-Davis, Upjohn, and Kellogg, for example, it will be fairly obvious that a company seven or eight times the size of MayDay has more buying power, financial resources, and systems in place. It will be very difficult for MayDay to thrive competing against Mays.

### BARRIERS

We never had problems getting insurance, even when most chemical concerns did. We were fortunate enough to go with Liberty Mutual when we first started. Our other insurance—medical, pension, et cetera—is handled by black agents, one from Massachusetts Mutual and one from Equitable. Product liability insurance, property, casualty, and general insurance are handled by Gregory and Appel, a strong insurance broker in this city.

Bonding issues only come up with contracts in certain cities, Cincinnati, for example. Our insurance company can write bonds; however, when something requires a bond, we generally use our $2 million letter of credit facility. Of that amount, about $200,000 is guaranteeing bonds for existing contracts. So bonding is not a major issue for us.

Some say that access to capital is the biggest barrier faced by minority businesses. I think understanding and managing a business is a bigger problem. Certainly recognizing an opportunity and getting access to capital are the biggest barriers to going into business.

### ADVICE TO FUTURE ENTREPRENEURS

If I were to give advice to an African American contemplating entrepreneurship, I would say that success requires three elements. You need (1) significant education related to your business; (2) experience, especially in a Fortune 500 company or some other business in your chosen field; and (3) money: begin identifying sources of money early on.

My best advice would be rather than starting a business from scratch, buy an existing business or part of a business. Then gradually buy more of it until you own a controlling interest. Businesses are for sale everywhere. Black folks don't manufacture very much, but look at what we consume—for example, tennis shoes. The technology for making tennis shoes can't be very complex, and the profit margins are high. Or look at high-volume consumer items like chewing gum or liquor.

I personally would consider franchises. Look at Magic Johnson and Earl Graves with Pepsi or Bruce Llewellyn with Coca-Cola. The manufacturing procedures are well documented. It simply requires the ability to manage a growing business with a big partner. Coca-Cola provides a lot of assistance. Another example is McDonald's. People buy one, learn to operate it, and then end up buying into three, four, or more.

### THE FUTURE OF MAYS CHEMICAL

I don't know what the immediate and long-term future holds for Mays Chemical. We want to stay the course. We already have the management skills and abilities we need to allow us to get to $100 million in gross annual revenue by 1995. I haven't decided what makes sense after that. It depends on a variety of factors.

After you conquer one hurdle after another, you have to keep finding new hurdles. The basic goal was to have a financially successful business, and we do. Next, we wanted the business to be respected in the industry and recognized by our peers. I think we've done that. Then, say, we want to be known and respected nationally. I think *Black Enterprise* magazine did that. So we move to other hurdles. Are we the largest minority business? Well, who cares? We're certainly substantial, so we quit preparing ourselves for that. Instead, we want to be the best. Not compared to other minorities, but the best anywhere. We are now looking on a more global basis to see who the best distributors in the world are as compared to the best in the United States. These are the companies that will ultimately be our competition.

The major chemical manufacturers are not taking on any new distributors. For example, we became the first distributor added by Dow Chemical in the last ten years. We look at that and think we have a bright future. But if someone offered a ridiculously high price for Mays Chemical just to buy into our market share or into our suppliers, we'd have no problem pulling the Mays name off the door.

### CASE 6
## MayDay Chemical—Bettye Daly

*Bettye Daly, age forty-three, is president and CEO of MayDay Chemical. Daly is divorced and has three children, David, twelve; Autumn, nineteen; and Jeff, twenty-three.*

## THE EARLY YEARS

I was born in Eufaula, Alabama, as were my parents, and I lived there until I was about seven. My dad was a noncommissioned officer in the air force, and we moved hither and yon. I probably attended sixteen, seventeen schools in I can't remember how many states. They were always on military bases or similar situations. But my roots are in the South.

I finished high school in Grand Forks, North Dakota, and went to the University of North Dakota. My first year in college was lonely because my family had moved away. The second year I transferred to Midwestern University in Texas to be with my mom and the rest of my family. My dad and brother were in southeast Asia.

That was the biggest mistake I ever made, going to live with my mother and siblings. She didn't understand that you just don't go to school, you study. She wanted me to either get a job after school or do housework. I also didn't have a car, so I had to bum rides.

Just to escape, I dropped out of college and got married to someone I had known less than three months. The three-year marriage ended in divorce in 1968, but I had a son, Jeff, who is now twenty-three. We ended up in Michigan because of the marriage. I was working full-time and going to school part-time. At age twenty-six, ten years after starting, I finally graduated from Western Michigan University. I enrolled in graduate school but had to work full-time, so I went to school in bits and pieces. I finished the course work for a master's degree in economics at age thirty but didn't do the thesis because I started MayDay Chemical.

My dad and I were not close, mainly because he was seldom around. My dad has a GED. My mom dropped out of school in seventh or eighth grade. Her greatest aspiration for me was to graduate from high school and get married after. We had a decent relationship, but after a certain age we had little in common. My mother is very subservient and docile, so our personalities clashed.

Both of my parents came from poor, rural southern backgrounds. My mother's father was a sharecropper with eighteen children. My dad came from a family of four children. His father wasn't well educated but was a carpenter and a tavern owner. They were much better off economically than my mother's family.

I have one older sister and one younger. When I was ten, my parents adopted my mother's nephew whose parents had died. He, too, was ten at that time. There has always been and continues to be a lot of sibling rivalry with the sister who is two years older. I have a mother-daughter relationship with my sister who is ten years younger. My brother and I have a good relationship. I think our family was close in its own way but never overly affectionate.

My father's father, the tavern keeper, became a kind of surrogate father when my dad was overseas. When we lived in the South, we lived down the road from him. He was the grandpa who fixed everything, took care of the family. He was the closest relative, the only relative outside of my immediate family that I can remember having warm fuzzies for. We moved around so much we never really had an extended family.

I went to my grandfather's tavern all the time. My mother tells me that I learned to count money before I learned to read. I'm actually writing a book and much of it has to do with my relationship with my grandfather. I force myself to remember those early years. What I do recall is that being the baby at that time, I was "grandfather's favorite" and got a lot of nurturing. I remember him as an old man who talked and related to me not as a parent but as a friend. He probably taught me a lot about interpersonal relationships that I certainly didn't realize until recent years—always pleasing your customer.

I'm a social being and so was my grandfather. I remember his interactions with his tavern customers. I know he wasn't wealthy, but he had one of the nicer homes in the neighborhood. Everybody knew who he was. I remember being in the limelight because he was my grandfather.

I was encouraged to become an entrepreneur when I was a teenager living in Mississippi. I saw abject poverty and ignorance, uneducated people trapped by public policy and an economic system from which they would never escape.

I immediately saw the flip side in Minnesota, where I was the only black student in the high school. Almost 90 percent of the people there were rich farmers with extended families of generations of farmers. Education was an expectation for their children. It was never whether you went to college, but which college you would attend. Strong family bonds were also important.

In moving directly from an all-black to an all-white situation, I had the chance to analyze the differences between the two. I didn't have time to build defenses; I was just there. I can truthfully say that my involvement with three white families in Minnesota and North Dakota probably helped me to survive in that system. They put the same pressure on me to get an education, to get ahead and succeed that they put on their children who were my friends.  These surrogate families challenged me and pointed me in the right direction. They taught me a different lifestyle; it wasn't necessarily good or bad, and I didn't prefer it over mine. They exposed me to different values. I think that made all the difference.

### DECISION TO START A BUSINESS

MayDay Chemical Company, Inc., is a full-line chemical distribution business. We mainly sell chemicals to manufacturers of food, pharmaceutical, and paper products, and we sell water-treatment chemicals. The company was incorporated in 1981 and became a subchapter S corporation in 1991. We are a "one-stop-shopping supermarket" for chemical producers. Because MayDay carries many products, customers can purchase, say, the ten products they need from me rather than from ten different producers.

Distribution is obviously a service business. Quite often customers can't afford to buy or are not willing to buy the volume a manufacturer requires. They can buy in smaller volume from me. We also custom blend and produce chemicals according to customer specifications, but we don't put a MayDay label on anything we manufacture. That's changing though. We've just started to produce our first proprietary product, a line of aeronautic maintenance cleaners that we ship to a government installation in Saudi Arabia.

I probably thought about becoming an entrepreneur when I was twenty-nine years old and totally frustrated in corporate America. I was doing very well, but not feeling very accomplished. There was nothing wrong with corporate life. I realized that the problem was with me. I just couldn't fit in.

At that time, I was taking a graduate management course in entrepreneurship at Western Michigan University. The course was taught by a wealthy gentleman from Kalamazoo, an advocate of entrepreneurship who happened to be the only surviving grandson of William John Upjohn, the founder of Upjohn.

After the second class he asked if I knew why I was taking the course. When I couldn't answer, he told me that in every tribe there's only one chief and everybody else is an Indian. "You're a chief, but you haven't found your tribe yet," he said. I understood what he meant. I had always felt misplaced. I actually had the classic entrepreneur's personality and outlook but didn't know it. I think a lot of black Americans are probably trapped in the same situation because they've never been exposed to it.

Entrepreneurs never say never. I don't hear no. I don't hear can't, and I very rarely hear won't. They are just not a part of my vernacular. I never met anybody I didn't like. I can eventually find some people distasteful, but I can't comprehend disliking anybody. Entrepreneurs are outgoing and optimistic, sometimes to their detriment. They have vision; they're dreamers. Entrepreneurs are not task-oriented people; they conceptualize, initiate, and then go on to something else. I see it every day.

Entrepreneurs are terrible people managers. They don't like fences and don't like to be fenced in. That was my problem in corporate America. Corporations have a structure and a system that requires conformity. If everyone was an entrepreneur, corporations wouldn't work. Entrepreneurs are really misfits in most of society's structures.

My first professional job, after I got my B.A. degree from Western, was in 1976 as a purchasing agent at the Upjohn Company. I had been working the previous three and one-half years in marketing for the Kellogg Company handling their West Coast brokers, who bought carloads of cereal and Pop Tarts for big grocery chains. I was the inside rep for the field reps.

That job financed my education. At that time, I was married and had two children. I worked at Kellogg from 4:00 to 8:00 P.M. and earned over ten dollars an hour. The job provided my first opportunity to go to school full-time during the day, pay for a babysitter, and contribute to the household. I was living in Battle Creek, so I commuted to Kalamazoo.

My husband was happy. I went to school, had a job, and was home at a decent hour, so I was happy. I had it all. It was the perfect job for me. So after I graduated, Upjohn recruited me to come to Kalamazoo for a professional job.

Upjohn provided excellent experience. When I was hired as a chemical purchasing agent. I told them I would accept the job with the understanding that I would stay five years. At some level, I knew the job was not for me, but I needed it and really wanted to work for them. During the last year and one-half, I knew that I would never make five years. I traveled all over the country for Upjohn, met many people, including senior-level management, and was exposed to many things.

I left Upjohn not because I was dissatisfied with the company, but because I had that "entrepreneurial itch." As I reached thirty, it was becoming an obsession. My biological clock was ticking, and I needed to leave that comfortable environment to satisfy an inner need.

I didn't have a clue about money. I didn't immediately start MayDay when I left Upjohn. Instead, I started a division of an existing Detroit company in southwest Michigan, which gave me a safe opportunity to exercise those entrepreneurial wings. We were starting almost from ground zero. They had few customers and had been calling on Upjohn and other big companies without much success.

Unfortunately, this opportunity did not work out. The owner also owned several other businesses, and this division had neither a high profit margin nor a high profile. His business ethics were questionable—not paying people, not treating employees well, shady dealings. I might never live down the reputation that I was developing there, so, I quit after six months. During that time, I picked up about a $1.5 million of business.

Today, everybody in the chemical industry knows me. In 1976, I was "different." Corporations had no black females in professional positions, and the chemical industry was totally male. I traveled. I had written articles about business issues published in industry journals. I chaired some national chemical industry functions held in Michigan. I immersed myself in my "professional peer group."

I didn't know what I was going to do after I quit this job. My second husband, an engineer, thought I was crazy quitting the job that I had quit Upjohn to take. By this time we had three children and no housekeeper. He was totally confused. I had given them two weeks' notice and I didn't tell my husband because he might have tried to talk me out of it.

### GETTING STARTED

I tried to decide what to do—I had quit out of total frustration. So the next day, I called Bill Mays. Bill and I had been working together since I was at Upjohn and he was with Specialty Chemical Company. When Bill started Mays Chemical Company, Upjohn had to decide whether to stay with Specialty or transfer their business to Bill. I was the one who said, "We don't know rip about Specialty Chemicals. We're really buying from Bill Mays, and if we want to support Bill Mays and his organization no matter what the name, we need to transfer that business."

Bill will tell you that I was the first customer to give him $1 million worth of business and the support of the Upjohn Company. I put Bill on the map. I knew that Mays Chemical was reputable, and because of their government contracts, Upjohn was interested in developing relationships with black entrepreneurs. I was helping them accomplish that in a meaningful way.

When I called Bill, I reminded him of last year's conversation, when he offered me a job with his company in Indianapolis. My husband said he was not going to be a Hoosier; he was a Wolverine. I told Bill I still couldn't move but thought we had a tremendous opportunity. I was going to start a business in Michigan. I wanted to offer him 50 percent of the business in return for start-up capital. I would do all the work. In less than ten minutes, Bill agreed. He asked me what I would need. I told him ninety thousand dollars and that it would be the best investment he ever made.

Bill knew me. Not only had he been my customer, but he was also my competitor when I worked for the new venture. He knew my contacts, reputation, and my abilities in my marketplace, Michigan. We had become friends over the years. I asked that his attorney draw up an agreement, because I didn't have the money to pay an attorney. By the next Tuesday, the documents were drawn and Fed Ex'ed. So MayDay started on my kitchen table; that's why I keep it in my office. I created the entire marketing plan and we were in business.

Bill owned 50 percent of MayDay for seven years. Now we're competitors again in Michigan. But you'll never hear anything bad from us. You'll rarely find two black entrepreneurs with a relationship like ours. That's how May-Day was born.

Bill's money was a loan, not equity. He actually got 50 percent of the business, seven years of interest expense. Entrepreneurs don't look at whether or not they're getting screwed on the downside. This was what I needed to get started, so these are the "opportunity costs." People can't believe I was willing to do it. What difference does it make? I'm still here.

I didn't take other classes or seminars, go to a business development agency, or seek advice about starting the business. I just took a basic marketing plan and adapted it to my needs. I told my customers they were doing business with me, not with the other entity. It was easy to transfer their business.

I developed a crude accounting system for myself and initially used Bill's accountant to do my bills. I already knew the products and the customers, and I was going to be shipping out of Indianapolis using Bill's warehouse and freight contacts. It was pretty elementary—get the business, figure out how I was going to pay the bills, identify the next customer I was going to call on, and sell. My business plan was very elementary, too, since I didn't need to go outside the company for funding. After about three years, I developed a formal business plan to approach banks about a loan.

Business capital for MayDay came through Bill, who borrowed money from his bank and entered the notes on his books. When his bank became curious about the notes receivables from a Michigan-based company, I met with his bank's loan officers. At that point, I wrote a business plan in the format that the bank was accustomed to seeing.

My husband was not involved in starting MayDay. I remarried in 1972 to a man of Irish extraction, one of the nicest people I've ever met, but not a risk taker. He just couldn't understand why I wanted to do this. We were both professionals and earned about the same salary. Our lifestyles were geared to two professional incomes. We had three kids and a huge house in the sub-urbs. And now, he also has a wife who's trying to find herself. Not only was he not instrumental in starting MayDay, but he was also threatened by it.

My children occasionally work in the business but are not regular employees. My older son, who is in college, works year-round for a few hours doing some computer work. My daughter has worked for us in the summer. She currently does some work for me in my home office. She also models. My kids earn $5 an hour through the business.

The business is located in the African American community because it was cheap. We also wanted it within Kalamazoo city limits, close to where I lived. Bill and I own the thirty-two-thousand-square-foot building, which we lease to MayDay.

### ACCESS TO CAPITAL

Loans of $90,000 to $120,000 for start-up capital came from William G. Mays, who received part ownership of the business in return. We did the loans in stages so the interest rates range from 14 to 18 percent.

We used Bill like a revolving credit line. We termed out the notes because, as a start-up, he too had to show those notes as assets on his books. So two businesses grew from one line of credit. I've repaid Bill Mays.

When MayDay was two years old, I went to commercial banks for a loan. I was well received by the loan officer. After looking at my financial statement, he said they couldn't lend to a business like mine that was highly leveraged and had no assets. I got the same answer from all the local banks. In a con-servative environment like Kalamazoo I wasn't going to get start-up capital without an asset base. I went to Indianapolis and piggy-backed on Bill's relationship with the bank. They got to know me during three years of work-ing with me. They looked at my financials and understood that the leverage was all debt financing.

I'm still in the same situation. When you start with nothing, it's hard to work out of the hole because everything you earn goes to pay interest. We had never put equity into the business in eleven years. We still have a neg-ative net worth. We need a year of tremendous profits or an equity infusion. The business can sustain itself, but it just can't compensate for the problems originally created by 18 percent interest.

The Indiana National Bank extended a revolving line of credit of about $250,000. Now Bill and I both had a working relationship with the bank. They understood entrepreneurial ventures. And, culturally, Indiana is much more mixed than Kalamazoo, Michigan, where a black walking into the bank looking for a loan might just as well be an "alien." Indianapolis, by contrast, has a history with minority customers.

Kalamazoo's conservative environment is a built-in business constraint. They weren't willing to lend on my negative net worth. I believe that they were applying the same guidelines to other business people. That could be untrue, but I choose to believe it. I accepted them as unprogressive and without vision. If race was a part of it, that's their problem. Gender may have been a part of it, too. As a black and a female, I can be compared to nothing in their port-folio. I just kept shopping until I got a loan.

Bill suggested that I talk to the Michigan Minority Business Develop-ment Council about the funds. The council led me to the Bank of Detroit, with-out success. I wanted to do the BCF program with MayDay's local bank in Kalamazoo. But BCF had no approved lenders in Kalamazoo. I said we would establish one. I went to another bank, where my attorney knew the pres-ident. With the bank's support, we brought the BCF program into the Bank of Kalamazoo. MayDay received $250,000 at prime, approximately 12 per-cent, payable over two years. They subordinated their collateral to the bank. So it was assets and receivables.

I talk about BCF to other entrepreneurs who are looking for capital and to corporations already participating in that fund. I tell them that we've taken advantage of the BCF funds and encourage them to continue their participation.

My overall experience with BCF was positive. It lowered my borrowing rate by about 2 percent for two years. Because my bank administers the loan,

I just write one check to the bank. It also brought new cash to my bank, which was then a start-up. Overall, it was a fairly painless win-win transaction.

We made our last payment on May 30, 1992, but we're going to borrow again. Although $250,000 is nice, we need more for a growth business. We could use private funding much greater than what BCF is willing to lend. With our age and size our needs are greater.

BCF funds gave me an opportunity to do 50 percent of my borrowing at a reduced rate and to acquire a new computer system and software. My bank was supercautious. They wanted us to participate in the BCF, but they wanted the BCF funds to replace or be part of the total loan package. So we didn't get their top line of credit. Our actual loan was reduced so that we never got more incremental money. That's another form of entrapment.

Bill and I were going to get 8(a) certified, but it required too much work. Other people who are 8(a) certified told us that SBA people who knew nothing about their business were telling them how to run it. It might be nice money, but I didn't want the controls they imposed.

About three or four years ago, we started to do business with government entities by competitive bidding. They send out an annual bid and we quote. If we're low bidder, we get the business. If not, we'll try next year.

We have one Department of Agriculture contract for about $150,000 for lab chemicals. We also have a contract with the city of Kalamazoo worth about $125,000. Government business is a very small part of our business.

So far, we haven't gotten any business as a result of government set-aside programs. If you hear of any, please let us know. The city of Detroit has a Sheltered Market Program that guarantees to make 30 percent of their purchases from minority businesses. Businesses are entered into a pool. Rather than bidding against major companies, you bid against other minority companies. The problem with the city of Detroit program is that the black folks already in power try to keep you out of the program.

The Sheltered Market Program application humiliates the business owners they say they "want to work with." Blacks, particularly in bureaucratic positions, try to keep you out, not bring you in. It's sad. We've been operating as a 100 percent black-owned business for eleven years and we're still not part of the Sheltered Market Program. According to them, we can't do the forms right. Can you believe that? The program is headed by a black female. That's the only set-aside that we know of, but it's set aside so that black folks can't get it approved. It needs to be challenged.

Here's my parting shot. Why does a city that's 80 percent black have a minority program for our own people? It's an interesting question, don't you think?

REVENUE, ACCOUNTING, AND INVENTORY

Our gross business revenue for 1990 was $7.5 million; for 1991, $7 million; for 1992, I expect about $8 million. We're about at the break-even point.

We're trying to get into more profitable markets and cut expenses such as interest expense. Now that our BCF funds are repaid, we're borrowing at prime plus two again. Insurance is another expense. My insurance bill jumped from forty-five thousand dollars in 1990 to eighty-two thousand dollars in 1991 because of federal and DOT [Department of Transportation] regulations, and the insurance industry withdrawing from chemical-related insurance. It takes a lot of sales to generate forty thousand dollars in twelve months.

The recession made the market supercompetitive. More people are trying to divide a much smaller pie. Our gross margins dropped by 25 percent. Expenses outside of my control are killing us. However, gross sales are actually growing.

The business remains current with FICA, IRS, and other withholdings. We have an outside auditing firm, a chief financial officer, and a full-time bookkeeper. Our accounting is computerized. I receive a financial statement every month and an external audit once a year. In addition, I have internal management meetings about two or three times a year. We keep about $300,000 in inventory on hand. Our inventory system is computerized, so I can monitor it daily.

COMMUNITY LINKAGES AND INVOLVEMENT

**Suppliers and Customers**

We try to use African American suppliers whenever possible. We were doing business with a computer services outfit, but they're no longer in business. We use some trucking companies. They simply do not exist in this community.

Our main customers are the big companies in Michigan—DuPont, Upjohn, General Motors, Ford, Georgia Pacific, Post Cereals, Warner Lambert, University of Michigan, Dow Corning, and a few little mom-and-pop platers. They plate items for the automotive industry.

138 LIFE STORIES OF ENTREPRENEURS

None of our current customers are African American. Over the course of this business, I think I've had four. I am now soliciting business with two; one in Flint and the other a start-up generic pharmaceutical manufacturing company in Detroit. Three of my four black customers have stiffed me on receivables. We treat each other worse than we treat anybody else. One owes me twelve to eighteen thousand dollars that I had to write off as bad debt.

### Employee Profile

We had two employees when we first started. We now have fourteen: one Korean male, two black females, three full-time black males, and the balance are Caucasian males and one female. We find employees by advertising and through employment agencies.

### Advertising and Marketing

Our market analysis showed that we could easily sell more profitable products, not necessarily more product. If I could increase my gross profit margin by 1 percent, we would be making great money; by 2 percent, I'd be ecstatic; and by 3 percent I'd be in the Bahamas on an extended vacation.

In our industry, personal selling is actually the most effective. So our advertising consists of company literature that is hand-delivered. We are also included in some industrial trade listings that come out annually.

### Principal Competition

Mays Chemical is certainly a competitor, and so are national distributors and billion-dollar companies like Chem Central, Ashland, and VWR. We compete with other distributors who are subsidiaries of huge companies with clout. They have state-of-the-art facilities, multiple locations, and nationwide distribution. I must buy in smaller quantities and try to compete with them on price.

I've tried to improve my competitiveness by staying close to home, providing the best service possible, and spoiling the hell out of my customers here so they won't go elsewhere. Because I stay local, my transportation costs are limited. I can ask them for a little bit of premium because I'm doing just-in-time deliveries for them. I'm building my business to accommodate them. We really only do business for customers in the state of Michigan, and that concept has worked for me. We don't have the resources to be in all fifty states.

### Community Activities

I sit on the board of the Kalamazoo Institute of Arts, and I am their volunteer marketing director. My objective is to integrate the Art Institute socially, because I think appreciation and use of art is one of the most enriching parts of life. I have also served on the boards of the chamber of commerce, United Way, and Junior Achievement.

In 1990, I started a program in Kalamazoo to mentor African American girls in public school grades four through twelve. I have thirty-two African American women who volunteer to provide the girls with a different view of life. It's that same view that gave me an opportunity to look outside my situation. I'm strongly committed to provide that opportunity for the girls in this community. I also belong to some other professional organizations.

We have an annual philanthropy budget of about $3,000 or $4,000. My accountant thinks that's too generous for our gross revenues. Last year we gave the black civic group twenty-five hundred dollars because they were in trouble. I was in trouble, too, but they were in bigger trouble. We support all the NAACP booklets and WISE minority programs for kids. We are the largest black-owned business within a wide radius, so we get solicited often. We've given the Little League team about $500 a year for equipment for the last four years, and they're Little League champions. I personally give to the church.

### Trade Association Activities

We belong to the state chemical group, the Michigan Minority Business Development Council, the Black Technology Association in Lansing, and the Kalamazoo Area Purchasing Association.

I've also contributed to professional publications in areas related to my work: how generic substitution would affect the pharmaceutical industry; how the oil embargo would affect American industry; and safety in loading and unloading hazardous chemicals and the resulting environmental consequences. Because I handle hazardous products, I am often asked to participate in surveys and forums and to contribute to journals.

### Role Models

I don't have a business role model or mentor. When we first started, it was Bill. We talked and interacted a lot, somebody to kick around ideas with. In day-to-day operations, I'm totally isolated. That's been a problem.

When I have a business problem or issue of concern I talk to my twelve-year-old son. He knows more about MayDay than perhaps anyone else. For Christmas, he bought me a book about how to energize an existing business. MayDay is his sibling; they're a year apart in age. He's been here since day one. When we talk about MayDay, you'd think he was talking about another person. He's next-generation entrepreneur. He has his own business making custom fishing lures he sells.

The attorney who helped me engineer the buyout has become extremely close. He's a father figure, an entrepreneur, a chemical engineer, and an attorney. We schmooze a lot. I talk to the professor who told me I was an entrepreneur before I knew it. He sits on the sidelines, my private cheering section. He, too, is a businessman and entrepreneur. We talk about business strategies, market trends, and related issues.

### Succession

I think, perhaps, my older son, Jeff, might take over the business. He's here quite a bit and is interested in what's going on. He's a nontraditional student. He spent four years in the marines, and now he's in college. Although I'm not grooming him for it, I think he is capable of running the business, whether by default or design.

Right now I'm trying to recruit the person I want to take over the day-to-day business operations. I know that person would have no problem selling the business if it became necessary in the future.

I want my children to find whatever makes them most happy and productive. I think my older son will first be a politician and then a businessman; he might do both simultaneously. My daughter, who models and is quite an actress and writer, is going to be a heck of an attorney. That's her professional interest. My younger son, I think, will be an entrepreneur.

### BARRIERS

One of the greatest barriers for African Americans is the inability to conceptualize that a business is not a job, it's a way of life. You have to live the life before you give birth to the business. It's called preparation, developing a mind-set. You suffer agony, poverty. Owning a business does not mean that you're going to wear designer suits, carry leather briefcases, and strut around like Mr. or Ms. Wonderful. Owning a business means doing a helluva lot of hard work with no rewards and nobody to give you an "at-a-boy."

It's total isolation. It's giving up self and a social life. It's almost like being buried alive, except that you like yourself so much that you really don't care. You, your business, and your immediate family are perhaps all you need for a time. You have to make a commitment. I don't see too many people willing to give up everything for an opportunity to develop something. If you're not willing, you just get a job.

I'm not sure that you ever overcome that barrier. People are always telling me that I'm so successful. What's success? We're not making any money. In economic terms, perhaps not. If you ask 95 percent of my customers whether I deliver product on time and if they're satisfied with MayDay, they will say yes. I'm successful in running my business by satisfying my customers. Am I happy? Have I been successful at life? I would say 90 percent of the time I am. So am I successful? I don't know. But I've never considered closing down.

I've been divorced so long I don't remember being married. I've been running this business and raising three children alone for years. The business definitely had a negative impact on my marriage. The "opportunity costs"— a stable home environment and a two-parent family—was the price I had to pay. In hindsight, it was a small price.

I've grown up with my children. This business is my fourth child. Although the minority population in Kalamazoo is about 13 percent, I have no peer group because, in general, entrepreneurs here are white males, older than fifty, and grandfathers. They have nothing in common with a black woman who has young children. Since I work for myself, I don't meet people in the workplace. I meet employees, but they talk at me, not to me.

I'm totally isolated. I have no extended family here, either. When I came here in 1977 to work with Upjohn, I had no traditional links with the community, particularly the black community. They call me Miss MayDay. They know who I am, but it's intimidating to the males. I'm a nonperson. It bothered me for awhile. Now, I've made peace with it and consider it one of the "opportunity costs" for living here and owning a business. It can either manage me or I can manage it. I choose to manage it.

My circle of friends consists of women who belong to my organization. But, then, I'm the president and organizer, so they put me at a different level. I can never be one of the "ace coon boons." I've made a few friends through business in other cities. But most of these people are customers, and you never really let your guard down around customers.

Since my extended family is out of state, my social life revolves around my children. I'm now wondering what I'll do when my twelve-year-old is gone. It will be the biggest divorce of my life.

## ADVICE TO FUTURE ENTREPRENEURS

Go for it! Everybody's going to say don't do it. If you think you can do it, do it. You might fail, but most entrepreneurs fail miserably two or three times. They get back up and try again.

If you want to start a business try one that you know something about. If you have a lot of money you can buy a business and hire people either to run it or teach you how to.

### THE FUTURE OF MAYDAY

My immediate business goal is to become profitable. Once we're profitable, we can secure capital in the commercial marketplace to actualize my long-term goal of building a new facility. We're out of space. The building is old and requires constant repairs. With a new facility we can become more vertically integrated in our product offerings. Then we can manufacture proprietary products so that we can make damn sure we'll be here for another twenty years, my other long-term goal.

I also want to have a division of MayDay in the Caribbean. Developing nations need water- and sewage-treatment products—one of our lines. The idea of doing business in black countries is exciting to me.

### CASE 7
## Exemplar Manufacturing, Inc.— Anthony Snoddy

*Anthony Snoddy, age forty-three, president and CEO of Exemplar Manufacturing, Inc. in Ypsilanti, Michigan, is married and has a seventeen-year-old daughter.*

### THE EARLY YEARS

I was born in Longview, Texas, and came to Pontiac, Michigan, at the age of five. My father came looking for employment in the automotive industry. After about six months, my mother, sister, and I followed. Like most poor families, we moved with another family into a two-room apartment in the low-income housing project. Later we moved into a garage, where we all slept in the same bed until we could afford another one. We moved again when the twins were born. We moved into a white neighborhood that was just starting to turn. It was a decent place with mostly hardworking adults and well-behaved children. Then, there were the others.

My father wasn't particularly happy when I joined a neighborhood gang. He had been an Eagle Scout and taught Boy Scouts, but I was never part of the Scouts. Gangs were one of the few organized activities. We hung out on the corner and were mischievous. By the time I graduated from high school, one-half of the neighborhood kids were either dead or in jail.

I can't say that I looked up to any one person in the gang, but I learned how to survive and get things done. My gang was nothing like the gangs of today. We had a few fights, but they were clean fights, no shooting. The worst thing that ever happened to me was when I was struck in the face with a broken bottle. The family was a little excited, but I got by. It was a good learning experience.

My parents emphasized education. Although my father never graduated from college, he was at the top of his high school class. I'm sure he wanted to be an engineer based on what he exposed me to. For instance, he gave me his Swiss drafting tools when I was in seventh grade. I learned how to use them and a T square and eventually won first place in Michigan's industrial arts drafting contest. My father was instrumental in getting me involved in those activities. Although my father worked at General Motors, he made his money in real estate renting out various properties.

My mother became a beautician out of necessity. With four daughters, she had to learn how to do hair. She started her own business in our house and then moved into another house that my father bought. Next, my mother moved into a larger building and employed five operators. She had one of the biggest beauty shops in the city of Pontiac before she retired.

I grew up with my parents. When I was born, my mother was seventeen and my father, nineteen. My mother had fifteen brothers and sisters. My father's family had seven children. I think my father was twelve when his father passed. My mother finally got her GED much later in life after a battle with cancer. She's also very religious.

I remember our first house, a bungalow with an attic in Pontiac. My father and I turned the attic into two bedrooms with a walk-in closet. We paneled the basement and added another bathroom. We built a two-car garage in the backyard. This experience helped me to develop certain skills and taught me how to make and put things together. My parents now live alone in a big four-bedroom house in Troy, Michigan.

I am the big brother to four sisters. I fought their fights, and they spoiled me. We had a close relationship. Karen is about eighteen months younger than I. Next are twins Neva and Norma, and then Marshilia, the youngest.

All of my sisters are college graduates and doing great. Since we were in college at one time, we all had jobs. My other relatives did this, too. My grandmother was a registered nurse. My father's brothers and his two sisters also went to college.

Education helped me, especially since most blacks shy away from math or science, subjects where I did well. At Eastern, I took courses in sociology, psychology, chemistry, energy systems, and plastics. I have a bachelor of science in industrial technology from Eastern Michigan University in Ypsilanti. I was probably the fifth black ever to graduate with this type of degree from that school. I never imagined that I would end up back in this city and in business!

My family is a study in self-help and independence. I have a great-aunt who made money in Texas oil. She didn't work but had a lot of money and maids. My great-uncle had a sawmill. Another had a grocery store. My grandfather was a mason who built sandstone homes. So in the back of my mind, I always thought I would do my own thing.

When I graduated from college in 1973, I didn't have to look for a job. One of my instructors who worked for Ford made sure I was offered a job without an interview, because he knew how good I was. I didn't like Ford, because I had heard about their layoffs. I was getting married, so I was concerned about keeping my job.

Then I went to talk with somebody at General Motors, but first I had to fill out an application. We talked for a long time. The interviewer said that he'd be interviewing at Eastern Michigan University and wanted me to sign up. I didn't. He called and asked me to come in. I didn't have on a suit or a sport coat, but he said come anyway. A few days later, he called me for another interview. I was interviewed for six hours straight by the top people at the Chevrolet division at General Motors. The next day they offered me a job. I told them I had to think about it.

I accepted the job, and the guy in purchasing who interviewed me said, "If you can read a blueprint, you'll do better than most of the people here. They have liberal arts degrees and they're buying automotive parts." I found that to be true. Most of the liberal arts majors didn't know what they were buying. But they were white, and they got the jobs. I later found out that most did not have degrees. The purchasing jobs were cushy, and you had to know somebody to get one. In the early 1970s, there was a big push to hire minorities. Only one other black guy was working there when I started. He thought he was the greatest because he was a buyer. They fired him and hired me and another black guy from Albany State College in Georgia. This was 1973. In 1975 both of us were laid off.

GM helped us get jobs elsewhere. That's when I understood the power of the automotive industry. Before we left GM, both of us had new jobs in a steel company. They weren't ready for us. It was 1975; they didn't like our mustaches, pastel-colored shirts, sport coats, or Afros. I was going to be the first black outside sales person for any steel company in the United States. They were taking bets that I would leave.

I went back to GM after about eight months. It was strange. Walking into the GM building I saw this white guy I worked with and I told him that I was fortunate to be back at General Motors. He said, "Anthony, you weren't fortunate. You were damn good. Don't you ever forget that."

The guy from Albany State, a predominantly black university, wasn't brought back. I later found out from some of the white guys that he hadn't learned how to deal with white people. He had been sheltered from their omnipotent ways and their underhanded approaches to blacks. I grew up in that environment and knew how to handle it. If they did things I didn't care for, I didn't rave and look like a fool. I might pull them aside and threaten them, which I have. Then it's a one-on-one scenario and nobody could prove it. That's one of the tools I used to get through General Motors.

I was now in General Motors' Detroit Diesel, Allison Division through personal recommendations from the Chevrolet directors of purchasing and personnel. I didn't know that until the interviewer showed me my personnel folder and said, "I guess I have to hire you. Who do you know?" I said I didn't know anybody, and he didn't have to hire me. I was very arrogant!

I recalled how I got the recommendation. The director, after the layoffs were announced, came along one evening when I was still working at 6:00 or 7:00 P.M. He asked why I was there so late. I told him I was working on a project and wanted to wrap it up. He said, "Do you know you're getting laid off?" I said yes. He said, "I'm not going to forget that. Everybody else left. You're the kind of person we want here, because you want to get the job done." I guess he really meant it.

At Detroit Diesel, they still thought that minorities had to have low-level jobs and couldn't assume greater responsibilities. The only way to move up was if somebody died or retired. I had met another white guy who said I should call him if I needed anything. So I did. He said he didn't have a position for me but would see what he could do. I was back at Chevrolet in two weeks. That's when things started to click for me.

I was working in the Purchasing Administration's Policies and Procedures group writing policies and procedures. I functioned as a statistical analyst. That was the best job for me, because I learned what was going on. Like in many corporations, white managers shuffled the work off to somebody else. I accepted it because I was learning; I absorbed everything. I saw this as an opportunity.

I started to realize that policies and procedures are a way to manage the masses. However, they helped me understand exactly what I could and couldn't do. I had an advantage because most of the buyers didn't thoroughly read or understand the policies or procedures.

### DECISION TO START A BUSINESS

My decision to go into business was influenced by what I saw at General Motors. In purchasing I did business with outside companies. Some of the successful people were idiots, dumb people. But they were white and had opportunities. One thing I noticed about them, dumb or not, was that they took risks. When I was growing up, my parents always told me to work hard and things would "turn out." That's true, but you also have to take some calculated risks. After awhile these successful business people started to feel comfortable with me. I'm a big guy, six feet, four inches, 250 pounds, and I can be intimidating. I've used it to help me achieve success. Sometimes you have to intimidate people; you have to have a demanding presence.

I found out that not many black people are in manufacturing. Before I left General Motors I was part of the vice-president's staff. I was giving presentations to the president of General Motors and his staff on how to buy powertrains, rubber parts, engineering services, machinery and equipment, et cetera. Over the years I developed an understanding of the industry, the people in it, and how things get done.

I had always been on the fast track. At age thirty, I was in middle management. Even my white peers didn't do that. Then my wheels fell off—I was too young, moving too fast, and I was black. I knew my job. I headed up purchasing for all the materials management activities for the second largest manufacturing complex in General Motors. One day I asked the material management director of the division I worked in if I would be the next director. He told me no.

Had I stayed at General Motors, I knew I would be financially okay, better than most. That wasn't good enough. I also knew they would never

148

give me what I really deserve. I realized that I had hit ʼ

time for me to get out. I was about thirty-six, thirty-

oping a plan. But first I had to build up my own n/

years later.

I was frustrated. I knew what I really wanted to do in ı..

pendent as possible. Eventually, I wanted to do volunteer work, ι

children and old people. At General Motors, I could only do that in a lim-

ited way. I had to make a lot of money to be in the financial position to help

others. I have to take care of my home and me first; then I'd take care of

everybody else. So I started building my net worth.

My intent was to buy an existing automotive company. Because I was

a buyer before I left GM, I knew what would be acceptable. I couldn't go to

General Motors and say, "I'm starting a business, would you do business with

me?" That wasn't going to happen. While I was in General Motors, I helped

minority supplier companies get started. I knew what made them and major-

ity companies successful. I asked my buddy Phil Pierce, a CPA, to look at avail-

able companies. He did the financial analysis, and I looked at operations.

I had always saved money, always hustled. When I was a kid I had two

paper routes. I cut grass, washed dirty pots and pans, and cleaned basements

to make money. I saved money, bought some stocks. As I got more sophisti-

cated, I did what my father did, bought real estate. The return was good. I would

buy homes inexpensively through HUD, fix them up, rent them out, and use

the cash flow to buy other properties. I didn't need cash. I wanted to build

assets. After I had a number of these properties, I had them reassessed. I was

able to turn a five-thousand-dollar investment into sixty thousand dollars of

assets.

Over five years I built a strong net worth, so that when I went to bor-

row money, I wouldn't hear what they usually tell blacks—"You have no net

worth." When I was ready to start the business, my personal net worth

appeared to be close to $1 million on paper.

Everybody said it was the worst time to go into the automotive indus-

try. But I've always made my most profitable investments during the worst eco-

nomic conditions. It's a risk, but that's how you make the most. I do it with

the houses. To get through rough times, make sure you have the right struc-

tures in place.

Over the years, Masco Industries, a conglomerate, was one of the big-

ger companies I had worked with. They own about thirty-five companies and e partnerships with others. They do about $1.6 billion a year, even though they traditionally play a passive role in the management of the companies. I was hoping that they would be my "big brother." They could also coach me in how to run a small business. That was important in selecting a company to buy.

My CPA buddy told me that a manufacturing company was available. The company did business with General Motors through a partnership with Masco Industries. I also knew that General Motors wasn't happy with the company and wanted to know Masco's plans. I made some discreet calls and decided to meet with them. I was the perfect guy to take over the company. I understood their products and people in the industry. I bought the company and named it Exemplar Manufacturing Company.

### GETTING STARTED

It took me four years to convince myself to leave General Motors. Once I announced the date, it didn't bother me one bit. My biggest concern was telling the GM vice-president of materials management that I wanted to leave with his understanding and support. He was in shock. He warned me about the risks and told me that no one else could do the innovative things I was doing at GM. Normally at that level they tell you to leave the same day, but they asked me to stay another thirty days. They also made a commitment in writing to my company as a supplier. He stated they were looking for good minority companies, and they figured if I can handle their money, I can handle my own.

When I left General Motors, Ford Motors called me and said that they were looking forward to doing business with me, too.

I wanted to buy a company that produced a free-spinning washer on a screw. My financial guy looked at the books and advised me not to unless I knew something else about the company. The company had lost about $2 million on this product over four years. But I looked at the equipment and talked to some of the people. I found out they were some of the best of the industry. They were doing unique things that no one else in the industry could do. They had a niche. But nobody managed the company. I knew the company's competitors and I knew we could be successful. I remortgaged the house and bought the company in November 1991.

I moved from a large corporation with responsibilities for billions of General Motors dollars into a small business that had $9.2 million in sales.

Under the circumstances, strong management was even more critical.

Exemplar Manufacturing supplies metal fasteners, screws, and bolts. We do precision machining of parts and assembly work. We are supplier to General Motors, Ford, and Chrysler, as well as companies like Steelcase, Cummin's Engine, and Black and Decker. I own 51 percent of the company with an option to buy the remainder. Masco Industries is my business partner with 49 percent ownership.

Masco Industries provides access to their legal staff and research and development facility whenever I need it. They are resources that only a company doing $150 million a year in sales might have.

You need a lot of money to buy into a company with these assets. In addition to money, you also need solid experience. Since I certainly didn't have the money to buy it all, I negotiated a value for my experience, a reasonable partnership.

The first thing I did was develop a business plan. Before starting the business, we made financial and other projections. Now, my business plan is an all-encompassing, living, breathing document that we continually update. It includes financial information; sales forecasts; markets or niches that we'll try to approach; where we'll invest our money, machinery, and equipment we plan to purchase; personnel requirements now and over five years.

I developed the market analysis internally. In fact, a lot of our customers want to see our business plan. Ford came in and did what they call benchmarking. They said I had one of the best business plans they had ever seen. A lot of people ask CPAs to prepare their business plan. I didn't do that. If employees know and understand what's in the business plan, they'll make decisions compatible with the business plan.

Some of the things I'm doing are only a theory in larger corporations. I don't have red tape to stop me. I give people whatever they need to motivate them whether its recognition, a pat on the back, writing them a special letter, sending them on vacations, or giving them cash. I can do these things. I drive here from Detroit every day, about an hour each way. When I get here, I go to the manufacturing floor, say hello, and see how people are doing. I try to know their names. I probably know about 80 percent. The previous owners were aloof. To them, the employees were just people who worked there.

We've got a vision and an operating philosophy that was developed with everyone's input. Our vision is to be a model company. We emphasize teamwork and continuous improvement in all areas of the business. Everyone agrees and understands that we're customer-driven. In some way, we're all customers and suppliers. Everything we produce must be top quality. If it's not, nobody will chastise you; just try to do better.

We look at attitudes and capabilities. The first group of people that I cut, and I cut very few, were the people with the wrong attitudes. If you don't mesh with the team, if you antagonize people or are abrasive, I don't have to tolerate you since I'm not bound by GM's corporate procedures. We can talk, try to help you work it out, and then have another talk. After that, you're out of here. It's not personal; it's just business. You don't fit. You had an opportunity. Working as a team is of the utmost importance.

The first team assignment was to identify the company's capacity to produce parts. Everybody had a different opinion. I told them that I wanted them to agree on the capacity. It took them more than three months, and they still couldn't agree. I told them they had to either influence the other team members or figure out some other way of agreeing. So, you just have to be demanding about things.

I compete against all of the major companies—Ring Screw probably does $150 million a year; MMP, about $105 million a year; Shakeproof; Camcar; Pioneer; and Federal Screw for example. To remain competitive we must outthink them. The strategy is simple—innovation and work hard. Since we're small, sometimes the only thing we can offer is our ideas. I show customers how they can reduce their costs. I am a whiz at buying things. I tell them how I can save them money.

Most companies don't know or understand their costs. The business people I worked with before made their money by happenstance. They fell into it, or they were able to sell their goods and make money in spite of themselves. In today's market, you have to know what the hell you're doing. The owner provides the leadership and the focus for the whole organization. You have to demand that people be accountable, make decisions. Embrace the concept of empowerment and diversity in your work force, because you can't do it by yourself. My employees are a rainbow of people.

We're current with IRS and FICA payments. This is a business with a controller and a staff of accountants. We also have an outside accounting firm, Dunn and Bradstreet, that performs an annual audit. Everything is checked. My partners and I share with the board of directors any information that might be out of whack.

## ACCESS TO CAPITAL

When I first started the business I had no problem getting a loan because I had net worth. When you don't need money, it's easy to get money. That was just for the initial investment.

A year later, I needed refinancing. I tried getting a loan from a local bank. Because the company I bought looked like it was failing, everybody said no. Everybody was polite and cordial, but all the top banks declined because my company had a negative net worth. I had to withdraw personal funds from my bank in Toledo, Ohio, to refinance.

I wanted to come back to Ypsilanti. It's a small town and money is exchanged between old friends. Unfortunately, I'm the new kid on the block. Even though I'm the third largest employer in the city of Ypsilanti—Ford Motors is first and Eastern Michigan University is second—none of the local banks would help me. They don't realize, understand, or care that their tax base is here. A lot of companies, minority or not, in small communities compete on a national and international level. They need money and support. I eventually got my money by networking with a group of white people at a cocktail party.

One guy was well enough placed in the banking community to make it happen. He took a look at our facility, talked to the people, and was impressed. We made a short-term agreement with no guarantees. If I don't perform at a certain level, he can withdraw the loan. The loan was for $200,000.

After four years of losses under the previous owner, I turned the company around in ten months. My company is now profitable. When I first started talking to Masco, I expected that it would probably take between two and three years before I could turn the company around. I did it faster than they ever dreamed possible.

About a year after that loan, I had a line of credit for daily operations, a line for old debt which is constantly paid down, and a line for growth. It was a better package than I had before. The local Ypsilanti bankers wouldn't consider anything like that. So, I went to Detroit, and it was at a better interest rate, too. The total amount of the lines of credit was about $3.8 million.

I'm not involved with BIDCO. I'm just getting familiar with them. I do know that their money is too expensive. Their lending rate is higher than what's available in the commercial market. They are like the loan sharks of my youth—every day costs big money. I served on a board with Catherine

Lockhart, the woman who is president of a BIDCO. The purpose of BIDCO is to encourage small businesses. If you need that kind of money, you can get it. In fact, BIDCO offered me about $800,000. But, I didn't want to pay their price for the money. They could take too much control over your company. I don't want that.

I went to an Entrepreneurship in America conference hosted by Dow Jones. A lot of people were talking about BCF as a way of getting your hands on money. It's interesting, and I intend to pursue it. The SBA is a hassle. I'm not gonna go through the SBA for anything. I don't want any governmental involvement and the paperwork is a hassle. If I get in a real pinch, fine, okay. But I'm not gonna have to do that.

## REVENUE, ACCOUNTING, AND INVENTORY

In November 1991, when I walked in the door we were doing close to $9.2 million. We did about $12 million in 1992, and about $14.2 million in 1993. That was about $2.2 million in growth. In 1994, we grew to about $18 million. In 1995, we gross about $25 million dollars. I also just put into place a nice little project in Rocky Mountain, North Carolina, that might turn into a $20 million project. We are doing fine.

## COMMUNITY LINKAGES AND INVOLVEMENT

### Employee Profile

I had 75 employees when I started in November 1991. We now have a multicultural work force of 105 people—Filipinos, East Asian Indians, Hispanics, Chinese, blacks, and whites. Before, the decision makers were primarily white. We changed the complexion of the company. There are a lot of minorities in business who are company owners and presidents, but they're the only blacks in the company. That's shameful.

Having a black business is important to me. I am responsible for ensuring that my company hires people who live in the community. If black people live in the community, I want to be sure they get the jobs. Too many of us don't do that. The spirit of entrepreneurship is to help your own community and your own people.

I don't believe you can't find qualified blacks. I do. They are responsible, and I'm proud of them. My right-hand man and director of manufacturing is a retiree from General Motors. He grew up in an apprentice program, became an assistant master mechanic, then a superintendent who assembles the rear axles and front ends for General Motors trucks. If he can handle that kind of work, he can handle screws and bolts. Plus, he's a professional man. One brother, a fastener engineer, is a helicopter pilot. I'm proud of what they're doing. I'm demanding, but I wouldn't ask them to do anything I wouldn't do. They all know that.

We became a casual-dress company for psychological reasons—to get everybody involved in the manufacturing floor. All personnel are there to produce the product or help the people who do. Here, if I wanted to go through the halls and say "Y'all," nobody would get upset.

### Community Activities

As a member of Kappa Alpha Psi Fraternity, I am very involved with all fraternity functions. The fraternity does a lot for the community—youth programs, cultural, and political activities. I'm involved with Springhill Baptist Church in Detroit. I support the Detroit School Board's math and science programs. I personally donate money for these programs and solicit money from other companies to make sure that children are encouraged to get involved in math and science. I sponsor basketball teams.

I'm on the Wayne County Intermediate School District's Board of Directors Foundation. We raise money for special grants for Wayne County school districts. I personally sponsor three guys, about age fifteen, who go to Cranbrook, a private institution in Bloomfield. Most of them come from broken homes, but they're intelligent children. I bring them into my home just to show them that you can be black and be successful and to encourage them to go to school. I try to be a positive influence. I get involved with anything to do with children. I think the total amount I personally contribute to youth programs is probably close to fifteen thousand dollars annually.

I have two scholarship funds at Eastern Michigan University, twenty thousand dollars over five years. I wanted the scholarship to go to a black male in the School of Industrial Technology with a grade point of 2.6. They usually require a 3.0. With that requirement, I wouldn't have graduated. I can relate to the plight of students. They deal with a lot of different things when they're in school. It's not that they're incapable, but they need money.

Exemplar also has a co-op program that brings kids in from the University of Michigan and Eastern Michigan to work for the company.

### Trade Association Activities

I'm more involved with kids than I am with professional or trade associations. They call me, but associations can't really help me since I already know everybody in the industry. I'm looking into the Young Presidents Club, a white group. Although I haven't been involved with them, I think I might. They told me that they have the ability to get ten to fifteen minutes minimum for any CEO in the United States.

I subscribe to various industry publications: *Automotive News, Cranes, Appliance Industry,* machinery equipment magazines, *Black Enterprise, Purchasing World,* and the *Wall Street Journal.*

### BARRIERS

The greatest barrier to African Americans going into business is the availability of money. If you're determined enough, I believe you can still get it. Maybe the biggest barrier is really racism. If I was white, I wouldn't have the same money problems. I'll get the money, anyway, but not all of us have learned how to manipulate the process to get there. Bottom line, racism is a business problem even after you get the money. My business could be supplying a plant, and they find out who owns this company and all of a sudden there's something wrong with my parts. This is racism; it's everywhere and it's institutionalized.

A lot of black business owners don't want their customers to know that they are black simply because they're afraid of the economic consequences. When I was at General Motors, a company was reported as a minority supplier and the amount of business they got immediately started to go down. Prior to that, when nobody knew he was a minority, his business was doing great.

I have black and white sales people. They all know who they work for. We tell our customers that we sell quality, cost-competitive products, and we deliver them on time, and, by the way, we are minority. If you've got a hang-up about it, tsk tsk. But, if you compare my product to anybody else's, you'll find that it's as good or better. I'm just one of these arrogant people who speaks up. I'm black; that will not change. I also happen to be one of the best businessman, regardless of color.

If you're black, you have to be better than they are. Even the company name says something—it's generic: Exemplar. It means: one worthy of imitating, one who sets the standard, the pattern for the model. We want to be the model company, I didn't say minority company. If you are the model, your customers are happy, your employees are happy, and you're making money.

## Summary

Each of the three entrepreneurs profiled in this chapter runs a successful business. Mays Chemical and MayDay Chemical are in the chemical distribution business. Exemplar Manufacturing produces metal fasteners, screws, and bolts. However, their experiences in acquiring capital to start operations are similar and mirror the results of the 1992 Roper Organization poll—access to commercial start-up financing eludes most African American entrepreneurs.

After exhausting all commercial avenues within their region, two of the three entrepreneurs used their own funds and/or noncommercial avenues to finance start-up operations. The exception is Anthony Snoddy, who easily found a commercial loan. Bill Mays established a personal line of credit with a white chemical distributor based in the same community and invested ten thousand dollars of his own money into the business. Bill Mays raised capital through his trade suppliers and buyers. By adjusting his billing cycles, he generated cash flow (his trade suppliers extended credit and payment terms to slightly beyond the normal thirty days; he asked his customers to pay net fifteen days). Bettye Daly started MayDay Chemical with loans from Bill Mays in exchange for part ownership in MayDay Chemical. Daly borrowed funds from Mays's line of credit whenever necessary. She then either retired or paid down the balance. This approach allowed Mays to grow two businesses on his single line of revolving credit. These entrepreneurs were able to secure commercial loans once their businesses were beyond the start-up phase.

Anthony Snoddy established substantial net worth within five years, at least on paper. He did so by buying homes inexpensively through HUD, renovating them, and either selling them for cash flow to buy other properties or renting them to build assets. Because of his fiscal health, he easily secured a loan when he wanted to start Exemplar. A year later, when Snoddy's business was the third largest employer in Ypsilanti, Michigan, he tried to refinance his commercial loan but was denied by every bank. Instead, he used his own funds. He eventually secured commercial refinancing at a cocktail party.

Agencies such as the BCF, BIDCO, and the SBA attempted to provide start-up and expansion financing to minority-owned firms to compensate for the lack of commercially available financing. Each of the three entrepreneurs had varying experiences with these agencies. Although Anthony Snoddy knew of BCF, he had not applied for a loan but thought it an interesting concept that he might pursue in the future. Bill Mays helped set up the BCF in Indianapolis. Although he did not need the financing, Mays borrowed $250,000 with the idea of repaying $50,000 each quarter. His reason for participating was to document the entire loan process. Bettye Daly convinced her bank to sponsor the BCF so that she could apply for funds; her experience was positive.

The entrepreneurs were unanimous in their criticism of the SBA. All found the paperwork necessary to qualify for SBA 8(a) programs onerous and time-consuming and did not recommend SBA as a lending source. Although Anthony Snoddy is the only one who mentioned BIDCO as a lending source, he did not participate. Snoddy considered their interest rates to be much higher than those available in the commercial market.

Overall, the three entrepreneurs found start-up capital more difficult to acquire than expansion capital. All had positive experiences with BCF loans and, in contrast, negative experiences with the SBA.

# 6

# Community
# Involvement

## THE WEST REGION

To what extent are African American entrepreneurs involved in the development of their community? Are they pillars of the community, exploiters of the community, or no more community-conscious than other people in business? These issues provide the central focus of this chapter.

Black business development during the post–Civil Rights era diverged: in one direction the traditional mom-and-pop businesses, small, community-based, and usually requiring little capital, minimal education, and few skills, and in the other direction "emerging" businesses, capital-intensive enterprises employing highly skilled and educated workers.

The literature suggests that many black entrepreneurs in community-based "traditional" businesses were viewed negatively by the community because they charged higher prices and provided poor service. In contrast, customers of "emerging" enterprises, because of the nature of their businesses, tend to be the national corporations rather than the African American community.

Chapter 2 documents both the increase in the number of black-owned businesses and a corresponding increase in the number of people employed by these businesses. But we know little about how these businesses interact with the African American community. Although a Roper Organization poll (*Wall Street Journal*, 1992) found that 86 percent of the black entrepreneurs polled in 1992 felt a deep responsibility to "give back" to the black community, do their actions correspond to their words? If "emerging" businesses, which tend not to target African Americans as customers, are the trend of the future, how important is the entrepreneur's relationship with the community? How important is community development to the entrepreneurs business and personal life? This chapter examines this issue through the experiences of four entrepreneurs in the West region: Ella Williams (AEGIR Systems), William Shearer (KGFJ Radio), David Lloyd (Bay City Marina), and Bill Alexander (G O Furniture).

### CASE 8
## AEGIR Systems—Ella Williams

*Ella Williams is president and CEO of AEGIR Systems, located in Oxnard, California. Williams had a somewhat unique experience getting her business started, but she maintains extensive involvement in the community. Age fifty-two, she is divorced and has two daughters, ages thirty-two and twenty-two, and two beautiful grandchildren, twelve and six. AEGIR Systems is an engineering systems service corporation.*

### THE EARLY YEARS

I was born in Jacksonville, Texas. My parents moved to Tucson, Arizona, when I was nine weeks old and stayed until I was about fifteen. My immediate community included three families: the Foleys, the Benefields, and my own. The three families had at least thirty kids. My mother had twelve children, the Benefields had about seventeen, and the Foleys had ten or twelve. There were a lot of boys. I loved being around the boys, because they always did exciting things—like hunt snakes and tarantulas, climb mountains, build playhouses or tree houses, and chop or pick cotton. My mother allowed me to do those things, too, because my brother was part of the group. I learned at an early age how to compete successfully with men. Competition is what it's all about. Some of the skills I have now, I learned when I was very young.

My father always had his own business fixing cars. I wanted to work with my dad, but he always told me to stay home and help Mom. He would let the boys work with him.

I also had seven uncles—all entrepreneurs—who lived in the Tucson area. I guess I was destined to be an entrepreneur; I learned through osmosis that you can start your own business. I had those examples of entrepreneurship.

We were extremely poor financially, but rich in family values, morals, and ethics. Our whole community was poor, but I never realized it until I had an opportunity to look back. My mother always gave us a lot of love and made us feel rich.

I believe that everything I am is because of my mother. My father worked all the time. We were twelve children, seven boys and five girls. My father left early in the morning and came home late at night. Mom was the cement that kept the family together.

I spent time in the kitchen with my mother. I realized early on if I stayed in the kitchen I would get more to eat. I loved being with my mother, and I loved all those wonderful kitchen smells. My mother used to talk to me about things in general. Once she told me that I made the cornbread better than she did, so that became my job. We had small farm animals, and I eventually became the one who killed and cleaned the chickens. I also worked with my mother in our family garden. But what my mother really allowed me to do was be myself.

My father did body and fender work. He was a master at fixing cars. In fact, people used to wait until my father could get to their cars. He always had old cars all around his building because people didn't want anyone else to fix their cars. My father always had a lot of business, always made money, even when nobody else did. But he was a poor money manager. My mother thought that buying property was a better investment. But in those days, a woman's place was really in the home, and he wouldn't let my mother manage his or the family's money. I remember my parents fighting bitterly because my mother wanted to buy the house we lived in, and my dad didn't. When we moved to Long Beach in 1955, my mother wanted to buy beach property. My father didn't. I really don't know how he made his decisions.

During the 1950s, I helped integrate the Tucson schools. I remember my mother being frightened for us. My parents had limited education—my father went to grade three and my mother to grade nine. She always emphasized the importance of education. I always saw myself going to college right out of high school.

I did go to college, subsequently got married, had a child, and then got divorced. I got an A.A. from El Camino College in Carson, California, while I was married. I later remarried and transferred to UCLA. During my last year at UCLA, I divorced again but couldn't finish my education because of financial considerations. I majored in political science with the idea of being a lawyer. While I was at UCLA, I was starting a business. I was doing a lot of things at the same time, trying to find my way, maybe.

Education always helps. Education plus your personal experiences help you deal with people and resolve issues and problems. I can't say that any one course was more helpful than the others. Everything that you learn is helpful.

I always believed in making money. I cleaned houses, ironed for my neighbors, and babysat. I realized early on that if I didn't do something to help my parents, like buy my own school clothes, I wouldn't get anything. So work and personal responsibility were important aspects of my upbringing.

When I was sixteen or seventeen I wanted to be a dancer. While I was taking dance lessons, I also worked in a Long Beach restaurant. I rented the big hall above the restaurant and taught kids dancing. I charged fifty cents a week. Whatever I learned, I taught to the kids in my community. So I guess I've always been an entrepreneur, even at seventeen. My mother always told me that I could do anything I really wanted to do.

In 1966, I started working at Hughes Aircraft doing data processing. The company was good to me. I got every job I ever asked for. I eventually worked my way through the corporate structure, where I interfaced with the division managers. Basically, I started talking to people and building a circle of friends and acquaintances whom I could occasionally call on for assistance.

### DECISION TO START A BUSINESS

I worked at Hughes for about thirteen years. And I always thought that, golly, these people aren't any smarter than I am. So if they can do this, why can't I do it?

Then I read an L.A. *Times* article about the SBA encouraging minorities and women to work in nontraditional fields. I thought that I could create a Hughes on a smaller scale. I could hire engineers and set up financial and marketing departments. So in my working at Hughes, I just said, this couldn't be this hard because I'm as smart as these people I'm working with.

I talked to people I knew at Hughes and elsewhere about creating an engineering services company. I also talked to Chips Sawyer, the marketing manager. I had no idea about how to market. I talk to Chips because he was a great marketer, and I respected him. And with my interface with him I gained his respect and I asked him, "You know, Chips, I think I could do this. Look at this article. I think I could do this." And he said, "You know, this is a great idea." That's basically how the business started.

## GETTING STARTED

AEGIR is a systems engineering company—we look at systems as a totality. We may work on a variety of issues to resolve engineering problems. My company basically started with the automatic test equipment group, and we work mostly for the government on major missile systems—HARM, AMRAM, Barrels, Sidewinders.

We incorporated in 1981, but it took about three years to get my first contract. I was marketing all that time. People were telling me, by the way, if my company was certified 8(a) through the Small Business Administration, which means that we don't have to compete with other companies if we identify work, people would tell me that they would give me a contract as soon as we got certified. Identifying work is the hard part. When I got certified, they gave some other reason why I couldn't get the contract. But I continued to market and market and market.

I got a building and furniture, and I was ready to go. In hindsight, if I had known then what I know now, I would have probably worked out of my house. As I speak across the nation, I tell people not to spend too much money until you see the whites of their eyes, contract is in hand and you're ready to sign it. So we had the trappings of a real corporation, and I kept marketing. However, people weren't giving me an opportunity. I was desperate; both of my kids were at home. It was scary.

I remembered what the Honorable Judge Schaffer said to me during my divorce proceedings: "Mrs. Williams, there are no more free lunches. You're going to have to take care of yourself." I'll never forget that as long as I live. I had worked all of my life, and I wasn't interested in free lunches. That wasn't part of my upbringing. In the back of my mind, I realized that I wasn't getting support from the court system. It was a rough time. Many nights when my kids were in bed, I would pray, "God, please let this happen," and cry myself to sleep. I didn't share this with my family because sometimes people try to rain on your dreams and try to squash your dreams. I carried this burden by myself. I was very frightened.

And then, like a bolt of lightning, I remembered something my mother said to me when I was young: The way to a man's heart is through his stomach. I started baking bread and cheesecakes, and taking them when I went to meetings. I would offer them a loaf of bread or whatever and say, "I was baking last night and thought you would enjoy it." And then when I came in, "Hi Ella, how are you? Did you get anything?" "You just hang in there because I know it's gonna happen." Sometimes that's all I needed to hear, that somebody maybe believed in me enough that they're gonna give me an opportunity or the chance to talk to somebody. After that, people were more encouraging.

### ACCESS TO CAPITAL

The key issue to starting the company was getting money. I already had a mentor in Chips Sawyer, and I knew many engineers at Hughes. Getting start-up money is extremely difficult. I got the money by taking out a sixty-five-thousand-dollar second mortgage on the house I owned in Carson as a result of my divorce, and I capitalized the company with about forty-five thousand dollars. I also used my credit cards.

In the business plan that I kept in my head, I thought our first contract would start in three to six months. This is the what people led me to believe. Wrong!

During this time, Chips died. I went into a deep depression. One day, I realized that Chips would want me to continue. So I started marketing again. By this time, I was running out of money. The forty-five thousand dollars was spent. Another thing my mother told me was that "if you're poor, you must have good credit and buy quality." I lived that philosophy. I started using my credit cards. Soon, I had about seventy thousand dollars in credit card debt at 18 to 21 percent interest. I'm sure the mortgage company thought they were going to eventually own my home. I took a helluva risk. I worked very hard to pay that back.

At that time, to qualify as an 8(a), you had to have been first turned down by two or three banks. I was readily turned down. Then I applied to the SBA.

The banks were very nice to me, but they didn't give me money. I think they had to go through a process to turn me down. They weren't interested in what I was trying to accomplish. I didn't get to talk to anybody. I left my package with somebody, and I never knew whether they looked at it or not. No one ever called to discuss it. They probably had some little guy sitting in the corner just turning down loans.

The relationship I have with my banker now is totally different. I discuss with them where we're trying to go and to anticipate capital needs. I know my bankers; I see them in town, restaurants, and different places.

When I was about to get my first contract, my attorney went to the president of Palos Verdes National Bank. They gave me a letter of credit saying that if I got the contract they wanted to work with me. Not really a commitment, but worded in such a way that SBA gave us the contract. It took me three years to get my first contract. It was for $8 million. In hindsight, it's not really that big, but it took me a long time to get it, and I hung in there long enough to get it.

I walked into one of the gentleman's office that I had been marketing for three years. And he said, "You know, Ella, I'm gonna give you a contract." And then he started talking to other people about what some of their needs were and this ended up a very large contract. Then it went to the SBA and they didn't know it was an $8 million contract before they accepted it for my company because I didn't tell them. And when they found out they said, "Well, you're supposed to start out at $25,000. You can't just have an $8 million contract, so you can't have this contract. You don't have a building." The SBA had not come out to inspect to see what I was doing. Their portfolio is so big, they can't give anyone the real attention that they need because there's just not enough people. So really you're on your own. They said, "You can't have this contract cuz you're supposed to start at $25K." I said, "Yeah, but nobody told me." They said, "You don't have a building." I had signed at that time a lease on a five-thousand-square-foot building. They said, "You don't have the people," and I had gone out and got signatures of engineers that if I got the contract, they would come to work for me. And they said, "You don't have any money." So I had gotten my letter of credit from the bank saying the bank would support me.

I got the letter from SBA on a Saturday. During my college years I had learned how to do briefs. So I put my package together like a brief. I said that the local SBA office is discriminating against me because I'm a woman. I had all of my documentation: signatures of employees, building lease, and a letter from the banker. I had kept SBA informed of everything I was doing, but nobody from SBA had ever come to my office.

Now that I had a contract, SBA wanted to take it away from me. No! At that time, Congressman Perrin Mitchell, known as Mr. Small Business, was in Washington. I had read an article about Perrin in *Ebony* magazine. I thought, "I've got go get to Perrin Mitchell because I know there's somebody in Washington who will help me." I intended to contact him and the national SBA to ask their assistance in making the local SBA do the right thing by me.

I told the local SBA office what I was going to do. I was still hoping to resolve this, because it would be expensive for me to go to Washington. Nothing was resolved, so I went to Washington. I remember the lady at the travel agency asked, "Do you want to go into National or Dulles Airport?" And hell I didn't even know the difference, so I just said Dulles. So I get up there that morning and hell, where is Washington? I'm expecting to see some high-rise buildings somewhere. But anyway, I get to Washington, D.C., with my ten packages. I went to see the senators from California at the time, Senators Hayakawa and Cranston and people on the Small Business Committee. The last place I went was Perrin Mitchell's office. His staff was impressed by my package, and they wanted to help me. They called me a month or two later to tell me that I was getting the contract. But I did realize early on that it's up to me. You gotta have all the tenacity and the drive to make things happen for yourself because people aren't out there for you.

I really feel SBA is understaffed. Their portfolio is over one thousand with a staff of twenty people or less. It's humanly impossible for them to handle this. I benefited from the squeaky wheel syndrome. Initially SBA did not support me in the way I thought they should. However, they have become my best supporter. If you're successful, you almost do it on your own, rather than with their help.

I did get some assistance under 7(j). Somebody came out to help me set up my books. That expense I didn't have to bear because of SBA. They also helped me get a brochure together. I think you have to find where they can really help you.

I think my problems have something to do with my being a woman. The man at SBA assigned to helping me said that they were "going to let me die a natural death." So I found somebody more supportive to handle my case. There, too, it behooves one to find the most helpful people in the organization. It's my responsibility to find the people I can work with.

The company has expanded to include three areas of expertise: systems engineering, multimedia, and software engineering. We started out in systems engineering, which includes avionics, figuration, data management, integrated logistics, reliability, maintainability, and program management on large programs. As the company grew, customers wanted more expertise. In the beginning we subcontracted some of those requirements. When we started getting so many requests we developed this expertise within our own company.

In the software area, we do application design and development, computer systems, and network design. We also do wide- and local-area networking. We've set up a couple of networks at the military base. One we did over a weekend, without any downtime. We are really proud of that job. We also do some embedded software applications within government systems.

We now have about ten very talented young men and women who do nothing but multimedia graphics. This grew out of a customer need. The company is building its expertise, and that's a real growing part of our business.

Our products are basically intellectual products. If you have a computer problem you want resolved or if you want us to design a finished product for you, we would do a requirements analysis and a feasibility study. Then we would tell you exactly what the end product will look like. So it's more intellectual rather than training or anything like that.

We're going after a huge contract at China Lake, a military base in the desert. They do research and development of exotic stuff. Almost immediately, we'll have over one hundred people. This contract is worth probably about $150 million. If we get the contract, we'll need an influx of money to cover salaries until we start getting paid from the government. So we've already alerted our bank. In fact, we gave them a copy of the proposal we submitted to the government. If we get it, they'll know exactly what we need.

We have a relationship with a small bank in Ventura County, the Bank of Levy. At different times I've borrowed money from the bank. I met a lady who works at some the Bank of America through one of the community boards I belong to. They actually came in and told us what they could do for us. They've been very supportive. We'll give them a chance to be our banker.

### REVENUE

We're a profitable company. You know, we were in business three years with no business. And then we got out first contract in 1984. So it took us about four or five years before we became profitable.

For 1992, our gross annual revenue was approximately $5.1 million; 1993 it was $5.5, and then in 1994 it dropped to $4.2 million; and for year end 1995, it will be about $3.2 million.

## ADVICE TO FUTURE ENTREPRENEURS

I've been taking classes all of my life. I take lots of classes at UCLA's Anderson School of Management. Several instructors teach a very good class on moving a company from being entrepreneurial to being professionally managed. Another UCLA instructor, Dr. Osborne, has been very helpful and instrumental. He is a wonderful guy.

I think it's important for people to find mentors. You'd be surprised how many people are willing to be mentors, probably 99 percent. But you've got to ask them. We think people are unapproachable; that they're going to look down at us. What I found is that most people will say, "I'm honored that you asked me." People really want to give back, but they don't know how. It's up to you to ask.

A business plan is extremely important. It doesn't have to be a formal plan, but it should be on paper so you can look at it and assess if this is really where you want to go. When we first started, Chips and I and a couple of other engineers talked about what we wanted to do. We wrote it down, so that we could change it as our focus changed. The business plan is a road map to where you're going. I also developed a business plan because SBA required it.

## COMMUNITY LINKAGES AND INVOLVEMENT

### Customers

Our biggest customer is the military. All of our contracts are with the government—Department of Defense, Department of Transportation, local governmental agencies, and the Metropolitan Transportation Association. We're currently teamed up with some commercial companies. With Northrop we're working on the advanced technology transportation bus, using new components. They call it the Stealth Bus to parallel the Stealth Bomber developed by Northrop. We also have proposals in with Siemens Duweg, ICM Kaiser, Morrison-Knudsen, and Bombardier. So the government is basically our customer.

We're also working closely with the Metropolitan Transportation Authority in the area of technology transfer. We're trying to get more work in this area because the Department of Defense dollars are diminishing as we speak. And so we're trying to move the company into transit and the environment. It's not easy to shift gears and still keep the company financially viable. Cost structures are so different.

### Advertising and Marketing

My secret for getting government contracts is perseverance, perseverance, perseverance, marketing, marketing, marketing! Take every opportunity you get to keep your name and your company's capabilities out there. It's a tremendous job. Knowing the customer's needs, how you can meet those needs and resolve some of their problems. Basically, people and the government don't want to do any work. They love it when you do it for them.

After we started getting work, people started hearing about the company. I won several awards that were noted in the newspaper. People become familiar with your name. I serve on several boards. I'm on the Boys and Girls Club of America. I meet people there. Predominantly white folks. I sit on the Commission on Human Concerns. I interface with a lot of these people. Then people give you awards. They hear about you. They see you at functions and they begin to think you're part of the community. So they extend a hand to you. I mean, that's basically the way it's happened.

We're a profitable company, but it took us about four or five years to get there. I worked like a dog and still do. It doesn't get easier. I think about business every waking moment, not because I want to, but because I have to. I've hired good people. That's not to say I haven't fired a lot of people. I can't afford to keep people if they can't do their jobs.

### Location

The corporate offices are located in Oxnard, California, because that's the first place I got work. We also have offices in downtown Los Angeles and in Washington, D.C. I also live in Oxnard. When I lived in Carson, I was commuting between Carson and Oxnard, a long drive. I had to drop off my youngest daughter at school at 8:00 A.M. drive to Oxnard, work fast, and come back to pick her up by 3:00 P.M. It got to be too much. In 1984, I moved my company and myself closer to the customer.

One of the best things I did was move to Oxnard. There were no other black companies in the area, so I was an anomaly. On the positive side, I was someone that people wanted to get to know. The other positive thing is that I got involved with the community. It helped my business. It's important to keep in touch with your customers. A couple of years ago, one of my customers warned me about an impending downturn. He suggested looking at some other areas if we wanted to continue to be successful. Your customers become your friends, and they begin to look out for you. You become part of their family.

### Employee Profile

It's very difficult to find blacks in this area. My previous human resources person, Renee Match, is a black woman. I try to hire African Americans whenever I can. I said, "Renee, I want another sister in this job." She looked, called agencies, and couldn't find anybody. So I told her to find the best qualified person regardless of color. Everyone in my company that needs a degree has to have a degree.

I tell Jill, the current human resources person, the same thing. I was just lucky when I found Karen. I was speaking somewhere and she told me that she had just finished college and wanted a job. I mean this girl is sharp, very sharp. So you have to expose yourself to those kinds of opportunities because people like Karen come in.

We have about eighty employees—engineers, technicians, computer scientists, and graphic design artists—about 50 percent white and 50 percent minority. My office in Los Angeles has more minorities than any other group. Oxnard is a different story. The Washington office has a staff of seven: two minorities, five women, and two men. I hire a disproportionate number of women, probably 70 percent. Do you want to know why that is?

For some reason, when you give women a task, they just do it. Give men a task, and they kill it, talk it to death. Maybe it's because I'm so impatient, but I have to leave meetings because they've already beaten this horse to death without coming to a decision. I can come back thirty minutes later, and they're still talking. They love to hear themselves talk. I hate to generalize like that, but that's my experience. If women need direction, they'll ask and then go off and do the job. Have you ever noticed that? Is it just me?

Sometimes I say, "God, I wish I could have just all women in this company because these men are driving me crazy!" In fact, I just fired my VP of operations because he was trying to pull some crap behind my back. He called my customers and told them that we lost our technical base. He's the loser. People are finding out what he's about. I won't lose any business because of him. I have good customers. That's why I think you have to pay attention to your customers.

Then you have the sexual thing. I mean you have that all the time. I was recently talking to one guy about something and he starts talking about a motorcycle. He made the comment, "Yeah, something warm between my legs." I got so angry that I didn't say anything. I called him the next day. I said, "I didn't appreciate that comment you made yesterday." He said he didn't mean anything by it. But he did.

This customer has given me $3 million worth of work. I want the work, so I have to handle it in a professional way. If I had said something then, I would have said too much, and I likely would have lost the work, too. This way, by stepping back, collecting my thoughts, and then coming back in a professional manner, I could deal with it. He'll never do it again.

That's why practically every woman in America was with Anita Hill. We've all been in that position. We all knew what she was going through. Women are always confronted with that. It's unfortunate, but it's reality. We deal with it, because we have to work.

One time, somebody was directing racial slurs to a Vietnamese woman, an engineer. I called an "all hands meeting," brought everybody in. I said, "Women and minorities will have opportunities in this company. If you can't handle that, then you need to find employment somewhere else." All the women thanked me after the meeting. If you do a good job here, there is a lot of room for advancement. We are a very young company; we can be anything we want to be here.

### Community Activities
Aside from keeping this business growing in the Oxnard area, I'm on the Boys and Girls Club Board, the Commission on Human Concerns, the African-American Chamber in Los Angeles. I've been so blessed, I do what I can to make other people's lives better, especially kids. What I really want to do is work with children. I was fortunate to have grown up in a community that cared about kids. Part of the reason I'm here is because you don't raise a child by yourself. It takes your whole community, your church. It's my way of giving back. It makes me feel good.

My commitment is still to inner-city Los Angeles, mainly because the need is much greater. I'm trying to start Ella's World Class Cheesecake, Bread, and Muffins. It's my plan for an inner-city bakery, a manufacturing concern. I want to work with inner-city kids, teaching them how to make cheesecake, breads, and muffins. I figure I'll need about $1.5 million. I've already identified a building owned by Penney's. I'm working through Rebuild Los Angeles to see if Penney's will either give me an attractive deal on the building or give me the building.

We want to open five retail stores in Beverly Hills, Brentwood, Palos Verdes, Westwood, and downtown Los Angeles. Next, we want to go to Washington, D.C., and, working from both ends, open stores all over the United States. It's a ten-year project. I've done my business plan. I had four students do it as a semester project. We taped it at UCLA, and it was shown on the television show *Life and Times.*

I work on this project every day. I met city councilman Mark Ridley-Thomas at the vendor fair, who told me it was time to get it moving! A couple of years ago, I brought a cheesecake when I went to talk to him about this project. I've been working on this for three years, and I've got a lot of people working with me, including politicians.

Southern California Edison and the rest of the L.A. Economic Development Council are helping me with this project. They introduced me to SE Rycroft, a concern that supplies food to restaurant chains and does layouts and building interiors for bakeries. They've worked with Wolfgang Puck and other restaurants. Mr. Sacks, of SE Rycroft, is charging me twenty-five thousand dollars to do the layout of the whole building once we get it. They're giving me twelve thousand, five hundred dollars in equipment, plus Mr. Sacks is not charging me for his time. But before I can go full on board here, I have to secure my business.

I contribute to a lot of groups. I seems that my name is on the damn master list somewhere. For the last four years I've given four to five thousand dollars to support Marion Wright Edelman's Children's Defense Fund. I've supported the Boys and Girls Club in Oxnard. I've probably given them about three thousand dollars. I help wherever I can and try to keep myself sane.

Right now business is not that good. If we get this big contract, I can give more. Someone just called the other day and wanted me to sponsor a women's conference with four thousand or three thousand dollars. I can't afford to do it right now. If business was better I'd be more than happy to sponsor it. So I try to give back wherever I can.

I support two children; one's at Berkeley. My responsibility is to get her through college, sixteen thousand dollars a year. I believe that charity starts at home. And one of my daughter's girlfriends couldn't pay her tuition so I paid her tuition for one year. I help my other daughter with my grandchildren. I take care of myself. So my responsibility is to see my own children through school.

I'm thinking about starting the Gertrude Anderson Foundation, in memory of my mother's name. If I put it into the foundation I'll have more money to give to charity instead of to the government. Lawyers are looking into that right now.

I do some mentoring with Jolene Godfrey, who started a company called An Income of Her Own. She works with young girls to teach them about entrepreneurship. We recently did a workshop at Loyola Marymount University, where I was the keynote speaker. I told them about my experiences, how powerful they are as women, and for them not to give their power to anyone. The *Wall Street Journal* wrote an article about it and someone on Oprah's show read about it and asked me to be on her show. That's just how it happened.

I'm also being honored at the Beverly Hills Hotel along with Maya Angelou and Dr. May Jamieson, Whoopi Goldberg, and Anita Hill. I won the AT&T Entrepreneur of the Year award. I'm just very honored to even be on the dias with these women. It's just fabulous.

I still bake breads and cakes. I just put that smile on my face and say, "Good morning. Guess what I baked for you last night?" It still works, and I enjoy doing it. I love to cook. Baking is my "therapy." When I've had a hard week, I'll call some of my customers and say, "I was in 'therapy' this weekend." They say, "How many loaves of bread did you bake?" "Fifteen," I say. They say, "I know I'm going to get one." "You've got one, that's why I'm calling you."

When I go into "therapy," I go to the store and get all the overripe bananas. They make the best banana nut bread, and I get them for ten cents a pound. So I bake a lot of bread, and I feel revived. It's amazing. Customers often request cheesecake. I've got a list of about twenty-five or thirty cheesecake customers. It's strawberry season now, and I'll go strawberry picking in the fields. I've got to make all these people a cheesecake during the season. They expect it.

It's a marketing tool. It opens up a lot of doors. When you go into a meeting with a big, beautiful cheesecake with strawberries on top, who won't give you business? They say how much business do you want!

### CASE 9
### KGFJ Radio—William Shearer

*William Shearer is the owner of KGFJ Radio in Los Angeles. Shearer is fifty-two, divorced, and has two daughters, ages twenty-five and twenty-three.*

## THE EARLY YEARS

I was born and raised in Columbus, Ohio. I graduated from East High School in Columbus, Ohio. My father died nine days after I graduated from high school. I had been accepted at Lincoln University in Pennsylvania, but when my father died I decided to go to Ohio State University, which was right in town.

I lived at home and spent the first two years playing cards in the student union. I was sixteen and not serious about school or anything else. Then my brother and I went into the military to get our lives in order. After two years I left the military and went back to school. It kind of matured me. I graduated from the University of San Francisco with a degree in behavioral science and management and went to Pepperdine for my M.B.A.

My father and uncle greatly influenced my life. Both graduated from college during the Depression and both became attorneys. From the day I could ever remember, my father never asked me was I going to college; we were told. It was, "Have you made up your mind yet where you would like to go?" College was never an option. Two things were certain: "You will go to college, and you will be an Alpha." Now I understand how important college is. High school graduation just signaled the next step. College was simply expected for me, my cousins. The family was so education oriented.

My father handled the college and education values. My mother delivered the manners and culture. I grew up when wives didn't work. She taught me the other part of my life: how to dress properly, keep your room clean, take a shower every day, brush your teeth, you can't go outside until your room's clean, if you don't go to church today, you can't go to the movies. I don't care how late you are for school, you don't leave your house 'til your bed's made. To this day, I never walk out of my house unless my bed is made. I'm very uncomfortable doing it, even if I'm late. Those things I can attribute to her.

We had a housekeeper from the time I was born. We were upper-middle-class blacks when it wasn't fashionable. I don't say it out of pride, because I had nothing to do with it. I was just a little black kid running around. Blacks then were segregated recreationally. The family belonged to the Links and Jack-and-Jills, and we had a summer home in Idlewild, Michigan.

Idlewild is not as popular now as it was then, because now you can go anywhere. Then blacks were segregated recreationally, and blacks in the Midwest went to two places for resorts: Idlewild, Michigan, or French Lick,

Indiana, where they had a resort for blacks. Blacks from Detroit, Chicago, Cleveland, Cincinnati, with a little bit of money all had cottages and cabins in Park Circle [Idlewild]. We would go the week after school was out and stay until the day after Labor Day. We locked up our city house, took our car, and my father would fly up on weekends. We spent the summers in our cabin, just doing nothing. We had a little boat we'd take out. A roller rink nearby.

My father's roots were in Lynchburg, Virginia. He believed that education was the black man's salvation. In high school, I was selected by the American Legion to go to Boys State, where we learned about government. I was also in the speech club and on the debate team. I was too small for athletics, so I learned the clarinet and joined the band because at least we got to travel with the football team in a bus behind theirs. It was a good high school experience. I was aggressive in high school and took aggressive courses. I took two or three years of Latin, two or three years of chemistry. My father wouldn't allow us to take courses like wood shop. We had to take "something of substance," as he called it.

### BECOMING AN ENTREPRENEUR

In radio, you don't start out thinking about becoming an entrepreneur; you say you need to become a general manager, which is a job. I become a general manager, which is a job, but it's also entrepreneurial in nature. A station is a certain size operation, the parent company was in another state, and I was running it for them. The process of actually becoming an entrepreneur begins when you say, "Hell, if I'm adding $1 or $2 million to the bottom line for them, why not for myself?" I think in radio, compared to any other business, I evolved into entrepreneurship.

Because as you become a sales manager, you're charged with achieving certain goals. Then every sales manager wants to become a general manager. "Hey, I'm making that cat rich. He's smoking a big cigar and I'm doing all the work. I want his job." I was making Willie Davis a lot of money while he traveled, did other things while I ran the operation.

We actually closed the deal to buy this station on December 31, 1986. We are incorporated in California as East-West Broadcasting with two stockholders: a black orthopedic surgeon and myself. I am majority stockholder at 60 percent. His 40 percent of the stock is an investment.

I've been in radio for twenty-one years. I started off in sales and have just taken the normal progressionary route upward.

## GETTING STARTED

Normally in radio you start in sales. Radio is divided into two sections, sales and programming. Programming is everything that goes on the air. And sales is the part that the public doesn't see, but brings in the dollars that pays all the bills.

The next move after general manager is owner. Every general manager—black or white—begins thinking about ownership. You're running the business for somebody who lives in Hawaii or in some other state, and you see how much profit is going to the bottom line. You begin to say to yourself, Why not me? The only handicap, normally, is financing. I would like to think that I'm still in sales, just at a different level. I spent seven years in direct sales; then I moved into management as a general sales manager. My next move was to vice-president of sales, then general manager, and now owner.

Radio is different, exciting, creative. You can write a commercial and hear it three days later, almost instant gratification. One day you can be meeting the guy who owns the pool hall or the hot dog stand, and two hours later you're sitting with the mayor or a corporate vice-president. It's not a boring business. Every day is different and exciting.

The fear that you won't have the telephone available any longer [is a factor to consider in going into business]. I worked with the American Broadcasting Company for about three years. I then went to work for the Inner City Broadcasting Company, a company owned by Percy Sutton and his family in New York. When I needed funds, I would pick up the phone and call the VP controller and would say I needed one hundred grand in the account. He would always say to me, "Mr. Shearer, as I am talking to you, I am wiring the money. I just wired $100,000 to your account." Your big fear is not having a telephone capability to call. You're in business for yourself, and when payday comes and the bills are due, there ain't nobody to call except your banker, and you can only call him so many times.

My consideration was strictly financial. I knew the business. I didn't have to ask if I was smart enough to run a station. I was being paid over $150,000 a year to do it for other people. But could I put together the significant dollars from the equity side and the senior debt side to make it happen?

## ACCESS TO CAPITAL

Once I decided to be an owner, it took about nine months' worth of work. The first thing you say to yourself is, will this go? That's a risky question when you're making a $10 million acquisition. It's not like starting up a hamburger stand at the corner. Those people wanted $100,000, nonrefundable deposit in escrow. When you wire the money to Bankers' Trust in New York, you gotta know you have a way to go. If not, you have just gone to Las Vegas and shot one hundred grand. Financing in radio is very tough. How can I structure the finances? Where will it come from? The lawyers can put the package together, but you have to give them the answers. You have to know that you're going to get the financing and that the price is right. And, second, do an analysis to know that you can service the debt. Borrowing money is one thing, paying it back in a timely fashion is another.

Since I was already running the station I'd bought, nothing much changed, not even my signature, which was already on the checks. It just became my responsibility. I stayed in the same office. The telephone numbers didn't change. I even worked the same fifty-, sixty-hour weeks. The only thing I had to change was the corporate name as the property owner.

I borrowed $4.5 million in a two-tier approach. I had senior debt with a major lender (Greyhound Financial from Phoenix) and seller financing under junior debt. You have to convince them that you're capable of repaying that debt. Borrowing in radio is different, because most major banks lend against assets. A radio station has few assets. If a radio station is sold for $20 million, only about $400,000 is hard assets, like boards and microphones. The rest falls into "good will." It's hard to borrow against good will because there's nothing to collateralize. The bank is really lending against cash flow. When they do, it means that the bet on the horse and the jockey is even more pronounced.

When they talk about radio station acquisitions and financing in seminars at conventions, there are three things that they tell all borrowers. The first thing they lend on is the management, the second is the facility, and the third is the market. Those are the three, in that order. So it is necessary to have a track record that is extremely positive and you're thought well of by your peer group. So that's the problem with so many minorities, is we have not had the chance and the exposure to be a general manager. You must show them. In my business plan, my accounting firm developed a trend chart to show my activity at every station I'd worked at. What the entry level numbers were, versus at the conclusion of my eight- or ten-year stay there, how we were doing financially. And that's the track record they bet on: the knowledge, because they have no assurances.

It's not like a house. The bank doesn't really care whether you make your house payments, because the house is worth more than the loan. It's not too risky for them. With a radio station, in addition to the risk of whether the station will make it and the lack of hard assets, you're also dealing with a government license that is not automatically transferable. Just because the bank forecloses on me doesn't mean that the Federal Communications Commission will automatically give my license to someone else.

That's why its more difficult, particularly for minorities coming in, to borrow in radio. Minorities have problems both on the equity side and on the senior debt side. The equity side, nobody will lend you more than 50 to 60 percent of the appraised price, the asking price, or the selling price. If the price is $10 million, and the bank lends you about $5 or $6 million, you still have a $4 million shortfall. The shortfall is covered by the equity side. If you put down $2 million, you're still short $2 million, which is the mezzanine layers or seller financing. Deals are tough to put together. That's why so many stations are owned by groups who can generate money by issuing stock.

I had a lot of things going for me, and I'm not at all ego-tripping. First, I was lucky enough to come to the party with whatever the big world wants. I started military service as a private and finished a colonel in the army reserve. I had an extremely attractive military background on a very fast track. I was the first black to be chairman of the board of the Southern California Broadcasters, an all-white industry group in this market. This area has 140 radio and television stations and no black had ever been on the board. I moved from secretary to treasurer to vice-chair to chair.

I played politics in the broadcasting arena at the national level at the National Association of Broadcasters. I'd been on four or five of their committees. At almost every convention every year, I would speak on broadcast management. I teach broadcasting at UCLA, at USC, and at Long Beach State. I'd been a general manager for fourteen years and made some extremely political acquaintances from the mayor on down. I also had the right education and an outstanding track record in radio. All of these characteristics made the borrower very comfortable.

Today, a lot of blacks are buying radio stations. But they made their money elsewhere and don't have hands-on experience. I started at the bottom and spent twenty years learning the industry. So a lot of station owners have never run them, never sold time in the field, never called on clients, and never written copy. Of the broadcasters I know, few have done it from the ground up. Some are outstanding lawyers who bought a station or two.

But I had what the banks were looking for. It would have been really hard to say no to me. They could have said it, but they wouldn't have been able to come up with an explanation of why. I'd been chairman of the board, not only of Southern California Broadcasters Association, but chairman of the board of the National Association of Black-owned Broadcasters, which includes all black owners and operators in the country. Those things speak highly that people respect you.

As a finance-type major with M.B.A.-type qualifications, I talked the language of a banker. People are more comfortable with you when you speak their language. That's not to say I understood everything, but I knew what they were talking about.

I've also had the right political exposure. I've been on maybe thirty boards in this city. I was treasurer of the Los Angeles Urban League, and even arranged to locate and buy the building that the Urban League now occupies. I had done a lot around here, and I am well known in the city, good or bad.

Our bankers love us. They spent two days here for our initial meetings. I brought in all the managers, and we put on a full presentation. It blew the white boy's mind away. I could have done it myself, but I wanted to show him the depth of our management. Each manager explained his piece of the game plan, and the guy was impressed! He called back two days later and said we had the money and was there anything else we needed. He was telling me that he knew this was a good horse and jockey to bet on. With any race track in this country, it doesn't matter how pretty it is, ain't but two things to bet on, the horse and the jockey.

The first thing I tell people is to really get to know your banker. Take him to lunch. If you do that, when you go back you just say, "Hey, Mr. or Mrs. Banker, this is my next need." Theoretically, they've already satisfied some need—they've gotten you whatever, a Master Card, a Visa card, a car loan, a little $10,000 line of credit. Next, you're going to need a $100,000 line of credit. If you develop your relationship right, it follows the next logical evolutionary step. So if you did it right, they'll evaluate your need, analyze your net worth, and say, "I can't give you $100,000, but I can give you $50,000."

It's smart to have a line of credit, because you're likely to have some downturns. That's when you can't borrow. If your $100,000 line of credit is already established, you push the button and the money is available. It's like insurance: nobody will sell you insurance when you're on your way out. Buy it while you're healthy.

When I speak on how to borrow, I always tell folks that SBA is a "court of last resort." I think you go there when you have nowhere else to go. Try to go with some of the regular, conventional, commercial institutions. SBA normally lends $600,000, with $800,000 tops. Also, because of First Amendment considerations, SBA was not allowed to lend to the broadcasting field when I was thinking about buying. That changed later with the help of our organization.

With the small amount that SBA can lend, you can only buy in one of the lesser markets, like Podunk, Iowa, or Columbia, Missouri. The major markets are too expensive. So the SBA will tie your hands. SBA is better than nothing, but I think you knock on that door only when you run out of places to go.

It's like MESBIC. I'm not anti-MESBIC; some of my best friends run MESBICs. I've never borrowed from them because they tie your hands, take equity, warrants, or stock, whatever they can beat you up to take because they're your partner. They fly in once a month at your expense, look over your books, and question every expense: "Why did you buy this guy pie and ice cream for dessert?" Banks don't do that. If you make your payments, the bank doesn't care about your travel expense or why you went to that convention. But MESBICs and especially SBAs get involved in your life. Traditionally with minorities, they'll tie up your aunt's property and your grandma's property. In my opinion, you have to want that money badly to go through them.

### PROFITABILITY

We tell our folks we're designed to be successful. I don't think success is luck; it's planned. We do a lot to ensure our success. We plan extensively. The department managers each write business plans that are consolidated into one corporate plan. We don't take chances. Excuse the language, but I'm always telling our managers, "We happen to be a black-owned business, but we're not a nigger operation." People expect us to be a certain way we're not.

We try to be top card. We have dress standards. In sales, we hire only college graduates with 3-plus averages. It's simple to me: if you're making here what you would make at IBM, I expect the same qualifications that IBM does. If I'm going to successfully outmarket and outsmart my competitor, I have to hire really sharp people who will represent us well. I want some University of Missouri–Columbia and UCLA graduates. We have about twenty-six people on staff and résumés are always coming in. A lot of particularly talented black people want to work for a professionally run black company. There's no shortage of qualified, distinguished applicants.

We're in a very major market that has great universities. Even if people graduate from University of Missouri–Columbia, they generally want to work in Chicago, New York, or L.A. People are always knocking on the door, particularly if they're black and they've knocked on so-called white company doors, where most can't get the time of day.

Both of my daughters work here. One is a business manager and the other is a sales rep. My brother's daughter works in production. Each is eminently qualified. My business manager daughter has an accounting degree and is awfully sharp. My other daughter, who has a communications degree and a 3.8 GPA, is twenty-five years old and makes $80,000 a year. She has never gotten a lead from me, she's done it on her own. My niece, who came out here to get into Hollywood, is twenty-five with a master's in theater arts and communications from a major university. These women didn't slide through the door because their name is Shearer. They are all well trained, which minimizes the element of nepotism.

## REVENUE, ACCOUNTING, AND INVENTORY

For 1988 and 1989, our gross annual revenue each year was about $1.6 million, and about $2.1 million for 1990 and 1991. From 1992 through 1995, its been about $1.7 million a year.

We produce a monthly P&L statement by computer and send it to our bankers. Since I have millions of dollars in loans, they want a monthly report. Once a year, the bank requires a certified audit that costs about twelve thousand dollars.

## COMMUNITY LINKAGES AND INVOLVEMENT

### Employee Profile

We have thirty employees, sixteen women and fourteen men. Two are Hispanic and the others are black.

This is an extremely people-oriented business. One of the very difficult things in black business is trying to get blacks to respect their managers as managers. They'll want to come in late and say, "Brother, you're supposed to understand, you know how it is." No, I don't understand a goddamn thing. Next Friday, you'll want your check on time. So we really run a different kind of ship here.

The people here are very professional, very well trained. They have to be, because people work here twenty-four hours a day, whether I'm home asleep, in Hawaii, or wherever I am. It's really like a hospital. The administrator is home asleep, and the nurses are up giving shots. And, it better be the right shot. Similarly, the on-air disk jockeys really have your license in their hands.

One of the mistakes that I think corporate America makes is that they demand their employees have a good education, good test scores, and all this. But once you're hired, they don't let you use it. They don't let you think for yourself. I think it's critical that our managers become managers; I force them to do it. When one comes to me with a problem, I look him dead in the eye and I ask what he thinks we ought to do about. So many people think that because you sit in a chair of a certain size and have a certain title, that you, in fact, must have all the answers.

I think the secret is teamwork. I have weekly staff meetings where everybody discusses something about their department. We have two rules: it can't be personal, and it must be of general interest to most people present. They just talk. So many organizations lack communication; the left hand doesn't know what the right hand is doing. I force them to be managers. I put pressure on them to think and to grow.

For instance, someone suggested that we have an on-air promotion and give away three twenty-one-inch color TVs. And I said to the promotion manager, "Let's back up. What goals are you trying to accomplish? Go to your goals and work backwards." Everything here is goal-oriented. What goals are you trying to do? If you're trying to build quarter-hour maintenance, which means you're trying to force people to listen longer, you may say, "Stay tuned," or "Coming up soon, we're giving away a pair of tickets to 'The African American.' " You're encouraging people to listen longer.

### Suppliers and Customers

We know our listening audience. We also understand how we earn our money, who our advertisers are. We're a black-owned business sustained primarily by the black community. Most of my people, including me, live in the black community. I assure you, I could have lived in Brentwood, but I chose to live in the black community. Our lives are here. My daughters both live around the corner from me.

This building is located in a predominantly black area. We were in another building, but when I saw this one, I knew it was what we needed: five thousand square feet on two floors. In broadcasting, it's ideal to put programming upstairs and sales downstairs. The landlord was willing to modify the building, and he spent about $160,000 making improvements. We have a twenty-year lease. I pay about $5,000 per month or $1.00 per square foot, an excellent deal.

Our retail clients are probably 50 percent black. The rest are advertising agencies that spend client dollars, usually the larger corporations.

Our advertising is by word of mouth. The station has been here since 1926, so we have franchise value. Anyone growing up in L.A. knows about KGFJ. When I started working for the company, the station was rated number two in the entire market, not just for blacks. Now it's number one. We've turned down offers to sell at a substantial profit, including offers that have been extremely large multiples of what we paid for it.

I came here in 1968. I've been here twenty-two years, which is how long I've been in radio. I left and came back as manager in March 1985 and then bought the company in December 1986.

### Trade Association Activities

I've continued learning since the day I started working in radio, twenty-one, twenty-two years ago. I've gone to seminars, training sessions, back to college. I also attend trade association meetings and industry conventions. It's hard to believe someone in any industry for twenty years not attending some seminars or meetings.

I serve on the board of the Broadcast Education Association. How I got there is an interesting story. I also serve on the board of the big white trade organization, National Association of Broadcasters, which is run by committees. After serving for three years on the Minority Executive Council, the affirmative action effort, I told the executive vice-president and president that I wanted to do something more visible, more important. I didn't want to box myself into an EEO corner. They suggested the Broadcast Education Association, and I agreed to try it. The communications departments of all of the colleges and universities belong to BEA.

NAB appoints six members to that board. Our purpose is to work on the convention each year to suggest to the academicians the skills and curriculum we're looking for. In the years when communications programs were expanding, we learned that these people were turning out folks we just couldn't use. What they were learning was irrelevant. I've hired people from USC's four-year degree program in communications who had never touched a board.

I just got Willie Davis's ex-wife a job at Long Beach State because she's a friend of mine. She pointed out that people with Ph.D.s who had never worked in a station were teaching communications and broadcast sales. So this BEA committee does curriculum oversight and all the colleges and universities are members. And we try to steer the committee to the schools where the curriculum is teaching what our employees need to know.

### ADVICE TO FUTURE ENTREPRENEURS

Anyone considering business should decide exactly what they want in life. Most people, whether its happiness or goals, don't know what they want. They spend their entire lives looking for that phenomenon called "happiness," without identifying what it is. The old Baptist preachers always say, "If He knocked on your door, would you have sense enough to let Him in?" You've got to want whatever it is that you want so much that you can almost taste it.

It's important to want to win. The three key ingredients in winning are planning, execution, and talent. I often talk about radio as it relates to sports. Take football. Each team has eleven players. They usually weigh about the same, are about the same height, use the same ball on the same size field. But only one team wins. The same is true for basketball and baseball. If everything else is equal, the difference between the teams that perennially win and those that perennially lose is talent. That's what I tell our managers: it's all about talent. That's why its critical to get the right people. That's how you beat the other team. It's that simple.

But I think you get the right talent when you have the right things to offer people. Most people look for the basics: a decent work environment and a decent salary. We try to have a first-class facility, and we pay competitive wages. We have an open, honest, family-style environment.

Many brothers get too carried away with their own importance. My business card only says "vice-president and general manager," even though I'm the owner. When people ask why I don't include "owner," I tell them it's not important. A second reason for not including "owner" is that it takes away my leverage when I'm with a client. Without it, I can say that the people back at the station wouldn't want to live with that. If I'm the owner, he'll say, "Who're you kidding?"

I meet brothers all over the country who have a corporation or a company with two employees and ten dollars in the bank. Their business card says "Chairman of the Board." I find that distasteful. We have no chairman of the board, just two stockholders. I'm president and treasurer, and my partner, an orthopedic surgeon, is vice-president and secretary. We don't have a chairman of the board, because "chairman" should indicate tremendous assets. If you're trying to survive and make your company grow, then you want to act humble and be humble. To hell with "chairman of the board." I don't believe in all that crap.

I have problems with people who make you talk to a number of people before they get on the telephone. I answer my own phone, and people are surprised. Even my home number's listed in the phone book. I don't believe you should ask the secretary to stop typing a letter that needs to go out just to answer your phone and make you sound important. We don't go through that crap here. I'd rather talk to you and get rid of you than have you call every day. When I call some buddies of mine, I go through all the "Does he know the nature of the call? Would he recognize the name?" I don't care if you're begging for one hundred dollars, I'd rather tell you nay or yay, get rid of you, and move on to the next project. But that's an individual thing.

## THE FUTURE OF KGFJ RADIO

Every manager here is being groomed all the time. Later, you zero in on one person. We have very bright managers, any one of them is capable, and they're all being trained. If we buy more radio stations, I won't have to be replaced here. I would send them to wherever the new station was located. We're working on something right now. When they close, we'll send some of our folks. It's better to start with people you know and you trust. I wouldn't go to Columbia, Missouri, and hire someone I didn't know; I'd send somebody from here, at least to get started.

My greatest accomplishment is maintaining a viable business that gives college-educated young black people an opportunity to have their shot at life. That's the reason why I won't sell the station. It would be very easy for me to walk away with $4 or $5 million, tell the world to go to hell, and move to my home in Hawaii. But I've got thirty people working here, and I know that twenty-four of them would not be in radio today if they didn't work here. Most radio stations want only one black and that's it.

CASE 10
## Bay City Marina—David Lloyd

*David Lloyd is owner of Bay City Marina, a shipbuilding and repair business, in San Diego, California. Lloyd is fifty-five, married, has two daughters, ages twenty-four and twenty-six, and two sons, six and nine. He had an especially unique experience starting and sustaining his business.*

### THE EARLY YEARS

I grew up in Linden, Alabama, located between Selma, Alabama, and Aurelia, Mississippi. It's a small, very rural town with no toilets and only about one thousand people. I went to seventh or eighth grade, as did my father before me.

I had one brother, he was killed in an accident when I was about seven or eight, and I have two sisters. I support them, and they think the world of their little brother. My mother died when I was five. My father worked in the sawmill grading lumber, a very prestigious job for a black. He made good money, thirty-two dollars a week or eighty-three cents an hour. The neighborhood people used to say they thought we were hot shit. If somebody ever needed ten dollars, they'd ask daddy.

My father was a religious man. He always told me that if you do the right thing, things would come. I didn't believe him at the time. I just wished that I could have gotten back to tell him that I'm sorry for not believing him, and that it was true. Unfortunately, he never saw my success. That's probably one of my biggest disappointments.

I had never seen a black person in business, other than the guy who had a little juke joint that sold barbecue and sodas on Friday night. I didn't think much of business. When I was about eleven, I started working as a house-boy in a wealthy person's home. I worked there until I was about nineteen. They had a two-acre estate and a lot of pecan trees and shrubs, so I started cutting the grass and raking the leaves. They had a big house with a swimming pool, a nice car, and they took their kids on vacations. This guy influenced me in business. I decided I wanted to live like that. Well, I've got all that shit now, of course, and I take my kids all over the world.

My first introduction to the ocean was at a young age, when I did a paper on the Suez Canal. When I came here from Alabama in 1955 at age nineteen, my only work experiences were picking cotton and washing cars. I went downtown to San Diego, and I was fascinated when I saw the bay, the yachts, and ships. That was the first time I actually saw the ocean. You can't be prepared for it, especially if you've never seen anything like it. It's awesome. I remember going to Point Loma. You can stand on the hill, and you can't see the end of it. I always dreamed about seeing the ocean. As soon as I could, I made a living on it; I was halfway to heaven right there.

### DECISION TO START A BUSINESS

I got a job working for a yacht company. My workmanship was such that people requested me to work on their yachts. I was good at varnishing and painting. That's my trade. I can do anything—bleach wood, simulate knots if that's what you want. I can make the wood look like you want it to look. I'm not a genius. I just spend the time required to do it. I've done a lot of "first" things, and I'm a mediocre, C-average type person. But I will spend whatever time it takes. I think it's important to complete the job right.

Then people started asking me if I would consider working on weekends. I said I would. Soon I was making more money on weekends than I was for the whole week. You know, you don't have to hit me with a sledgehammer! I bought an old van and went into the business of painting and varnishing right here on this old pier in the San Diego Harbor Boat Shipyard. It seemed risky to quit a good job to do your own thing, but there was no risk.

### GETTING STARTED

I didn't take classes, but I borrowed library books on different subjects: The *Fundamentals of Business, Estimating, Painting and Varnishing, How to Unlock the Winner in Yourself.* You've got to be motivated and stimulated. Places like IBM or General Motors have weekly or monthly sales meetings to reinforce motivation. You can't go into business, read something once, and say, "I got it." You don't. Without reinforcing it, you can drift back into old habits. I always keep a book in the bathroom or in my car. If traffic is tight, I read. I read about economics. I always read *Reader's Digest* because it's condensed.

I also talked to business people. To this day, it surprises me that people will not ask questions. Right now, if you said to me, "David, I'm thinking about going into the ship-repair business. What is it like?" I could tell you everything I know in two hours. But people won't ask. If you don't know the profit margin or how much you can chart, all you have to do is ask. You could go to any business right now, ask to talk to the manager, and he will tell you how he did it and what it's about.

I'll tell you another important step when I started my business. At the time I didn't realize the impact it would have. I picked a very dilapidated-looking boat down near the beginning of the marina. I estimated what it would take to do the work, the materials, everything. The I contacted the owner, which is easy to do: you go to the marina and find out who owns which boat and made an appointment to meet him at his boat. The boat really needed repairs. I told him I was starting a painting and varnishing business and that his boat needed the kind of work that I could demonstrate my skills on and get noticed. I said, "Here's what I'm proposing to do: you buy the material. Here's a list of what to buy. I will paint and varnish this boat. I'll do it just for the cost of the materials. Then, I would like to take pictures of it before and after I do the work to show people what I've done." Naturally I didn't have to twist his arm.

That was the smartest thing I've ever done. I put in about two hundred dollars' worth of labor on that boat and, back in those days, that was a lot of money. I've painted, I would say, fifty boats in that marina from that job. He was a very wealthy guy, he just didn't take care of things. I also painted his house and got a lot more work. He was a doctor, and I got to paint the houses and boats of all his doctor friends. He felt obligated. He was proud of what I had done. See, people like to help somebody that's willing to help themselves. The guy helped me for years. It got so that I hated to hear him call. He kept getting me so much work. You know how it is. People are always asking for something. How many times do you think this millionaire ever had anybody give him anything?

I actually started the business in 1968 and incorporated in 1971. I'm the sole owner. I think the reason that I was successful in this business is that I didn't see how hard it was.

I love the ocean. I saw it and got a job at a shipyard within three or four days. I've been here ever since. I've worked on a lot of yachts. And I loved it so much it never seemed like work to me—long hours, sanding, varnishing, and all. I work until seven o'clock at night, but there's no need for me to be here. I have managers who have been here eighteen, twenty years. They can certainly handle everything, but it still isn't like work to me.

San Diego is the largest ship-repair facility. Because of the navy, we have more ships in this port than in any other. It averages between $280 to $500 million a year. Only ten companies have an M.S.R., master's in ship repair license. It's like a driver's license is to cars. Only people with the M.S.R. can bid on $3 to $500 million jobs. The M.S.R. is difficult to get. I'm the only black who has an M.S.R. Right now, we're repairing two aircraft carriers and building two hotel ships.

I'm not the only guy working on these. Of the ten companies, I'm sure six are working, too. A carrier's so large, they can't bring it to your facility, you've got to go do it. They have many decks and what they call packages, or articles. It may be five hundred of them. I might bid on fifty of the five hundred and another contractor bids on thirty or one hundred. The bidding goes on weekly. So even if you have a big facility, maybe only 5 percent of the work is done there. The other work is done on the ship. Ninety-five percent of my business is repair work for the navy.

I help build commercial fishing boats, too. I remember building three commercial fishing boats that accommodated crews of seven. They had about six rooms below, each fifteen feet by fifteen feet, where they stored the fish. Each could handle one hundred tons of fish.

It took a long time before I qualified to get an M.S.R. Back then, I worked on commercial fishing boats and yachts only. I'm also a general contractor. I built some high-rise buildings, shopping centers, and bridges.

In 1979, I designed and built that lifting device all space shuttles use. It mates the space shuttle to the 747—puts it on and takes it off. I built one and Rockwell International built one. Mine cost $5 million; theirs cost $10 million. Mine works better.

I made the decision to go into business about eight or nine months before I quit my job. I prepared my plan based on what I'd already done. I kept track of how much time it took to sand a boat, putty it, the best time of day to do it, the weather. All of this information helped take the gamble out of the business. The one drastic mistake that I made was not communicating the plan to my wife.

She was supportive, but she wasn't aware of how long it takes. That's why so many people give up. They assume success is going to happen overnight. The reason for her disappointment was my fault. I told her that we needed $150 a week, and I showed her how we were going to be making about $300 a week. But I hadn't prepared her that $150 of the $300 had to go back into the business. Sometimes, $300 wasn't coming in every week. Maybe, one week I'd get nothing, and next week I'd get $400. She didn't handle this part well at all. The ups and downs made her insecure. Since we'd been married, there was always a weekly paycheck. All of a sudden he's in business, and now there's no money.

She accused me of being caught up in this business thing, the business cards and going to different things. She thought I was enjoying that instead of the reliability of a secure job. We had two kids at the time, and she was young. So she became very insecure. We were married in 1957 and divorced in 1969.

We never lacked money, but she had always worked so that we could have a better lifestyle. My wife had gone to college and was a librarian. She had a prestigious job that made her feel secure. When I met her, she had a kid and was independent. She was comfortable with that.

She was supporting the family. I always had money coming in, we could pay the rent, make the car note. It was the inconsistency that she didn't understand. Then, I would get a big job and make one thousand dollars that week. When I'd come home, I'd be excited and tell her I bought four new sanders or an air compressor. That didn't go down right, and we started fighting over that. I got one real big job and made twelve thousand dollars. And she thought, now I can get new furniture and overhaul the house. I said no, now I could move into a facility and buy the equipment I needed. That's what I did, and she didn't like it.

Then she started to think, you said we were going into business to make more money, to have a better lifestyle. Well, you're making more money, but it's all going back into the business. But, you see, that's how I was able to grow my company. I don't believe in debt. I've got equipment, cranes, everything I need. The only money I owe is $800,000 on the Harbor Drive property. I'm going into escrow with it right now. The total purchase price of the property is $8 million.

I think long range. I took the property and used it. We went from $1.5 million to $12 million a year for about five years. I made all that money and the property also increased in value. It was still a good investment. But to a wife, the $57,000 monthly payment was a lot of money.

Look at what's come back. Now, I own a lot of property and a lot of different things. I bought a lot in Fairbanks Ranch for $200,000 and just sold it for $1 million. I'm not struggling. I've got a million-dollar home and a $400,000 yacht. That's still very conservative compared to some of the other guys in this kind of business.

Both of my daughters work in the business. Lisa, twenty-four, just got married. Laurie, twenty-six, is married and has a family. I've since remarried and have two young boys. Lisa works full-time, Laurie works part-time, and her husband used to work here. Unfortunately for me, he quit to start his own business but is not doing well. That was something he had to try. I tried to talk him out of it, but he's an ambitious, good kid. I like him.

Lisa does the billing and tracks down accounts. In government work, you're always looking for money. And you're going after so many jobs. It's a full-time job keeping up with how much they owe and whether they paid.

Laurie is in charge of delinquent accounts, making sure that we get all of the money we deserve. You're getting guaranteed payments on government jobs for thirty days, ninety days, two years, so it's hard to keep track of it. Many times I've had orders done where they never sent the five or six hundred thousand dollars, because you never sent them a bill. You can't afford to have that happen.

We're working on one job for General Dynamics. We're doing the tooling on their $5 billion project. We're not doing the tooling in Marietta, Georgia, we're doing it in Alabama. These things have to mesh. If they find one problem with A in Alabama, everything stops for six months, eight months, a year. Well, you don't get paid when everything stops. Or they might contact you and say we're going to scrap that project, break down everything you've done, and we'll pay you for that. Or we'll continue. You do so many of these jobs, a lot can fall through the cracks.

### ACCESS TO CAPITAL

I started this business with two hundred dollars in 1968. I didn't borrow money because I didn't need to. I was the one doing most of the work.

About 1970, I borrowed twenty-five thousand dollars from the SBA for ten years. I paid it back in three. Then I assumed the SBA loan of another company because I wanted the equipment. I was lucky on that deal. When I first went to borrow the money I wanted, they turned me down as unqualified and I wasn't. They told me I needed more management experience, that my business plan was incomplete. You have to do a lot of little things for them to see how realistic you are.

And when they told me I didn't qualify, I asked why. I thought that these people were doing it because I'm black. But I changed the stuff they said was wrong just to see what lie they tell next time. Instead, they handed me the money. That was a valuable lesson for me.

I needed a forklift and an air compressor. About ten thousand dollars of the twenty-five thousand dollars was going to be used to purchase the equipment. The rest of the loan was to help me cover operating expenses. I didn't need the other fifteen thousand dollars. My business did well.

From that experience, I learned you cannot assume anything, and that they asked all the questions for a reason. You really have to listen to what people are telling you, rather than draw conclusions from what they say. I concluded that they had turned me down because I was black. It didn't have anything to do with it. I just assumed that it did.

That attitude has helped me many times. I have bid jobs and not been the low bidder. But I never assumed it was because of me. I go back and ask for information on how on the low bidder got the job. Normally, they won't give you a copy of the winning bid, but they will let you see an earlier one.

When the bank asks about your track record, it's in your best interest. They want you to succeed so you can repay the money and hopefully borrow more. For instance, the SBA 8(a) is a good program, but it isn't as good as people think. I never would have gotten a $50 million contract to build a ship without the 8(a). But I did get a contract for $15 million and another for $3 million.

See, at that time, I only had about $1 million in cash. No way under normal circumstances could you get a $50 million job with only $1 million in cash. They just wouldn't do it. But the 8(a) program is different. You've still got to be the low bidder, and demonstrate your ability, but you get progress payments a little faster. The disadvantage is that you have to justify every dime. It's a negotiated contract, and they can question everything. When you're the lowest of three bidders, they question nothing.

For instance, I got a job for $15 million that would have gone for $19 million if it had been on a bid basis. I took the job way too low. They went over every little dime and quarter. How much was steel? They weighed it and said, "Well, we can get the steel for this price." How much for that? There was no cushion anywhere. That's the disadvantage of the 8(a). It's negotiated and the officer looks at every thing you've got.

The annual profit for a low bid job may be $2 million, maximum. In non-8(a) contracts, you can deal with that guy and pocket the money. You can't if it's an 8(a) project; the government benefits from the deal. That's a disadvantage. I made, at the most, $2 million on that $50 million contract. If I didn't have to negotiate so tight, I would have made a minimum of $6 million. But I looked at it as getting in 8(a).

Now I can bid on any job, because I've got the expertise and all the different things to show. Once I bought all the equipment I needed to do the contract, I was in another league. So my benefit wasn't that contract, but it came five or six years later. Right now we're working on seventeen boats and doing very well. I wouldn't have got those without 8(a). I've built seven hotel ships for the navy at about $8 million each. I also wouldn't have had that. You learn. You're not going to make money doing many of the jobs, especially in the early years, because you swap dollars to buy material and equipment.

### PROFITABILITY

I made money from the beginning, because I had taken most of the gamble out of it. To give you an idea, I get $42 an hour from the government. My direct labor per man based on one hundred employees is $12 an hour. The rest is overhead. When I go above one hundred employees, that overhead cost—the biggest cost—becomes profit. So there are many times you show no profit but you get the overhead. I still buy equipment at auctions. Like the eighty-ton crane out there; it cost $1 million. I paid $300,000 cash. I have six of them, yet my cost is as if it were new.

### REVENUE

Business with the government really dropped off in recent years. We usually gross around $20 million, but that has been down recently. In 1990, we did about $14 million. In 1992, it was $8.4 million; for 1993 and '94, it dropped to around $2.2 million with the downsize and base closings; and for 1995 we will do only about $3 million. The military has downsized, but there was work to be done. They've moved it to other places and that has hurt our gross average.

My company is one of the stronger ones because I have been more diversified than others. I haven't had as many navy contracts in the 1990s, but then I had a big job from Martin Marietta and General Dynamics building a Minute Man missile. I built the first one of those. And Exxon rented over one hundred big carriers and freighters from the navy to accommodate people working on an oil spill. When Exxon finished with the ships, I got the contract to put them back into like-new condition.

I enjoy the work. I had the most employees when I had this $40 or $50 million contract to build a Coast Guard ship administered by the navy. I went from 150 to 300 employees. I had a lot of other contracts at the same time. It was a very difficult time for me, too, because I had so many new people. We had to hire new people for the ship, and I had one hell of a time with it. I was glad to see the end of that project. As a matter of fact, there were three more, but I wouldn't do them. And even though I would have made money on them, it wasn't worth the wear and tear on my employees.

I built my first Coast Guard ship in 1983. The job was for three ships, and each took about two years from signing the contract to finishing the work. It takes a year to order materials. You can't buy a ship's engine off the shelf. It takes a year to make it. Then there's six months of testing after it's built. It only takes eight months to actually build the ship, but it's stretched over two years. On that project, I went from 150 to 300 employees. Right now, I have 200 employees.

I had another facility in Seattle, where I built the first two. I didn't have space in San Diego. It takes five acres of space to build a ship.

## COMMUNITY LINKAGES AND INVOLVEMENT

### Suppliers and Customers

I have used few black suppliers. They mostly sell insurance. A lot of black people here have a contract on me because I won't take their insurance. But one of the toughest things is getting the right bonding insurance. That is L&H, Longshoreman and Harbor Insurance. You must have it when you're on the water, and to get insurance for your equipment.

The insurance company just about blackmails me. When I bus a guy from here to the ship, he requires three different insurances, depending on where he is. One insurance covers him when he gets on the bus right here in the yard. Another one when he gets on the street. A third when he gets to the ship. Now, if something happens, either one of those insurance companies will say it's the other one's fault. Black people can supply the insurance near the office, but they don't supply the others. They get angry because I won't buy it. My present agent has all three insurances. They write $200 million in insurance for me.

In twenty years, I've never had a black customer. Never.

## Employee Profile

I try to only hire people in this field. My average employee earns about $700 a week. They make $500, but there's about $200 a week in overtime. You need guys who will work overtime. People from the private sector who do construction jobs won't work overtime.

When I get a contract, I get a time limit for completion. It's not unusual to get a $2 million job that's got to be done in thirty days. The average private sector contract takes six months. A navy ship can't be out of service that long. So when the ship is in port, you're working twenty-four hours a day.

There are about thirty different welding certifications. So when we need people, we hire them from our computer list. We try to hire guys with the proper certification. Most people have two or three. The QA [Quality Assurance] department tells us how many we need for a job.

My workforce is 60 percent minority—black and Mexican. Over the years, it's strange that I've seen that you can't hire the average white guy. Some white guys can't work for a black company and they don't know it. They're not aware of it at first. At first it's a novelty, "Oh, I'm working at this black shipyard." Nice guy, wonderful. But then he starts to get into the company, and he sees things. Like, I make $500,000 a month on the Exxon contract. He starts to resent that and you can see it.

Like when the first guy first started work there: "Hello, Mr. Lloyd. How are you?" Because I walk through the yard every day and pretty soon they see you coming and he turns his back. It's getting to him a little bit. Because he doesn't think that it's fair. And he still thinks it's some kind of giveaway program. Because he looks at it and he identifies an intellect with my level. And it just don't seem right that he's out there busting his butt for five hundred dollars a week, plus maybe a couple of hundred overtime, and he knows what I'm making. He resents it. Resentment has set in.

And pretty soon he maybe starts to talk to somebody about this guy he works for. "Well, what's this guy like?" "Oh, he's kind of a regular Joe Blow." "Oh, really? Went to college?" "No." "A regular guy and making all that money."

He starts to think and to take it personally as an insult. "I'm the white guy with the intelligence. I should be making that." And I can come in and write on my calendar: In two weeks we'll have to fire him. He'll start to get irritable, lose his respect for authority or everything in the company. And he doesn't even know what happened. Over twenty-some years you'd be surprised at how many times I've seen it.

### Role Models

I guess my role model was that little white guy in Alabama. I was his houseboy, cut his grass, fed his horse, et cetera. They had a black maid, too. But I did the hard work, like waxing the floors. In those days the nice houses in Alabama had hardwood floors. So I saw he had a beautiful home and was very successful. He owned car dealerships and sold Oldsmobiles, Chevrolets, and Cadillacs. He was the "richest" guy in this little town, probably making a $100,000 a year. That's nothing today.

I remember one time he ordered a lawn mower for me to use but couldn't assemble it. Since I've always been mechanically minded, I told him I could put it together. He said, "Okay, then put it together, boy." I did. Several other times I saw he couldn't do things, so I did them. That's when I started to gain confidence, little by little. That's why when I came to California I was intimidated, but I realized I could learn. You see, it's the informed guy who get's the work, not necessarily the smart one.

He was a nasty guy. He had the Little Caesar's complex. He was a moody person. He wasn't a wonderful guy, and lovable and all like that. That's why it was hard for me to say he was my mentor. You picture your mentor as somebody you respect and all. Well, I did respect him, but I didn't like him.

### ADVICE TO FUTURE ENTREPRENEURS

For any young African American person thinking about business, I would say: be prepared, be aware, learn about business, and when you talk to people, listen. I learned a lot from reading books. You still have to do that, and you still have to prepare.

Assume—especially if you're black—that it's going to be difficult. You don't know everything you think you know about business. You're a rookie going into business and that's difficult. You're in competition with people who have more money, more knowledge, more everything than you have. It's like being pushed into the ring with Mike Tyson and someone says, "Win, David." Now, if somebody told me today, "You're going in the ring with Buster Douglas tomorrow," I'd say, "I'll be ready. But I'm going to have with me an assault rifle, a couple baseball bats, and a plan to win."

Don't expect to compete against Bay City Marinas. My foremen have twenty years' experience. Not one of them will work for you because he's worried about his salary and I'm giving him a $50,000 bonus a year above his salary. You can't match that. So you won't get a guy like that.

However, there is something you can do that I can't—give personal service. Like, what I did fixing up that first boat, taking pictures to the next person to show them what you do. I can't do that now. The company's too big. Just to open my doors costs $2 million a month. You won't have that $2 million a month obligation either. Those are things that you have to use. My cost is $42 an hour. You can start with a cost one-third of that. So you can't beat me in the ring, but you can offer a lot more service. Every businessman wants personal service at a better price.

Another barrier is convincing your customer that you're prepared. Because you just don't see many positive things about blacks, people have a myth about us—we don't follow through, we want something for nothing, and we can't compete. All this has to influence that white customer you're trying to get. He may not even know it influenced him, but it does. We've got to get rid of the negative things. And one thing I found out is that being the low bidder isn't the end of it. You have to convince the people you can do the job, that you have the know-how. The pre-award phase is when a lot of blacks lose the job.

I think it's because there are so many things white people want to know, and they can't ask. For instance, if I get a job on his yacht in his community, he wants to know what kind of people I'm bringing to work on his boat. He won't ask you if they're white or black. Or how much money you have in the bank, and can you finance the job or will you be in his office the next day asking for money. He can't ask those questions because he's afraid of hearing "discrimination."

So I tell him up front. I've got pictures of my equipment, like the brochure, a list of materials I have, my banking, my line of credit. I give them that. White folks don't have to; we do. If a white person sees ten negative things about a white person, he doesn't remember them. If he sees one negative thing about blacks, that's all he'll remember. If he saw ten whites defraud somebody, he'd give the eleventh one the job. Let ten black guys defraud a guy and heaven help that poor eleventh black guy who asks for a contract. We've got to be aware of these things and address them so that they become an advantage. If you don't, they will be your disadvantage.

What made me aware of this was the test for a trash collection job when I first came here. I failed that test. That humbled my butt. I became aware that you don't know everything you think you know. Now, I ask questions and I read. I assume I don't know. I assume the job will be hard. Once I do that, I am pleasantly surprised that it isn't as hard as I thought it was going to be because I'm prepared. Most people do just the opposite.

I'm very disappointed that my daughters are not as aggressive as I'd like them to be. I loved it when they were daddy's little girls, and so I made them like that. On the other hand, I'm raising my sons to be aggressive like I am. I should have treated my girls the same way. I didn't give them that option. So I'm disappointed in myself because they both are very feminine. They don't have the drive and determination to take over the business. They weren't taught to be that way.

My older son has been skiing for two years. He skis everything on the mountain. He's on the soccer team and Little League three years on a row. Every year he's been number two. But I raised him like that. There's no reason I couldn't have done that with my daughters. That's one of the reasons why blacks only have 1.5 percent of the wealth. They weren't raised to "take over." I was raised: "Do this so you can get a job working for Mr. White Boy." I was raised to be a soldier because my father didn't know that I could be the general. Most blacks weren't raised to be generals, and then we're surprised that they're not.

The point is: we were raised to be workers instead of entrepreneurs. It never occurred to me I was going to be a millionaire. Not in my wildest dreams. Let me tell you how I discovered I was a millionaire—this is shocking.

I was banking with a bank here and just doing my work. I always cared what people thought of my workmanship, so I always did good work. I'd never borrowed from my bank, except for fifteen thousand dollars or so. And all of a sudden my lending agent comes up and says, "David, the president of the bank wants to meet you." The president of the bank wants to meet me? Who ever met a president of a bank? All you ever meet are VPs, senior VPs, you know. "And he wants to have lunch with you. He's going to be in town next week."

I said, "Sure, what date?" He said, "No, no, no. The question is, What day do you want to have lunch with him?" I said Wednesday. "Okay," he said, "And what do you like to eat?" I said chicken. "What do you like to drink? Do you want wine? What kind of wine do you like?" And what kind of this, that. I didn't know much about wine. I said, "I like white wine." "What brand?" I said, "I don't know, any kind, it's okay." So he said, "Okay, Wednesday. Would quarter of twelve be okay for you to be picked up?" I said, "I'll drive!" "No, no, no! We pick you up." And he said, "David, I know you're a working kind of guy, but could you wear a tie? I mean, you don't have to, but just so you'll feel comfortable because everybody else will be wearing a tie."

Okay. So this girl comes to pick me up in a limo. And she picks me up and takes me down to the Westgate Hotel. I forget the name of that restaurant right on the top. It's private. She's taking me up there and we get on the top floor, and then this long table, and my name all up there and setting there right beside me was this president, and on the other side of me was this girl who picked me up. And then on the other side of the girl was my lending agent and his boss. And that was it. I said, "What kind of lunch is this?" So I get there and sit down. The president comes in and gives me a really warm handshake. And I'm looking totally confused. This is a working guy, I had my jeans on earlier.

And he said, "Mr. Lloyd, you seem a little perplexed and I can under-stand that, so I will explain." And he says, "You have become in this bank a cash millionaire." And he says, "What that means, is that your balance is never less than a million dollars and that's just your checking account!" And I had five or six CDs, because my lending agent said, "Hey, you've got excess cash in there, you should buy another CD for six months." I said, "Okay, okay. What-ever you say." I did it. He said, "And the bank makes a lot of money from this because normally the bank borrows money from the government, and they have to pay a lot. So once you get that status—and it's been over a year—you get special privileges. And from now on, you never have to come to the bank anymore. See, this lady here is assigned to you. If you need money orders, a check cashed, you tell her how much and she brings it down, you just hand her the check and she gives it to you. From now on, we will never bounce one of your checks. You can write up to (I can't remember what it was) over whatever you have in the bank and we will still honor it." Before then, if I needed to borrow those little loans—fifteen, twenty thousand, whatever I needed—I had to come down and get it. He said, "From now on, you don't have to do that anymore. You can just make a telephone call and it's done." A cash millionaire! He showed the print out to me. I don't even have it now, but I was the largest depositor in Crocker Bank, now Wells Fargo.

And the only time that money had ever been an issue was when I got divorced. At that time I was getting twenty-five thousand dollars, which wasn't quite enough, so I had to live tight. So I gave myself a ten-thousand-dollar-a-year raise. So I was living off of thirty-five thousand dollars a year and I had a million dollars, average, in the bank. I had a lot more than that, but

I mean, that was just there. And that was the last time that I had even tried to increase the business for financial gain. That was in '75, something like that.

The thing that has meant the most to me—given me the warmest feeling —had nothing to do with money per se. My father was a very tall man, and athletic, six feet, six inches. I've played basketball and I've been in sports all my life. I jet ski, water ski, or skydive. You name it: tennis, golf, every sport. And I was always good, just a little bit less than great. And that's how I was going to make my success: playing sports. But I stopped growing at six feet and I just knew I was going to be tall. I was going to be the first Michael Jordan. He was going to copy me. But I stopped growing. And I remember being so disappointed, living in this little country town, and I couldn't see any way out. Because I looked at my father, grandfather, aunt, and they'd never been out of that little rural town—Linden, Alabama. I didn't even know how to flush a toilet until I was twenty-one years old.

And I just didn't see no way out. Because sports was a way. I had heard of the Joe Louises and all of them. I couldn't sing and dance, but I could play sports because that's all we had to play was sports. I'm sure you remember when you went to school, you knew five or six kids just as good as you were. That humbles your butt. You need some kind of edge. So, I can remember walking down the railroad tracks, and I came to the conclusion that I wasn't going to grow anymore. And I wasn't going to be able to do what I needed. And I was thinking I just shouldn't even get out of the way of this train.

The SBA recognizes minority businesses, and I didn't know what that was about. They called, I went back to Washington, and they had this dinner and all the different stuff. Dave Bing and all those big shots were there. And I was one of those. I was chosen by Elizabeth Dole. That's what this is! And I remember, we were there in the White House with the president. It happened to be Reagan, but it wouldn't have mattered. And when they had the twelve of us standing up there and they said, "These are the *most outstanding minority business people in the United States.*" And it hit me like a brick, the day I was walking on the train tracks saying I would never make it anyplace. And standing there right in the rose garden and the Lincoln Monument was facing us. And trying to be brave, and the tears . . .

You know, it seemed like from that time on the railroad track to that day, it was just like a month or so. And I'm saying, "Please hurry and give us this award. Let me get the hell out of there." I don't want them to see me lose it here! And this was a breakfast, at ten o'clock in the morning. And each one of us got to sit down and talk with the president and share some stories about how we'd done it. Media was there from all over the world. We were stars! Then they had this big ball and all that. We were treated royally. I was just so overcome by it. I had no idea it was going to be like this. I didn't even take my family with me. It was just me. And that night, I was catching the red-eye to come back. And I went out there to the Lincoln Monument. And I sat there and I couldn't get up. I mean, every little thing that ever happened in my life, and all of the times teachers told me—my father told me—you can be whatever you want. You've just got to work hard, and you've got to do it. I could just hear each of those influential people in my life telling me that. And I remembered the time I was in the bank and I thought the guy wouldn't loan me money because I was black. And all of these things just kind of bam, bam, bam! One after the other just went through my mind. I missed my plane sitting there. That was the highest that I've ever been. And after that I don't think I touched the ground at all. And that was the highest I've ever been.

## CASE 11
## G O Furniture Manufacturing Company—Bill Alexander

*Bill Alexander is a major stockholder in G O Furniture Manufacturing in Vernon, California, a Los Angeles industrial park. Alexander is married and has one son, Brian, who is age twenty-five.*

### DECISION TO START A BUSINESS

In working for extremely large corporations, particularly those with government contracts, people experienced certain frustrations. We all, at one time or another, put in many overtime hours, burned the midnight oil to produce something the government ordered, only to find that the order was canceled and put in a dead file because of an arbitrary or, usually, political decision. So you sometimes concluded that earning a paycheck was all you had accomplished over a given time. You were paid reasonably well and had good fringe benefits. But in terms of weekly or monthly achievements, sometimes you shrugged your shoulders and said, I'm not sure I really did anything worthwhile.

Like others who have worked for very large corporations, I often daydreamed about getting into a small business, not necessarily owning it, but being involved in some way. So, somewhere along the line I suppose I picked up some aspirations about small business.

That's one of the things that certainly influenced my leaving. Fortunately, I had security, initially at least, because I took a leave of absence. That was important to me at the time. Although I probably would have made the same decision, regardless of the leave.

I had taken a couple of general business courses in adult school, thinking they might be handy in my career. When I finished my degree in mechanical engineering at the University of Illinois, I had no business background per se. But I think I began to develop an interest in business, perhaps because of the frustrations of doing work that was technically interesting but administratively frustrating.

When the opportunity came along, I suppose I was ready for it. My wife was supportive. She said, "If that's what you want to do, then go for it."

### GETTING STARTED

G O Furniture is a California corporation owned by several other corporations and individuals. John Ketch, the chief executive officer, and I are majority stockholders holding about 70 percent of the outstanding shares. G O manufactures wood office furniture. The business started in April 1968, and I joined the business in August 1968.

G O Furniture was started by the Green Power Foundation, an organization established shortly after the Watts riots in the 1960s. Norm Hodges was the prime mover. One of the foundation's goals was to establish businesses that could employ large numbers of blacks, particularly those who were unemployed or underemployed. One of the first product ideas we discussed was the manufacture of a baseball bat called the "Watts Walloper." The bat was highly publicized and manufactured by the company initially called California Golden Oak Products.

The foundation wrote proposals and attempted to borrow start-up capital from banks. At that time, as an employee in the aerospace industry, I was responsible for writing portions of proposals. The foundation asked me to help them develop this proposal, and I did. After the loan was approved and the corporation opened for business, they asked me to become the general manager.

I understood the business from putting together the bank proposal; however, I didn't know anything about baseball bats. They didn't either. We would learn together. In August 1968, I took a leave of absence from the North American Rockwell Corporation, thinking nothing ventured, nothing gained. John Ketch, with a background in sales and marketing, joined us in September or October as a sales manager. At that time, he worked for a manufacturer's sales rep firm representing a number of products and traveled across the country selling those products.

We started studying how to produce and sell these baseball bats. After three or four months of investigation, we reported to the corporate board of directors that we didn't think the bats were a viable product. The board told us to do some more study. We put together more data that proved that bats were not economically viable.

The cost to buy ash, the wood used for baseball bats, and to ship it from the Midwest was about a $1.05 per billet, as I remember. A billet is a rectangular piece of dried ash, not yet a bat. At that time bats sold wholesale for about $1.50. We could spend only 45 cents to cover manufacturing and selling costs, and to produce a profit. That wasn't enough. We couldn't make money with that kind of margin. The board of directors told us we didn't know what we were talking about. And at that point we offered our resignations because we couldn't run the company under those conditions.

Some of the community-oriented people on the board offered wonderful theories, such as selling the bats for $3.00. I suppose we could have sold a few as a novelty, but how long would you sell bats for $3.00 when everybody else is selling them for $1.50? Eventually reason prevailed and the product was terminated.

Next, we went into the wooden toy business. Frankly, we needed a product to survive. The toy business turned out to be tough because it was seasonal. Between 70 and 80 percent of all toys are for the Christmas season. We manufactured and actually made money from August through November, but virtually shut down and starved the rest of the year. So we began looking for products that we could sell all year long, not just on a seasonal basis.

Richard Nixon became president and showed great interest in minority business enterprises. He got the SBA very active and activated the 8(a) program. We decided to get involved. John Ketch went to Washington and enrolled the business in the 8(a) program. Our first 8(a) contract was to make plywood packing crates for the General Services Administration.

We were, of course, very excited. We had our first product that was not a toy. However, we lost our butts because we failed to anticipate the rapid increase in the cost of raw materials. We also made mistakes in learning to conform to government standards. The government standards are such that if the staples in a plywood crate vary more than a fraction of an inch, the GSA may reject the whole lot. You have to be extremely careful in meeting government standards. Our people weren't trained to do that. So we learned a lot but lost money on that first contract.

I think our next contract was for wardrobes, also an 8(a) contract for the General Services Administration. Then we got a postal service contract to provide self-service kiosks, little houses where you buy stamps and other postal supplies from vending machines. We had a few contracts with them that were reasonably successful. We did a couple of other products that I've forgotten. During that time we were still producing some toys, but we were also manufacturing for the government.

Our first break into furniture came when John was in Washington marketing our capabilities. Someone told him that the Department of Commerce was about to award a contract for dormitory furniture for the Merchant Marine Academy at King's Point, New York. They were considering giving it to a minority business for their first 8(a) experience. John immediately said, "We have that capability. Consider us." They sent us the specifications. We determined the pricing, my area of expertise, and submitted it. We got the contract.

We were finally in the furniture business! Then, a week or two later, we got a phone call from Washington telling us, "Sorry guys! It's disappointing, but you're not going to get the contract. We're going to award it to a tribe of Indians out West." They said we hadn't done anything wrong. It was just politics. A senator from New Mexico or Arizona had clout. He came in and said, "By God, my state's going to get this contract. We promised those Indians something and this is it!" So we were disappointed.

A month later, we got another phone call from Washington asking if we are still interested. They were ready to award the contract when the Indians told the Department of Commerce people they couldn't visit their plant because it wasn't built yet. Needless to say, they promptly yanked their contract.

The catch was that we had to guarantee delivery of the product on the original schedule. The Merchant Marine Academy cadets go on a cruise every summer, and the new furniture had to be in their rooms before they returned at the end of August. We recognized that it was impossible to meet their schedule because of the lead time required for raw materials. We had two choices. We could tell the truth, not get the contract, and they'd award it to somebody else who would have the same problem. Or we could lie and say we'd meet their schedule, get the contract, and then try to make up for it as best we could.

We guaranteed to meet the deadline and got the contract, and just as we predicted, we were about a month late delivering the product. The cadets came home from their cruise to find the furniture still not in place. We, of course, got beat across the head and shoulders on a daily basis by several government agencies. The Merchant Marine was calling us, the Department of Commerce was calling us, and the SBA was calling us. And of course they were telling us that we were going to cause the whole entire 8(a) program to have a terrible black eye because of our nonperformance. But we of course learned a long time ago to have thick skin and we withstood all this abuse and got the product there about a month behind schedule. But when they got it, it was accepted well. The quality was good and so the end of the story turned out to be a happy one.

The Green Power Foundation exists today only as a memory, but it had a significant impact because it started a number of other black businesses. One located in the Watts Industrial Park for some years manufactured printed circuit boards. They are no longer in business. The foundation helped start a company that had the first franchise on luggage carts at the Los Angeles International Airport. They must have started at least a dozen other businesses; I've forgotten how many. Unfortunately, most of them, for one reason or another, did not survive. Norm Hodges, the president, and a number of people that were active in the organization came out of the aerospace industry and sparked a lot of interest and activity.

### ACCESS TO CAPITAL

The start-up capital was borrowed from the United California Bank, now First Interstate Bank. There was no equity in the business. Looking back, the loan was granted on the basis of information regarding the manufacture of baseball bats, which we later found to be unrealistic. Someone knowledgeable about industry could easily have blown holes in it. So I think that the initial loan was more of a social loan than anything else.

Before we found our initial product not viable, we had already expended funds, hired people, and produced some bats. The company was at the point of bankruptcy. We undoubtedly would have gone out of business without the Arcata MESBIC, California's first MESBIC.

The Arcata people, headquartered in northern California, are big in printing and lumber. The fellow running the Arcata MESBIC either heard about us or somebody called him. But regardless, he came to talk to us and liked what he saw. So he made a combined equity and debt investment and spearheaded getting funds from other individuals in the form of equity.

That was the second round of financing, probably between $200,000 and $250,000. The first round was the bank loan of $150,000 to start the corporation. Arcata gave John Ketch and me the right to purchase equity in the corporation. This was very helpful. Arcata's theory was that people need to have a piece of the action to feel personally the fortunes of the company, whether up or down. The Green Power Foundation's board of directors initially resisted. They didn't really want us to have a piece of the action; they wanted to maintain full ownership. But Arcata essentially gave them an ultimatum. We got options and purchased shares. That's how we began acquiring equity in the corporation ourselves.

Overall, our experience with SBA has been positive. We've certainly gained some benefits that enabled us to survive, particularly in the early years of the business. We've used most of the SBA's resources, other than technical assistance. We had one or two direct loans of $100,000 or less from the SBA, and we've had SBA-guaranteed loans from a bank. And, of course, we've participated in the 8(a) program. The 8(a) program turned out to be very positive for us. We were doing 8(a) contracts for several agencies from the time the baseball bat was deep-sixed until we started into the commercial wood furniture business. The most successful contracts we got were to build wood desks and credenzas for the General Services Administration.

Once we got through the start-up problems in producing the desk on that first GSA contract, it really wasn't difficult to maintain the high standards required by the government. We found that we could refine our manufacturing process to where we could make a reasonable profit. We were lucky that we got into that market when the federal government could not get enough desks and credenzas from their regular sources. As a result, once we got the start-up, the General Services Administration gave us a series of back-to-back contracts.

GSA increased the size of the contracts to the maximum level that we could produce. They would take as many as we could manufacture. We began expanding and, at our peak, we produced approximately one hundred desks a day for the federal government. We produced and shipped over sixty thousand units over four years. As we continued to refine our manufacturing process, we made an acceptable profit and had some good years.

We knew the 8(a) program would not last forever. At that same time, we began developing our commercial line of the desks, credenzas, and seating. There were problems with operating in the 8(a) program during that time. We were adversely affected by several organizational changes within the SBA and the GSA. In fact, a couple of times, our contracts were stopped or frozen because of things out of our control. But overall, 8(a) was clearly beneficial. And we probably would not be where we are today without them.

### PROFITABILITY

We had our first profitable year somewhere between 1973 and 1975, when we began producing desks for the government. Then the 8(a) program changed. We added other products but found it difficult to support both the government and commercial markets. By then we were heavily into the commercial market. Since the government market requires different priorities and additional time, we dropped the government market. In essence, we just graduated ourselves out of the 8(a) program, which was the goal of the program.

The early years in the commercial business were not profitable. Our commercial business really didn't produce enough volume to sustain the corporation when we lost the 8(a) business. So for a few years, we lost money on the commercial market. But finally we again became profitable.

We've done some advertising over the years, but not much. We get business mainly by knocking on doors, talking to people. We use outside, independent sales representatives who do some door knocking for us. We also send out catalogues and printed literature from time to time. It's a people business, and basically you have to be in front of the people who make decisions about buying furniture at the right time.

We've considered closing down a few times simply because we thought we had no choice. But Ketch and I are stubborn enough to believe that "I'm not dead until I quit breathing." We've thought about it a few times only when we felt we were at death's door. But fortunately, we've learned to live on the edge, because we've been there many times.

### REVENUE, ACCOUNTING, AND INVENTORY

Our best year was in the early '80s, when we grossed over $12 million. Our gross annual revenue was $10 million in 1988 and a little over $10 million in 1989. In 1990, it was somewhere around $11.5 million in 1990. The recession hit in early '90s and business dropped off dramatically. In 1992, our gross annual revenue was $5.4 million; 1993, it was $6 million; and in 1994, we began to recover at $7.5 million.

We use an accounting system that's probably fairly standard for people in manufacturing. We have a financial vice-president and an accounting department of four reporting to him. They are responsible for keeping our financial records.

Our inventory turns somewhere between sixty and ninety days. Inventory is a combination of book and physical inventories. Some items are inventoried weekly; others we only physically inventory annually. We inventory all materials at the end of our fiscal year. That information is included in our annual audited financial statements, which are done in conjunction with a CPA firm.

### COMMUNITY LINKAGES AND INVOLVEMENT

**Location**

We are located in the city of Vernon, which offers very competitive lease rates. We pay about fifteen cents per square foot for 120,000 square feet, a very good rate compared to other areas.

Since Vernon is an industrial city, its municipal services are geared to serve industry. We have excellent fire and police protection and a reasonable tax rate. Fewer than two hundred people actually live in the city. We have showrooms in the Chicago Merchandise Mart, the Atlanta Piedmont Center, and the Los Angeles Pacific Design Center. But all manufacturing is done in Vernon.

**Suppliers and Customers**

Our customers are large corporations nationwide. A significant portion of our business is in southern California. The second strongest region for us in terms of sales is the greater New York City area. Since we're looking for a concentration of corporate end-users, we go to where the corporate buying organizations are located. We also have some accounts in Kansas City, a couple in Chicago, and a scattering in other locations. We go to the customer's buying location.

A very small percentage of our customers are minorities. We do have one African American dealership and one Puerto Rican dealership in New York that buy our furniture. We've also got a couple of Asian organizations here in southern California. But overall, our minority customers probably represent less than 5 percent of our business.

Most of our major suppliers are within a radius of twenty miles. Some are scattered over southern California and other areas. Given the opportunity we would certainly try to give African American suppliers a chance. However, most of the materials we buy are not supplied by African Americans, at least not that we're aware of. For example, we buy large quantities of particle board, veneer, and hardwood lumber. I'm not aware of any large African American suppliers of these materials.

### Employee Profile

When we first started in 1968, we had about 30 employees. It varies; we've gone up and down as our fortunes have also gone up and down. We've been as low as 10 employees and as high as 240. At our peak, we ran two shifts.

We get a lot of referrals from current employees who bring in friends. But we've also used newspapers ads and headhunter search firms. During the first year or two, the workforce was predominantly African Americans, in some instances from other parts of the world, particularly the West Indies. But over the years the workforce became more Hispanic. Today, 90 percent of our workforce up to and including first-line supervisors is Hispanic. That's true of our industry in general in southern California.

Excluding John Ketch and myself, our top management is now primarily male Caucasian.

### Trade Associations

We're still members of the Black Business Association, but we're not active anymore. We're fairly active in the Minority Purchasing Council. Ketch is on the board of directors of the Minority Business Council. We're not really active in any industrywide trade organizations at the moment. We are probably going to join BIFMA, an office furniture industry organization headquartered in Michigan. I am a former director of the National Association of Black Manufacturers, now defunct.

I read *Business Week* and several trade magazines, like *Wood Products, Wood Digest,* and so on. I subscribe to a number of trade magazines related to our business. I think Ketch subscribes to *Contact Magazine* and the *Wall Street Journal.*

### Role Models

I didn't have a role model. I grew up in St. Louis and was in high school during World War II. Black business, for me, was a barber shop. I remember a black woman who had a hair-care establishment and did well. As a matter of fact, she owned a couple of buildings. But in general, black business was a shoe-shine stand or a laundry shop. I did know a couple of brothers who were in the insurance business, but that was about it. As a kid, I had no black business role models.

Although I didn't recognize it at the time, maybe something did rub off. My dad, a schoolteacher, was also involved in several little side businesses. At one time he and a partner had a heating and ventilating business installing heating equipment on weekends. I wasn't involved at all, but perhaps something rubbed off. At that time, if you wanted to achieve something in the community, you had to be a preacher, teacher, doctor, civil servant, or postal worker—the lawyers didn't do very well. My mother's family were also schoolteachers.

### Succession

We're beginning to look at succession and hiring some people who will be in place when we're ready to leave. We brought in a new chief financial officer in his mid-forties. We're going to bring in a vice-president of operations, who is around fifty. We're also looking at adding another person who's around forty years old. I'll probably be leaving first because I'm ten years older than my partner. None of the potential successors are related to Ketch or myself.

I have a twenty-five-year-old son who's working in the health-care industry. However, he hasn't decided whether he wants to make it his full-time career. I've always told him that I will support his decision on virtually any positive career choice that makes him happy.

### BARRIERS

The things that are most likely to cause you to be unsuccessful in business have nothing to do with race. They have to do with the economy in which we live. Business is highly competitive, and your competitors would really like to see you go out of business. Your competitors will do everything they can to make sure that you close your doors. And that doesn't necessarily have anything to do with your color. Our system says, if I am on top of the hill, I'm not going to do anything to make it easier for someone to stand beside me on that hill. In fact, I'll do everything I can to grease the hill so you can't get there. That's how I can continue to enjoy all the fruits of success.

### ADVICE TO FUTURE ENTREPRENEURS

You have to make sure you control your marketing, have a solid financial base, watch your bottom line, manage your people properly, and do all the things you learned in business school.

There is still another factor you're going to encounter from time to time, sometimes very subtle, sometimes overt. Someone won't order from you because they don't like the color of your skin. More often than not, it will only be a suspicion. You won't be positive. It may be true, but it's difficult to prove it one way or another.

The solution? See if you can get around him. Wait for him to retire, or give up on that corporation and move on to the next. Look for individuals who don't necessarily have that kind of bias, someone more inclined to make the decision based on the quality, service, or price. These are the factors you want him to base his decision on anyway.

### EPILOGUE: THE DECLINE OF G O

Business began to drop off in 1991 when the recession hit. This was the longest and worst recession we experienced. It affected every segment of the economy in which we did businesses. Previous recessions were segmented. If one was down, another was up. But not this recession. It lasted four years.

We signed a contract with U.S. Sprint in 1991 with the expectation that 1991 would be a good year, that Sprint would expand. Their business went to zero. The contract was canceled. Furniture is always something that can be deferred. Businesses began to buy used furniture. The effect was catastrophic. We went from usually $10 to $12 million in sales to about $5.5 million in 1992 and no more than $6 million in 1993. Every thing was down.

We did everything we could to wait it out. We cut personnel, overhead, and our own salary trying to wait it out. In 1992, G O went in Chapter 11 bankruptcy. Some of our competitors closed their doors before we did. By 1994 we began to see some upturn; we grossed $8 million, but it was too late. The straw that broke us was that, in early 1994, our landlord decided they wanted to do something different with the building. We had been there since 1972. "I want you out," he said. We thought about moving, but that would have been too expensive. In late 1994, a Cuban American–owned firm in Chino, California, called M&M Manufacturing purchased our assets out of bankruptcy for $500,000. They also hired many of our employees, so we were pleased about that.

We were in business from 1968 to 1994. I consider that success, because we gave a number of employees an opportunity that they would not have had otherwise. We provided minority people an opportunity to be managers that they would not have gotten. Winston Bowman was a militant from Chicago when we hired him as an assistant buyer. When he came to us, he talked to people abruptly, harshly. But he grew and mellowed. He was offered a job with in sales with another company and became one of their top sales persons. He went from militant to ultraconservative and he said to me that if we hadn't given him the opportunity he would have never gotten to where he is now. We made a difference for a lot of blacks and Latinos.

Often we were the only African American firm in the industry. We made an impact on the industry. The ending wasn't as I would have written the script but we had the chance and we made the most of it. One thing about capitalism is that you have the chance.

## Summary

Community involvement for the entrepreneurs interviewed from the West region range from very substantial to none. Of the four, William Shearer and Ella Williams continue to maintain and nurture strong ties to the black community. In large part because of the nature of their business, Bill Alexander and David Lloyd do not use African American suppliers or have black customers.

Shearer, through his business and personal life, remains immersed in the African American community. The company's two stockholders, almost all of his employees, and one-half of his customers are black. The company's building is located in the black community, and he, his daughters, and most of his employees choose to live in the black community. His involvement in the community goes beyond this fundamental level of support. His is a proactive vision of providing an environment that both nurtures and nourishes the next generation of successful black entrepreneurs and professionals. The managers on his staff are being groomed and trained to operate their own radio stations.

He considers his greatest accomplishment to be the ability to maintain a business that gives young black people who have prepared themselves "their shot at life."

Ella Williams's approach to "community" is somewhat different—she neither lives nor does business in the black community, but her commitment to the community is evident. Although all of her customers are government agencies, she makes an extra effort to seek out, hire, and do business with African Americans whenever and wherever she can. In the company's Los Angeles office, one-half of her employees are minority; in Washington, two of the seven are. "Giving back" is what Williams does when she serves on several boards. She considers herself to have been blessed as a child by the support and love of her community, and she wants to do what she can to help other children, especially those growing up in the inner city of Los Angeles. Her most grandiose project for the benefit of children is Ella's World Class Cheesecake, Breads, and Muffins, a business to teach inner-city kids how to manufacture and market bakery products. She has already written a business plan and identified the plant site and the location of five retail stores in upscale neighborhoods. She is also generating interest for funding through local development councils and industries as well as twisting the proverbial arms of contractors to provide reduced-cost or free construction-related services.

Bill Alexander's roots as an entrepreneur are grounded in the 1960s, following the riots in Watts. African American individuals created the Green Power Foundation to foster employment within the community by establishing local businesses that would employ large numbers of blacks. Although most of the businesses spawned by the foundation did not survive, one eventually became G O Furniture, a manufacturing concern headed by Bill Alexander and John Ketch. G O manufactured furniture for corporate clients such as the American Express family of companies. Less than 5 percent of their customers were minority, and none of their suppliers were African American; however, Alexander says he would certainly use African American suppliers if any supplied the materials he needed.

The ethnic composition of G O work force has varied over the years. Today, 90 percent, up to and including first-line supervisors, are Hispanic. "That's true of our industry in general in Southern California,"

notes Alexander. With the exception of Alexander and his partner
Ketch, top management is white male. Thus the line of secession in this
business does not seem to indicate that the business will remain African
American–owned.

Other than his early activities with the Green Power Foundation,
Alexander did not indicate during the interview any present-day involvement in or with the African American community.

David Lloyd builds and repairs ships. Considering the nature of
his business, it is understandable that his only customers are the navy
as well as government contractors and large corporations such as Martin Marietta. His work force is 60 percent minority, mostly Mexican and
African American. Lloyd seldom uses black suppliers, except for those
who "try to sell me insurance." Like Alexander, during the interview
Lloyd did not indicate an involvement in or with the African American community.

With the exception of William Shearer, none of the entrepreneurs
profiled in chapter 6 targeted the African American community as
their customers. To some degree all four employed African Americans;
however, Shearer and Williams actively recruited and train African American employees to become top-level management.

None of the four can be accused of exploiting the African American community. However, only Williams and Shearer expressed a need
and an obligation to contribute to the community with the ultimate goal
of improving the quality of life. Both did so in substantial ways.

PART 3

# The Outlook
# for Black
# Business
# Development

# 7

# **The Future**

This book illustrates *what it is like to be an African American entrepreneur in the post–Civil Rights era.* Although the level of economic rights accorded to blacks has increased substantially over time, they still do not enjoy full economic rights. Indeed, an economic detour composed of artificial barriers appears to influence success or failure as much as or more than business acumen.

The era of the unskilled mom-and-pop owners of corner store businesses in a segregated community has all but come to a close. In its place, highly skilled and trained entrepreneurs operating within the expanding fields of national markets are emerging. To what extent are the entrepreneurs included in this study representative of the top .5 percent of the 620,912 African American–owned businesses earning $1 million or more annually?

These twelve life stories clearly illustrate that race-based institutionalized barriers to full participation in the economic arena still shape the African American business experience in the post–Civil Rights era. Put differently, the kind of economic detour that negatively impacted the growth of black entrepreneurship in the pre–Civil Rights era has transformed itself but, nevertheless, continues to negatively impact the entrepreneurial experience of African Americans in the post–Civil Rights era. The life stories of entrepreneurs included in this study show that considerable thought, preparation, and planning are required to circumvent the economic detour and succeed as an entrepreneur.

How does one become a successful entrepreneur in the post–Civil Rights era? Derrick Bell (1992), in his book *Faces at the Bottom of the Well,* warns that "racism is an integral, permanent, and indestructible component of American society." Extreme power differentials designate African Americans as the group at the bottom. From Bell's perspective, African Americans will never have the rights routinely enjoyed by other ethnic groups. He argues: "Black people will never gain full equality in this country. Even those herculean efforts we hail as successful will produce no more than temporary 'peaks of progress,' short-lived victories that slide into irrelevance as racial patterns adapt in ways that maintain white dominance. This is a hard-to-accept fact that all history verifies. We must acknowledge it, not as a sign of submission, but as an act of ultimate defiance" (1992, 12).

In the face of relentless racism, how do African Americans "still rise," as Maya Angelou implores? I concur with Bell that racism, in the form of limited economic rights, continues to constrict full participation of African Americans within the American economic arena, despite their herculean efforts. Bell further argues that white Americans can neither identify with nor empathize with the experience of black Americans, and therein lies the American Dilemma.

Although polite circles invoke the currently popular rhetoric of a "color-blind society," the fact remains that the United States is a race-centered society in which most white Americans fear that blacks will outpace them. As a result, policies that would benefit most whites are unsupported and undermined for fear that blacks would also benefit. The standardization of employment criteria required under affirmative action regulations clearly illustrates this point. Affirmative action policies actually enhance the working conditions of all workers, but much of its potential impact is eroded by the myth of reverse discrimination.

How do African Americans still rise as entrepreneurs in a race-centered private enterprise system designed to keep them at the bottom? This is an increasingly crucial question, but the determination of young African Americans to become entrepreneurs signals a new promise. Commissioned by the U.S. Department of Commerce, Minority Business Development Agency, James Chase (1993) recently conducted a national study that examined the awareness and attitudes of minority youth and young adults ages eighteen to thirty-five toward owning a business. Chase found:

1. Black young adults had the highest expectation of owning a business (38.1 percent), followed by Asian (37.6 percent), white (35.5 percent), and Hispanic (25.5 percent) young adults.
2. Overall, males had higher expectations of business ownership than females. Black urban males had the highest average expectation (50 percent), and Hispanic females, rural and urban, the lowest average expectation (21 percent).
3. Respondents of each racial/ethnic group felt that the major advantage to business ownership was the freedom associated with being one's own boss. The expectation of high financial rewards was a distant second.
4. Respondents of each racial/ethnic group felt that the major disadvantage to business ownership was the possibility of failure, followed by the excessive demand for hard work. Black young adults identified hard work as a disadvantage less frequently than did the other racial/ethnic groups.
5. A strong relationship existed between having role models for business ownership and expecting to own a business in the future. Only 51 percent of the young adult respondents without a role model expected to own a business, whereas 70 percent of those with one role model and 82 percent of those with at least two role models said they expected to own a business.
6. Almost one-half (45 percent) of the respondents indicated that they had at least one relative or friend who was a business owner. However, less than 10 percent of this group were black or Hispanic, but 21 percent were Asian and 21 percent were white.
7. Minority young adults were less likely to have access to five to ten thousand dollars for start-up capital from relatives or friends.
8. Less than one-third of all young adults knew where to go in their community for advice on starting a business.

The Chase study confirms a burgeoning entrepreneurial spirit among African Americans, as does the 46 percent increase in business starts for African Americans between 1987 to 1992, a rate greater than for

Americans as a whole. Young adult African Americans, especially males, expect to go into business and are willing to do the work necessary to succeed.

In the face of indestructible racism, which over time has undermined economic development and wealth accumulation, the entrepreneurial spirit among African Americans continues to burn hot. The hurdles are many—too few role models in business, a lack of access to start-up capital, and limited knowledge of sources for business advice, all circumstances created by limited economic rights. Nevertheless, the hopes and the entrepreneurial spirit among these young adults persists.

How do African Americans "still rise"? The life stories presented in chapters 4, 5, and 6 serve as *pathways* to full economic rights. The common threads within the life stories light the pathway around the economic detour to successful entrepreneurship.

## The Pathway of Successful Entrepreneurship

### SOCIALIZATION

A strong association exists between having a parent, close relative, or friend in business and selecting entrepreneurship as a career path early in life. This study tends to support this connection, but with significant variation.

For two-thirds of the entrepreneurs, either one or both parents were involved in some business activity, but this was almost always a form of "moonlighting." For the most part, parents were full-time teachers, dentists, lawyers, ministers, noncommissioned military officers, postal service workers, social workers, and assembly-line workers. In addition, typically the father and sometimes the mother, also, had a part-time business as restaurateur or club owner, owner of apartment buildings, beautician, furnace installer, caterer, or painter for construction projects, or in auto body repair or the refuse-disposal business. In the pre–Civil Rights era, parents needed both full-time employment and a side business in order to sustain their families and provide a middle-class standard of living or better. Some parents simply worked two full-time jobs to provide necessities for their families.

An interesting perspective about parental moonlighting activities surfaced. Entrepreneurs did not consider their parents' moonlighting as a factor influencing their own decision to become entrepreneurs until required to do so for this study. Although the parents of these entrepreneurs generally lacked opportunities to engage openly in private enterprise, they created a foundation for today's generation of skilled entrepreneurs.

What parents told their children regarding entrepreneurship is unique and interesting. Few of the entrepreneurs' parents explicitly encouraged them to go into business. But all inspired their children with the attitude that they could be anything they wanted to be and do anything they wanted to do if they just set goals and worked toward them. Parents also urged their children to get a solid education as preparation for a worthwhile career, although the range of career choices was usually unclear to the parent.

## DECISION TO START A BUSINESS

How does one make the decision to start a business? This question is especially important for those overwhelmed by the fear of starting a business. Before the Civil Rights era, most African Americans did not expect to engage in private enterprise in an open market. Their lack of expectation stemmed not from lack of desire or tradition but because institutionalized race-based laws and customs made it clear that African Americans were unwelcome and would meet strong resistance, including death.

Instead, African Americans aspired to the "good job": a management job in a major corporation, teacher, doctor, dentist, lawyer, social worker, or postal service worker. Others aspired to work on the "good paying" assembly line. With such a collective outlook at that time, how did the entrepreneurs of this study make the decision to start a business?

Nearly all of the entrepreneurs in this study commented that they "had never thought about being an entrepreneur." None acknowledged it as a lifelong dream. Entrepreneurship was often thrust upon them as a result of colliding with corporate America's "glass ceiling" or being uncomfortable with the nine-to-five routine. For some, it flowed naturally from their professional interests.

The typical entrepreneur in this study worked in a professional occupation within the corporate or public sector for five to fifteen years. During this time, he/she realized the incompatibility between the desire for advancement and the organizational culture that defined the positions and levels of authority available to African Americans.

The experience of Anthony Snoddy, Exemplar, illustrates the point. By age thirty, he was a middle manager and headed up the second largest manufacturing complex at General Motors: "Even the white boys don't do that." But he knew that he would never achieve his goals there. As one of the top purchasing people, he should have been a division director. When he asked his division director if he would be the next division director, the man answered no. He had hit the glass ceiling. "And that's when I said it's time for me to get out," Snoddy says.

Ella Williams, AGEIR, had a somewhat different experience in corporate America. Her mother had convinced her that she could do anything if she really wanted to. When she worked for Hughes Aircraft, Williams quickly realized that the people she worked with were no smarter than she: "So if they can do this, why can't I?"

At that time, Williams read that the SBA was encouraging minorities and women to enter nontraditional fields. She studied Hughes's organization and said, "This couldn't be too hard, because I'm as smart as the people I'm working with." She talked to others at Hughes, particularly a friend in the marketing department, about trying to create an engineering services company, a smaller version of Hughes. Once the friend agreed that she could do it, Williams realized that she was ready to start after thirteen years of valuable experience at Hughes.

The decision to start a business tends to come during midlife rather than in early adulthood. Each of the twelve entrepreneurs were over thirty years of age when they launched their business. Each considered a variety of factors before making the decision to start a business, but money or financing was not always their primary consideration. Entrepreneurs more frequently cited issues related to personal happiness, freedom from harassment, technical aspects of operating the business, what to sell, what to charge for services, adequate market research, lack of consumer confidence, fear of failure because blacks only get one chance, desire to provide leadership, and desire to contribute to their community.

## EDUCATION

Entrepreneurs in emerging businesses tend to be well educated. Eleven of the twelve entrepreneurs have at least a four-year college degree; eight have an M.B.A. or another advanced degree. All reported taking adult education or extension courses dealing with various aspects of business management in order to stay current in their field. In stark contrast to the images of pre–Civil Rights era entrepreneurs, emerging entrepreneurs prepared themselves educationally and are committed to a program of continuing education.

## GETTING STARTED

After making the decision to start a business, one must identify and take the appropriate steps. Although entrepreneurs did not plan to go into business as a lifelong goal, once they made the decision, they thoroughly planned its initiation.

Starting a business appears to be a three-step process. The first is to hire an attorney to incorporate the business as a subchapter S corporation. This form of organization allows businesses to derive the maximum benefit from the tax laws and provides protection from frivolous litigation.

The typical second step is to prepare a business plan. This document describes the entrepreneur's business vision and serves as a baseline against which to measure business growth and development. To prepare a business plan, one must research industry conditions, identify the competition, and identify the anticipated market share. The business plan usually includes a marketing strategy and cash-flow projections.

When Albert DeMagnus started Computer Management, his first step was to incorporate, and his second step was to formalize a business plan, which included a financial plan and a marketing plan. Once the plans were written, he began marketing. The business plan focused on narrow goals. The financial plan indicated a "get out of bed number," the amount of work to be accomplished in a particular amount of time. The plan also included a "win" number ("If we get this much, then, heck, we're well on our way"). DeMagnus's business plan helped him to define and clarify where he wanted to take the company and to organize and target his ideas. "It's nice to know that you are headed in the right direction," he notes. "The plan basically let me know the direction I was headed."

Some of the entrepreneurs developed their plans only after their businesses were in operation for several months or a few years. In contrast, Bill Mays, Mays Chemical, has never developed a formal business plan—an ill-advised and not-recommended approach. He indicates that "the business plan was probably in my head." However, when asked how he could establish a successful company without writing a business plan, he responds philosophically: "I was living it and dying it as I was doing it. I didn't need a road map."

Mays was also in the enviable position of acquiring start-up capital from a friend rather than from a commercial institution; consequently, he was not required to write a business plan. The people with a financial stake in the business already knew the business and had faith in him. Today, some phases of Mays Chemical have a business plan of sorts, but Mays notes his stronger interest is a sales plan that projects revenue and bottom-line profits.

Step three in starting a business is to actively begin the marketing process. For African Americans, marketing is not always straightforward.

David Lloyd of Bay City Marina took an innovative approach to getting business. He identified a dilapidated boat docked in a visible area, contacted the boat's owner, and offered to repair the boat if the owner paid for the materials. In return for his labor, Lloyd wanted to take "before" and "after" pictures of his work to show other prospective customers: "I painted, I would say, fifty boats in that marina from that. That was the smartest thing I've ever done."

After incorporating, writing a business plan, and initiating a marketing strategy, entrepreneurs annually update their business plans. The updating process allows entrepreneurs to evaluate their progress toward reaching revenue goals and the effectiveness of their marketing strategies.

## ACCESS TO CAPITAL

Many prospective entrepreneurs are immediately concerned about gaining access to capital for start-up. The respondents in this study indicated that *personal savings is the most important source of start-up capital for emerging entrepreneurs.* The entrepreneurs used between

$1,200 and $500,000 of their personal savings and retirement funds as the source for start-up capital. This indicates, contrary to popular belief, that emerging black entrepreneurs are self-supporting. Table 6 in chapter 3 illustrates that of all African American entrepreneurs who borrowed money for start-up, 10.7 percent borrowed from what might be referred to as personal sources: spouse, other family, friends, credit cards, and second home mortgages. Nearly 10 percent report having borrowed start-up capital from a commercial bank. Four of the twelve entrepreneurs reported borrowing between $2,000 and $120,000 for start-up from personal sources such as family members, friends, credit cards, or a second mortgage. G O Furniture Manufacturing and KGFJ successfully borrowed $150,000 and $4.5 million, respectively, for start-up from commercial sources.

Gaining access to capital through commercial banks is particularly difficult. Entrepreneurs frequently do not even apply for commercial financing for fear of being rejected summarily or for having insufficient assets. For instance, Bettye Daly, MayDay Chemical, said although she was well received by bank loan officers in conservative Kalamazoo, they "could not lend to a business like mine that was highly leveraged with no asset base. They were just not into venture capital." Daly suggests that in addition to her race, the loan officers might also have been uncomfortable with her gender: "They have nothing in their portfolio to compare me with. They just deal with statistics and comparison charts."

Entrepreneurs with sufficient assets felt that their loan applications were not reviewed fairly. This perception was strong and consistent in each region, for men and women, regardless of the business longevity. The case of Harold Martin of MVP Products is a clear example. Martin's market survey indicated that the athletic footwear industry, growing at a rate of 35 percent, was strong enough to support new companies. He had sufficient net worth, and to differentiate his company, he found a niche in personalized footwear.

Martin first approached the National Bank of Detroit for financing and then heard the same story from forty-nine banks in a number of cities: the company was a start-up venture and the principal did not have the necessary background. So he scaled down his business plan. Even then, he was refused by the banks and the SBA. Even with the support of J. C. Penney and the visible signs of impending success, the banks insisted on offering Martin much less than the business required. "To me, something big-time was going on," he says. "We definitely qualified, we should have had the opportunity."

Entrepreneurs' experiences with commercial banks emphasize the considerable difficulty African Americans have in gaining access to capital in the commercial market. In contrast, consider the beliefs and experiences of William Shearer, KGFJ Radio, who was successful in obtaining a loan for $4.5 million to purchase a radio station. Shearer started with seller financing under junior debt and senior debt with a major lender, based on his ability to convince them that he could repay the debt. Persuasion is especially important, because a radio station's only hard assets may be $400,000 worth of equipment. The rest is "good will," which is hard to borrow against.

Shearer found it necessary to have an extremely positive track record and to be respected by his peers. His accomplishments were well known. He had been promoted from private to colonel in the army reserve and had worked his way up to become the first black chairman of the board of the Southern California Broadcasters. He was active at the national level in the National Association of Broadcasters, served on numerous committees, and spoke annually at the convention. He teaches broadcasting courses at UCLA, USC, and California State–Long Beach. Shearer has been general manager for fourteen years and counts the mayor as one of his friends. In addition to having an M.B.A., he is well versed in finance: "I had what they were looking for. I had the right exposure. It would have been hard for them to say no."

### ALTERNATIVE BUSINESS FINANCING: BCF, BIDCO, SBA

Alternative sources for financing for small and ethnic minority-owned businesses have developed to fill the capital gap created by the traditional banking establishment. To be successful, alternative sources must be attuned to the issues that small and minority-owned businesses must address in order to survive. The Greater Detroit Business and Industrial Corporation and the Business Consortium Fund of New York City are two sources of alternative financing.

The Detroit BIDCO, which operates only in Michigan, is similar to an SBA Specialized Small Business Investment Company (SSBIC).

BIDCO started in January 1990 and provides financing for start-up, operation and expansion activities. By December 1993, BIDCO had offered sixteen investment loans totaling $4,277,000 to minority businesses.

The BCF, founded in 1989, takes a different approach to meeting the capital needs of minority entrepreneurs. BCF provides only contract financing when a minority business has won a contract to provide goods and/or services to a Fortune 500 corporation or other eligible government unit. By June 30, 1994, BCF had made a total of $40,176,736 in contract financing loans to minority businesses, which in turn created 3,488 full-time jobs. Employment generated as a result of BCF financing further encourages the economic development of ethnic minority communities in America.

The data I collected clearly indicate that entrepreneurs have had overwhelmingly positive experiences in obtaining BCF funding. When asked if they found the BCF representative helpful, 100 percent of entrepreneurs surveyed (n = 33) said yes. Of those who were asked if they found the BCF experience as a whole helpful (n = 18), 67 percent said the experience was excellent, 22 percent said it was good, and 11 percent said it was fair. When asked if they found the BCF application process fair or unfair (n = 35), 97 percent said it was fair. Ninety percent of those surveyed (n = 18) said they have told others about the BCF.

After a number of unsuccessful attempts to locate approved lenders willing to participate in BCF, Betty Daly of MayDay Chemical responded with "We're going to establish one." With the assistance of Daly's attorney and his contacts, the lending program came to the Bank of Kalamazoo. She received a $250,000 loan at 12 percent for two years secured by MayDay's assets and receivables.

Based on her positive experience with BCF, she encourages other entrepreneurs searching for capital to consider the fund. Daly credits BCF with reducing the cost of a portion of her borrowing and considers it "not painful at all," because her bank administers the loan— a one-stop-shopping approach. The loan also brought new cash to her bank, which was then a start-up. She views her BCF activities as "a win-win transaction" but believes the amount of money available through BCF is insufficient: "We could use funding much greater than what BCF is willing to lend because we are at an age and size where our needs are just greater."

As the experience of Daly illustrate, BIDCO and BCF provide innovative approaches to financing small and minority businesses that the traditional banking community is unable or unwilling to consider. Banks appear to either ignore or disregard the business goals of African American entrepreneurs. Faith Ando's (1988) empirical research documents that banks tend not to lend to qualified African Americans. BIDCO and BCF provide much-needed financing to minority businesses, which in turn creates jobs in minority communities across the country.

Another alternative source of financing small and minority businesses is the U.S. Department of Commerce's Small Business Administration. Experience with SBA is mixed. Some respondents in this study report having a positive experience, and some respondents had negative experiences. David Lloyd, Bay City Marina, felt fortunate about his experience in applying for an SBA loan to buy equipment. The first time Lloyd applied for an SBA loan he was refused: "They told me that I needed more management experience and to fix my business plan." Lloyd's initial reaction to the refusal was "these people are doing this just because I'm black." He made the changes they requested, reapplied for the loan, and "they handed me the money. SBA is on the up-and-up; I wasn't prepared for that." His experience with the SBA taught Lloyd a valuable lesson about one's "track record" and about banking in general. When a bank asks an entrepreneur about his track record, he notes, "it's in your best interest. They want you to succeed so you can repay the loan and hopefully borrow again."

Although Albert DeMagnus has no SBA loans, his company is qualified as 8(a). He feels that SBA's reputation as not being helpful is unwarranted; they are understaffed. In addition, 8(a) companies are plagued with a tremendously negative image that needs refurbishing. DeMagnus considers it "unfortunate" that he has received business as a result of government set-aside programs. He wants to be considered a business like any other: "We provide quality service to our clients each and every time."

As an example of the problem and the need for consideration, DeMagnus tells of a situation in which his company was very competitive but was not awarded the bid: "They told us that we did not lose the bid. We were just weren't selected. We won, but they gave it to someone else. They told us that nothing was wrong with our cost, our technical qualifications, or our presentation. That's just the way this game is played in the real world. Think about it. It shows that these programs are necessary."

Hamilton Bowser, Evanbow Construction, was an SBA 8(a) contractor in the early days of the program. The company's work mostly involved redoing and repairing work completed by another minority firm: "We fixed it up, patched it up, and tried to keep the program looking good." Bowser encouraged the SBA to offer "better work" rather than "small, dirty jobs." The program was reasonably successful in the early years, according to his assessment, because "there were firms like ours that had experience, capabilities, and technical knowledge. Some people were upset that they couldn't prove SBA wasn't doing a good job." One of the problems SBA faces, Bowser says, is their lack of enough top-notch people to replace those looking to secure a pension. Some are caught between wanting to advance in government and not wanting to alienate the wrong people.

In the past, Bowser has used SBA's direct-loan program, loan guarantees, and the Treasury collateral program. But now the funding pool has substantially decreased and Bowser uses other SBA programs, especially the 7(j) program for surplus equipment, because Evanbow Construction is an equipment-intensive business. Another feature of the SBA 7(j) program that Bowser found beneficial was technical assistance. Consultants knowledgeable about his business area visited regularly, offered advice and suggestions, wrote reports, and made follow-up visits. He was pleased by this and other services provided by SBA.

One-half of the entrepreneurs in this study had negative experiences or perceptions of SBA's program to assist minority entrepreneurs. A frequent comment targeted SBA's restrictions and requirements of "tons of paperwork." Many entrepreneurs simply opted not to participate in the program.

Shearer, KGFJ, considers the SBA as the "court of last resort," the place to go when no other options exist. In Shearer's estimation, the SBA is too demanding. SBA takes equity, warrants, stock, "whatever they can take, then fly in at your expense to look over your books and 'beat you up.' With minorities, in particular, SBA ties up your aunt's property and your grandmother's property. You have to really want the money to go the SBA." In contrast, the bank's only concern is that loan payments are paid promptly.

Ellen Sanders of Sumanco Office Equipment did not seek SBA assistance. With her business located in an incubator, she was able to communicate with a number of other entrepreneurs who could share experiences and insight. She found from their experience that working with SBA "takes a long time and is restrictive." She perceives SBA methods of operation to differ from hers. Neither would Anthony Snoddy, Exemplar Manufacturing, consider an SBA loan. He characterized the process as bureaucratic and a hassle. Bill Mays of Mays Chemical shares that opinion: "I filled out tons of paper and got to the point where the requirements to qualify for SBA 8(a) participation were so onerous that it wasn't worth it."

Many emerging entrepreneurs are strongly opposed to government involvement, of any kind, in their business. This sentiment is frequently based on a fellow entrepreneur's negative experience with the SBA, the SBA's restrictive guidelines, or the onerous paperwork usually associated with government involvement. Such entrepreneurs compete and succeed in the open market solely on the quality of their products and services.

On the other hand, entrepreneurs recognize quite clearly that the "playing field" is not level and that racial discrimination can effectively exclude them from access to capital, markets, and business services. In an attempt to neutralize the persistent inequality, many entrepreneurs use the programs and services offered by SBA—technical support, loans, and procurement. Their experiences with SBA range from very negative to very positive. For many, SBA made the difference between business success and failure.

Some entrepreneurs felt that the effectiveness of SBA was hampered by some large-scale political forces that may have tried to subvert the program's goal. The African American entrepreneurs profiled here hold various beliefs about government involvement in their business and have had a broad range of experiences with SBA.

## Community Linkages and Involvement

To what extent do entrepreneurs contribute to the development of African American communities? To what extent are entrepreneurs linkages for the perpetuation of business activities within their respective communities? Are their businesses located in a predominantly black community? Do they hire African American employees? Do entrepreneurs purchase goods and services from African American suppliers? Who are their customers? Do entrepreneurs support community organizations? Are entrepreneurs preparing for business succession to perpetuate their business traditions? These issues frame the discussion of community linkages and involvement.

### LOCATION, CUSTOMERS, AND EMPLOYEES

Half of the entrepreneurs interviewed located their present business facility outside the African American community. This should not be considered as evidence that the entrepreneurs are abandoning their communities. Businesses operating on a national level often select locations closest to transportation or closest to a central business district. Those who located their business within their communities expressed the need to support the community even though revenue was derived elsewhere.

Only two businesses, MVP Products and KGFJ, provide products or services to a predominantly African American customer base. The overwhelming majority of these businesses count Fortune 500 corporations or the government as their primary customers. A major distinction between African Americans doing business during the pre– versus the post–Civil Rights era is that top entrepreneurs in the latter era provide goods and services to a national market of Fortune 500 corporations and government agencies.

Regardless of business location or customer base, African American–owned businesses exhibit their community commitment by hiring talented African American employees. The number of employees vary from as few as three to as many as two hundred. But in almost all, the work force is predominantly African American, with a substantial representation from European and other ethnic groups. In most cases, the work force reflects the diversity of the country but with an African American majority.

The comments of Anthony Snoddy, Exemplar, reflect the employment policies of most of the entrepreneurs. His 105 employees are multicultural, a veritable rainbow of people—Filipinos, Indians, Hispanics, blacks, and whites. "When I got here," he said, "this company was primarily white. We changed the complexion of the company." Not all entrepreneurs share his drive for diversity: "Many minorities, brothers in business, are presidents and owners of companies. They're the only ones who are black. That's pathetic, an embarrassment, and they ought to be ashamed of themselves." Snoddy feels a responsibility to hire the people who live in the community, and "if black people live in the community, I want to be making sure they get jobs. The spirit of it is to help your own community and your own people."

## COMMUNITY ORGANIZATIONS

Entrepreneurs are active citizens of their community and contribute substantially to its social, political, and economic development. Community involvement falls into two categories: participation in organizations that focus explicitly on the African American community and organizations that focus on the wider community.

Only G O Furniture and Bay City Marina reported having "not too much" involvement in community organizations. The overwhelming majority of the entrepreneurs reported considerable involvement both in organizations that focus on African American interests and the interests of the wider community. Entrepreneurs participate in and sit on boards of the chamber of commerce, the Convention Center, YMCA, YWCA, Boys Club, Girls Club, Institute of the Arts, United Way, Junior Achievement, American Heart Association, state music commissions, child protection services, Children's Legal Defense Fund, children's hospitals, Commission on Human Concerns, and school boards.

Of the organizations that focus on the African American community, entrepreneurs are most frequently involved in and support the NAACP, the Urban League, and the United Negro College Fund. Entrepreneurs are also involved in speaking publicly on entrepreneurship and youth development, and in sponsoring activities such as a youth entrepreneurial academy, sickle cell research, Little League baseball, tennis leagues, internship programs for college students, scholarship programs, high school science and math programs, church activities, black expos, Ebony Talent Associates, and Mama Said (a parent mentoring organization for young mothers). Entrepreneurs also participate in the National Association of Negro Women, brotherhoods and sisterhoods, Kappa Alpha Psi Fraternity, and Delta Sigma Theta Sorority.

In addition to participation, entrepreneurs financially support organizations. Although no entrepreneur reported an organized system or schedule of contributing, each supported special interests and other organizations that asked for support. First-generation entrepreneurs in business a short time tended to give less than long-established, second-generation entrepreneurs. Annual contributions ranged from a few hundred dollars to fifty thousand dollars.

When Ella Williams, AGEIR, was asked the number of organizations to which she made financial contributions, she replied, "How many? I don't know. Is my name on the damn master list somewhere? A lot." For the four years prior to the interview, Williams gave about four to five thousand dollars to the Children's Legal Defense Fund and about three thousand dollars to the Boys Club and Girls Club in her area. She also paid one year's tuition at the University of Southern California for her daughter's girlfriend, who otherwise could not have remained in college. Her attitude is, "I try to give back whenever and wherever I can. In fact, I'm thinking about opening up the Gertrude Anderson Foundation, in my mother's name. Rather than giving my money to the government, I'll put it into the foundation and then have more to give out."

Through their involvement and support of projects focusing on both the African American and the wider community, emerging entrepreneurs are conscientious citizens with significant links to their communities. Their participation and financial support make the much-needed projects listed above available for the benefit of all.

## SUCCESSION

Clearly an enduring tradition of entrepreneurship flourishes and wealth accumulates when a successful business is passed from one generation to the next. In traditional wisdom, the progeny of the entrepreneur grows up in and learns the business, gets a relevant education, and takes over when the parent retires. Traditional wisdom does not seem to hold with emerging entrepreneurs. About half of the entrepreneurs are either planning for or grooming a successor to the business when they retire. The plan is quite likely long range and neither specific nor documented; and not every entrepreneur plans that their progeny will either take over their business or start their own. Indeed, entrepreneurs tend to allow their progeny to chart their own career choices while providing support and encouragement.

First-generation entrepreneurs in business for less than ten years are primarily concerned with expanding their business and simply have not had the time to plan for succession. Some are neither planning succession nor retirement. Albert DeMagnus, Computer Management, age fifty-one, discusses a vision in which he expects to build factories in the inner city that will employ both the educated and uneducated African Americans: "I lack the confidence that the majority groups cares enough to do it." He is unwilling to consider retirement until his vision becomes a reality. Business succession is the least-developed aspect of planning for emerging black entrepreneurs.

## Summary and Conclusions

The study of ethnic entrepreneurship is moved toward an indigenous frame of reference as a result of the profiles of African American entrepreneurs in this book. Specifically identified are: (1) factors that entrepreneurs consider in choosing to start a business rather than to remain in traditional employment; (2) the specific steps entrepreneurs take to initiate their business; (3) entrepreneurs' experiences in gaining access to capital for start-up, operations, and expansion; (4) entrepreneurs' experiences with business development agencies, such as the Detroit BIDCO, the Business Consortium Fund, and the Small Business Administration; and (5) the extent of entrepreneurs' community linkages with respect to philanthropic activities, hiring coethnic employees and suppliers, organizational involvement, and succession planning. Because accurate assessments of black businesses have been unavailable in the past, the experiences of these entrepreneurs in emerging business fields can serve as a guide for future entrepreneurs.

### LONGEVITY HYPOTHESIS

The longevity hypothesis argues that first-generation businesses in operation for less than ten years would benefit from Civil Rights era legislation. Furthermore, it claims that it would be easier for them to gain access to capital, to initiate, and to sustain a business than for owners of second-generation businesses in operation for more than ten years.

The case histories do not support a longevity hypothesis. First-generation businesses appear to have the same difficulty in starting and sustaining a business—including lack of access to capital—as did their second-generation counterparts. Business development agencies such as the SBA, BIDCO, and BCF have become more common and institutionalized within the last ten years. However, the level of difficulty in initiating and sustaining a business in an emerging field remains substantially unchanged and still requires considerable planning and resource accumulation, as was true for businesses longer in operation.

### REGION HYPOTHESIS

In a similar vein, the region hypothesis ask the question, Would entrepreneurs in one region have a less difficult experience starting and sustaining a business than entrepreneurs in another region? There was no support for this contention. In each region entrepreneurs report negative experiences in trying to gain access to capital, markets, and products. Race remains a critical and inhibiting factor for African Americans trying to initiate and sustain a business in all geographic regions of this country.

### GENDER HYPOTHESIS

The gender hypothesis contends that gender bias makes it more difficult for African American women to gain access to capital and to initiate and sustain a business than for African American men. Most of the women entrepreneurs handled issues of gender and race by turning a negative into a positive.

Ellen Ann Sanders, SUMANCO, sees gender and race as "red flags" to her suppliers/wholesalers of office equipment: "If the newcomer is a black person, people see color before they see anything else." However, Sanders will not be deterred: "I think we can turn it into a positive, since so few of us are really out there, and we're becoming fewer in number."

For Ella Williams, AGEIR, sexual politics is just one of many delicate issue that must be "handled" in the business marketplace. When a client that provides Williams's company $3 million in business addressed a sexual remark to her, she waited to tell him it was offensive instead of responding in anger. "I want the work," she said, "so I have to handle this professionally. Had I responded right away, I would have said too much. I would have lost the work, too. This way, he'll never do it again. You have to deal with it because you have to work."

The evidence suggests that gender does, indeed, make a difference. To deal with gender-based barriers is an additional burden for black women doing business. To their credit, black women entrepreneurs consider this a moot issue and see any bias, regardless of the source, as just another impediment to navigate before conducting business. African American women entrepreneurs are adroit at turning negative situations into positive outcomes for their business. Moreover, the evidence suggests that they do so with integrity and professionalism.

### THE FUTURE OF BLACK ENTREPRENEURSHIP

The outlook for African Americans in entrepreneurship as a means of accumulating wealth remains turbulent. Artificial barriers preventing to access to capital, markets, and products, and being viewed as a viable business person cut across business longevity, region, and gender. Women have the additional burden of dealing with gender and race issues. Nevertheless, blacks are starting businesses at a greater rate than Americans in general. And black entrepreneurs are starting businesses in fields that are more capital- and skill-intensive, fields that are expected to grow in the next twenty-five years.

### INTERNAL BARRIERS

In order to circumvent the economic detour, African Americans must overcome two types of barriers—internal and external. The internal barriers are being sure that you want to be an entrepreneur, having the confidence to know that you can do it, and the willingness to commit to entrepreneurship.

Americans love to be Number One, the best. However, we frequently fail to understand the level of sacrifice necessary in order to accomplish a goal, especially in business. The sacrifices are formidable. One entrepreneur put it this way:

> First, you have to get through the barrier in your own mind. This is not a corporate job. There is no paycheck on the 1st and 15th. You must be willing to make the sacrifice; shed the blood, sweat and tears; take the bitter with the sweet; persist even when you have no money and you think nothing is going to work. But if you can hold on to the vision of what you want, the people you need, the resources you need, the money you need will come to you. You have to live it. You have to say this is what I want, and I'm willing to go against the odds to do it. (Kenneth Carter, Focus Communications Group, Dallas, Texas)

Similarly, Bettye Daly of MayDay Chemicals put it this way:

> This is not a job, it's a way of life. You have to live the life before you give birth to the business. It's called preparation. You have to understand that you are going to suffer a lot of agony, a lot of poverty. Owning a business does not mean that you wear designer suits, carry leather briefcases, and strut around like Mr. or Ms. Wonderful. It means a hell of a lot of hard-ass work with no rewards. Nobody to give you an "at-a-boy." It's total isolation. It's not having a social life. It's almost like being buried alive, except that you like yourself so much that you really don't care. You and your business are your immediate family and all you need for a length of time. If you don't want to give up everything for an opportunity to develop something, just go out and get a job.

In addition, entrepreneurs frequently suffer from fears and self-doubt concerning their chances of success. Most develop confidence by being thoroughly prepared for business and by emulating other successful businesses. Hamilton Bowser Sr. of Evanbow Construction emphasized the importance of preparation—getting administrative and business background within a company or getting technical training in school: "I think our greatest weakness as black folks is not having sufficient business experience and business training." African Americans themselves must take full responsibility for eliminating internal barriers to entrepreneurship.

### EXTERNAL BARRIERS

Entrepreneurs more frequently mentioned the external barriers to business development. As expected, the most common external barrier was *lack of access to capital or unfair treatment by banks,* followed by the *perception that blacks are not bona fide business persons and lack of access to markets.* These issues are obviously intertwined and appear to be manifestation of the limited economic rights accorded to African Americans.

Charles McCampbell, Heritage Paper, said the greatest barrier was the availability of finance and capital. He described, as a powerful second barrier, getting an opportunity to compete in a particular field on an equal footing: "To my knowledge, only three or four minority companies today distribute paper on a direct-mill basis. In the past twelve years, only two major mills were willing to sell directly to us. It's a closed game. By not giving minorities an opportunity to buy on a direct basis, they can't compete with the established dealers who've been out there for a hundred years."

Anthony Snoddy, Exemplar, sees racism as a major external barrier that impedes an entrepreneur's ability to acquire financing: "If you're determined enough, I believe you can still get it no matter what. Now, if I was a white boy, I wouldn't have the same problems getting my hands on money." In his estimation, racism is "institutionalized, it's everywhere." He explains that many black business owners protect the viability of their businesses by not publicizing their ownership.

Snoddy, however, without ignoring his ethnicity, touts the quality of his products: "We sell quality, cost-competitive products, and we deliver them on time. And, by the way, we are minority." To be a successful black business, "you have to be better than they are. Exemplar aspires to be a model company. I didn't say minority, but a model company."

## Mo' Better Business Policy

### OVERCOMING INTERNAL BARRIERS: SELF-HELP

In order to sustain economic development, African Americans must persist in forming and growing incorporated businesses in capital- and skill-intensive fields. Despite increasing numbers of role models in these emerging fields, internal barriers still hamper business development. Specific and deliberate actions must address and begin to diffuse these barriers.

First, African Americans must reorient their culture so that the "successful entrepreneur" becomes as honored a career path as having the "good job" was in the past. To do this, African American parents must explicitly include entrepreneurship in the mix of career options presented to their children. Fortunately, entrepreneurship is now part of the curriculum of some high schools, offered as an extracurricular activity and available through community-sponsored entrepreneurship academies.

Business development agencies and business incubators are also available to assist those who express an interest in business ownership. Individuals must locate these opportunities and take advantage of them. If such programs are unavailable, parents and business owners should either insist that they be created or identify opportunities in another community.

In the post–Civil Rights era, African Americans now have economic options that extend beyond the good job to business opportunities in the marketplace. However, thorough preparation and planning are absolutely essential to increase the likelihood of success in a highly competitive business environment. The foundation for business preparedness is a B.A. or B.S. degree in a relevant field, followed by graduate-level course work in business or entrepreneurial studies courses leading to an M.B.A. or advanced entrepreneurial studies degree. Formal education provides the entrepreneur with a firm conceptual and theoretical foundation on which to build a successful business. However, a continuing education program affords the opportunity to stay abreast of technical innovations and to learn the latest management and business operation practices.

In addition to educational preparation, work experience is a necessary condition for business success. Indeed, entrepreneurs require five to fifteen years of work experience to learn the technical aspects of the chosen business. The time in service provides the entrepreneur with a depth of knowledge and technical expertise not attainable in any other way. Relevant educational and work experiences give entrepreneurial hopefuls the confidence and the knowledge that ensures the success of a new business.

Finally, save, save, save! The evidence clearly illustrates the obstacles in obtaining commercial bank loans for start-up businesses.

Therefore, African Americans must either save the capital required or rely on personal sources for loans.

African Americans can minimize and overcome internal barriers through relevant education, experience in the field, and by saving substantial capital for business start-up. By successfully negotiating the internal barriers to business development, entrepreneurs will have developed armor to better deal with the external barriers to business development.

## OVERCOMING EXTERNAL BARRIERS: EQUAL BUSINESS OPPORTUNITY POLICY

Even after properly preparing oneself to start and expand a new business, African Americans must still overcome a set of external barriers associated with race: unfair treatment by banks that blocks access to capital for qualified borrowers, a stereotypical perception that blacks are not bona fide business persons, and a lack of access to markets and products.

A renewed commitment to an Equal Business Opportunity policy is required to overcome persistent external barriers. For instance, the commercial banking community should adopt at least two strategies to increase access to capital for qualified African American entrepreneurs. First, regulatory agencies must invoke full legal sanctions against banks that violate equal opportunity lending statutes by using practices that summarily deny African Americans, or any other group, a fair evaluation of loan worthiness. The Community Reinvestment Act (CRA), as presently construed and implemented, cannot serve as an effective deterrent to ill-meaning bankers. The CRA simply does not provide adequate sanctions for unfair lending practices.

Second, the banking community must initiate an industrywide "Diversity Lending Intervention" conducted by external consultants trained in diversity and entrepreneurship. Such an intervention will provide an opportunity to examine bank policy and practice as well as the attitudes of loan officers with respect to evaluating the commercial loan applications of African Americans. It is necessary to continue to expose and reorient the commercial banking tradition of redlining in order to ensure access to capital. An industrywide Diversity Lending Intervention will reorient the banking community to view African Americans as bona fide business persons who have the economic right to an unbiased evaluation of their loan worthiness. Such an industrywide diversity intervention would neutralize the horrific "capital" experiences of qualified entrepreneurs and ensure that they will not be repeated in the next generation of African American entrepreneurs.

## ACCESS TO MARKETS AND PRODUCTS

Being in business is a challenge, a kind of "war" experience. Successful businesses compete for the largest share of the market and attempt to eliminate competition by any means possible. Marketplace competition is fierce without regard to racial issues, and competition is equally fierce among African Americans in the same industry. However, historically, race has been the criteria to almost totally exclude African American competitors from the "open market."

The experience of African American entrepreneurs in the post–Civil Rights era clearly indicates that race persists as a barrier to markets and products. Set-asides in contracting were developed to provide African Americans and other minority groups access to a limited portion of lucrative markets that were historically closed to them. By use of set-asides, less than 10 percent of government contracts go to minority firms. But set-asides to disadvantaged groups have been under constant challenge in the courts. Now the Supreme Court, in the Croson and Adarand decisions, has invoked the concept of strict scrutiny in awarding contracts, which severely curtails minority access to these markets. For example, after Adarand, and in the face of significant threats from Republicans to use the racially charged issue of affirmative action against Democrats in the 1996 presidential campaign, President Clinton began a review of all 150 to 200 federal affirmative action programs. The review concluded that set-aside programs are indeed needed to redress past discrimination, but they must comply with the Supreme Court ruling that affirmative action programs must be narrowly defined and address specific grievances.

As a result of this review, the Department of Defense, the biggest government contractor and an agency important to minority businesses, eliminated its "rule of two" policy used since 1987 to award contracts. In 1994, $1 billion in federal business was awarded to minority firms. Under the "rule of two," if at least two qualified small, disadvantaged businesses express interest in bidding for a contract, only disadvantage businesses can compete for it. The Adarand decision effectively challenges the constitutionality of the "rule of two" and the Department of Defense, Department of Labor, and NASA no longer use the rule.

At the close of the twentieth century, African Americans are experiencing another institutionalized retraction of economic rights, as they did at the beginning of the century. The end product of Croson and Adarand, and the ensuing retreat from protected economic rights for African Americans, is that white American male entrepreneurs will have a near monopoly on government and corporate markets while talented black entrepreneurs will be excluded because of their race.

Derrick Bell's (1992) words appear to be prophetic: "Black people will never gain full equality in this country. Even those herculean efforts we hail as successful will produce no more than temporary 'peaks of progress,' short-lived victories that slide into irrelevance as racial patterns adapt in ways that maintain white dominance." In other words, the economic detour appears to have mutated into a post–Civil Rights form in attempt to deny African Americans even limited access to markets.

Like Bell, I am not optimistic that sustained and herculean efforts will achieve more than short-lived successes for individual black entrepreneurs in the era of the Angry White Male. Thus the life of a black American entrepreneur in an emerging business is not for those with limited determination or for the faint of heart.

Competition in the free-enterprise system ensures that consumers get the best quality of goods and services at the best price. Excluding entire groups from the marketplace based on race or any artificial criteria is detrimental to our society. Through the Civil Rights movement, African Americans demanded inclusion and a national policy that created the Small Business Administration and its programs.

The SBA's guaranteed-loan program has increased access to capital for many entrepreneurs of color. The SBA 8(a) program tremendously increased access to the largest American market, the government. Despite their burdensome paperwork and other faults, the SBA programs substantially contributed to the formation and stabilization of black-owned businesses in America. They provided opportunities for black businesses to gain access to capital, to grow in a protected government market, and then to move into the open market after nine years.

Without the continued support of the SBA programs, many small African American businesses will succumb to the strong undertow of racial currents prevalent in the business war. To continue its supportive role, the SBA programs should be enhanced by streamlining the required paperwork, adding adequately trained staff to address the needs of entrepreneurs, and strengthening and broadening the 8(a) and 7(j) programs. In American society, where race continues to be a salient basis for including or excluding entire groups from economic opportunity, a strong and firmly enforced national policy is imperative if we are to achieve the ideal of equality of opportunity.

## INNOVATION IN ACCESS TO MARKETS AND CAPITAL

In addition to a commitment to an Equal Business Opportunity policy, innovative strategies to improve minority access to private-sector markets and capital are required. While under constant challenge, private corporations still sponsor barrier-abatement programs because it makes good business sense. The BCF represents an innovative collaboration between private sector corporations and a major philanthropic entity, the Ford Foundation, to provide minority access to capital and markets.

The BCF, and similarly the Greater Detroit Business and Industrial Corporation, are a beginning. Until the economic detour is eliminated and African Americans experience full economic rights in this society, additional creative solutions will be needed. Similar to the Ford Foundation initiative, some other entity must now step up to help fill the gap in access to capital and markets that persists for qualified African American entrepreneurs.

The evidence clearly suggests that the entrepreneurial spirit burns fervently among African Americans. Persistent artificial barriers cannot extinguish these entrepreneurial flames. Indeed, while also supporting their community, African Americans increasingly rise to choose business as a career path to success and wealth.

# BIBLIOGRAPHY

Angelou, Maya. 1986. "And Still I Rise." In *Maya Angelou: Poems.* New York: Bantam Books.

Ando, Faith H. 1988. "Capital Issues and the Minority-Owned Business." *Review of the Black Political Economy* (Spring): 77–110.

Bates, Timothy. 1993. *Banking on Black Enterprise.* Washington, D.C.: Joint Center for Political and Economic Studies.

———. 1985a. "Entrepreneur Human Capital Endowment and Minority Business Viability." *Journal of Human Resources* 20 (4): 541–554.

———. 1985b. "An Analysis of Minority Entrepreneurship: Utilizing the Census of Population Public Use Samples." Minority Business Development Agency Report. Washington, D.C.

———. 1981. "Black Entrepreneurship and Government Programs." *Journal of Contemporary Studies* 4 (Fall): 59–70.

———. 1973a. *Black Capitalism: A Quantitative Analysis.* New York: Praeger.

———. 1973b. "An Econometric Analysis of Lending to Black Businessmen." *Review of Economics and Statistics* 55 (August): 272–283.

Bell, Derrick. 1992. *Faces at the Bottom of the Well.* New York: Basic Books.

Bonacich, Edna. 1972. "Theory of Middleman Minority." *American Sociological Review* 3, no. 1 (Fall): 22–45.

Bonacich, Edna, and John Modell. 1980. *The Economic Basis of Ethnic Solidarity: Small Business in the Japanese American Community.* Berkeley and Los Angeles: University of California Press.

Bowser, Georgia W. 1981. "Who Seeks Minority Assistance? A Study of Minority Entrepreneurs." *Journal of Small Business Management* 19 (October): 24–28.

Brimmer, Andrew. 1966. "The Negro in the National Economy." In *American Negro Reference Book,* edited by John David. Englewood Cliffs, N.J.: Prentice-Hall.

———. 1968. "Desegregation and Negro Leadership." In *Business Leadership and the Negro Crisis,* edited by Eli Ginsberg. New York: McGraw-Hill.

———. 1971. "Small Business and Economic Development in the Negro Community." In *Black Americans and White Business,* edited by Edwin Epstein and David Hampton. Encino, Calif.: Dickinson Publishing.

Butler, John Sibley. 1991. *Entrepreneurship and Self-Help among Black Americans.* New York: State University of New York Press.

Butler, John Sibley, and Kenneth Wilson. 1988. "Entrepreneurial Enclaves: An Exposition into the Afro-American Experience." *National Journal of Sociology* 2, no. 2 (Fall): 127–166.

Chase, James. 1993. "Awareness and Attitudes of Minority Youth and Young Adults Toward Business Ownership." Contract No. 50-SABE-200084. Washington, D.C.: Minority Business Development Agency, U.S. Department of Commerce.

Douglass, Merril E. 1976. "Relating Education to Entrepreneurial Success." *Business Horizons* 19:40–44.

Du Bois, W.E.B. [1899] 1967. *The Philadelphia Negro: A Social Study.* New York: Schocken Books.

Durand, Douglas E. 1975. "Effects of Achievement Motivation and Skill Training on the Entrepreneurial Behavior of Black Businessmen." *Organizational Behavior and Human Performance* 14:76–90.

Foley, Eugene P. 1966. "The Negro Businessman: In Search of a Tradition." *Daedalus* 95 (Winter): 107–144.

Fratoe, Frank. 1986. "A Sociological Analysis of Minority Business." *Review of the Black Political Economy* 15, no. 2 (Fall): 5–15.

———. 1988. "Social Capital of Black Business Owners." *Review of the Black Political Economy* (Spring): 33–49.

Fusfield, Daniel, and Timothy Bates. 1984. *The Political Economy of the Urban Ghetto.* Carbondale: Southern Illinois University Press.

Gomokla, Eugene. 1977. "Characteristics of Minority Entrepreneurs and Small Business Enterprises." *American Journal of Small Business* 2:2–21.

Green, Shelley, and Paul Pryde. 1989. *Black Entrepreneurship in America.* New Brunswick, N.J.: Transaction Publishers.

Jacobs, Jane. 1969. *The Economy of Cities.* New York: Vintage Books.

Light, Ivan. 1972. *Ethnic Enterprise in America.* Berkeley and Los Angeles: University of California Press.

———. 1980. "Asian Enterprise in America." In *Self-Help in America: Patterns of Economic Development,* edited by Scott Cummings. Port Washington, N.Y.: Kennikat Press.

Light, Ivan, and Edna Bonacich. 1988. *Immigrant Entrepreneurs: Koreans in Los Angeles.* Berkeley and Los Angeles: University of California Press.

Marble, Manning. 1983. *How Capitalism Underdeveloped Black America.* Boston: South End Press.

McCelland, David C. 1961. *The Achieving Society.* Princeton, N.J.: D. Van Norstrand Press.

Oliver, Melvin, and Thomas Shapiro. 1995. *Black Wealth/White Wealth: A New Perspective on Racial Inequality.* New York: Routledge Press.

Osborne, Alfred E., Jr. 1975. *Emerging Issues in Black Economic Development,* edited by Benjamin F. Bobo and Alfred E. Osborne, Jr. Lexington, Mass.: Lexington Books.

Pierce, Joseph. 1947. *Negro Business and Negro Education.* New York: Harper and Brothers.

Portes, Alejandro, and Robert L. Bach. 1985. *Latin Journey*. Berkeley and Los Angeles: University of California Press.

Sexton, Donald, and Nancy Bowman. 1984. "Entrepreneurship Education: Suggestions for Increasing Effectiveness." *Journal of Small Business Management* 22 (April): 18–25.

Shapero, Albert, and Lisa Sokol. 1982. "The Social Dimensions of Entrepreneurship." In *Encyclopedia of Entrepreneurship,* edited by Calvin A. Kent, Donald L. Sexton, and Karl H. Vesper, 72–90. Englewood Cliffs, N.J.: Prentice-Hall.

Sowell, Thomas. 1975. *Race and Economics.* New York: Longman.

Stuart, M. S. 1940. *An Economic Detour: A History of Insurance in the Lives of American Negroes.* New York: Wendell Malliett.

U.S. Bureau of the Census. 1974. *1972 Survey of Minority-Owned Business Enterprises.* MB72-1. Washington, D.C.: GPO.

———. 1979. *1977 Survey of Minority-Owned Business Enterprises.* MB77-1. Washington, D.C.: GPO.

———. 1984. *1982 Survey of Minority-Owned Business Enterprises.* MB82-1. Washington, D.C.: GPO.

———. 1990. *1987 Survey of Minority-Owned Business Enterprises.* MB87-1. Washington, D.C.: GPO.

———. 1991. *1987 Characteristics of Business Owners.* CB87-1. Washington, D.C.: GPO.

———. 1995. *1992 Survey of Minority-Owned Business Enterprises.* Advance Report. Washington, D.C.: GPO.

Walker, Julia E. K. 1983. *Free Frank: A Black Pioneer on the Antebellum Frontier.* Lexington: University of Kentucky Press.

*Wall Street Journal.* 1992. "Black Entrepreneurship." April 3, sec. R, 1–20.

Wilson, Kenneth, and Alejandro Portes. 1980. "Market Experience of Cubans in Miami." *American Journal of Sociology* 86:295–312.

Wilson, Kenneth, Alejandro Portes, and A. Martin. 1982. "Ethnic Enclave: A Comparison of Cuban and Black Economies in Miami." *American Journal of Sociology* 88:135–159.

Wilson, William J. 1973. *Power, Racism, and Privilege.* New York: Free Press.

———. 1980. *The Declining Significance of Race.* Chicago: University of Chicago Press.

———. 1987. *The Truly Disadvantaged: The Inner City, the Underclass, and Public Policy.* Chicago: University of Chicago Press.

Woodard, Michael D. 1982. "Ideological Response to Alterations in the Structure of Oppression: Reverse Discrimination, the Current Racial Ideology in the United States." *Western Journal of Black Studies* 6 (3): 166–175.

Yancy, Robert. 1974. *Federal Government Policy and Black Business Enterprise.* Cambridge, Mass.: Ballinger Publishing.

# INDEX

Adarand decision, 29–30, 239
affirmative action, 30, 105, 181, 216;
    effect of Civil Rights movement
    on, 30–31
African American(s): access to
    mortgage lending, 32; business
    ownership, 7; cultural constructs
    of, 37; exclusion from free
    enterprise, 7; middle class, 31,
    172; in military service, 23;
    purchasing power of, 31, 32;
    research on entrepreneurship of,
    34–38; stereotypes of, 8–9; as
    targets of marketing campaigns,
    32; in traditional businesses, 8
AGEIR Systems, 158–171, 220, 231,
    234
Alexander, Bill, 199–210, 211, 212
Allen, Richard, 10
American Broadcasting Company,
    174
Ando, Faith, 34, 101–102, 226
Angelou, Maya, 170–171, 216
Attucks, Crispus, 23

Ball, Thomas, 10
Banker's Fire Insurance Company, 19
banks, 5, 52, 64–65, 74–76, 109, 151,
    162–163, 175–176, 189–190, 200,
    203–205, 223

barber shops, 51
barriers: bonding, 59, 79, 126; to
    capital, 6; competition, 208–209;
    economic, 208–209;
    environmental, 22; ethnic, 6;
    exclusion from opportunity,
    69–70; external, 235–236;
    financial, 21, 59, 79, 154, 236;
    gender, 7; institutional, 6–7, 22,
    215; insurance, 59, 79; internal,
    234–235; isolation, 140, 141; to
    markets, 239–241; overcoming,
    236–239; racial, 6; segregation, 22
Bates, Tim, 9, 26, 27, 32, 34, 101
Bay City Marina, 184–199, 222, 226,
    230
Beard, Jimmy, 122
beauty parlors, 51
Bell, Derrick, 216, 240
benchmarking, 149
benevolent societies, 12
Bernoon, Emanuel, 10
Bettis, Byron, 108, 109
Bing, Dave, 198
Black Business Association, 207
Black Code regulations, 13
Black Technology Association, 139
*Black Wealth/White Wealth* (Oliver
    and Shapiro), 32
blocking, 65

Body, Henry, 11
bonding, 59, 79, 86, 87, 126
Bowman, Winston, 210
Bowser, Hamilton, 53, 80–98, 98, 99, 100, 227
Boyd, Henry, 14
Boyle, Robert, 15
Breedlove, Sarah, 17–18
Brimmer, Andrew, 31, 33
Broadcast Education Association, 181, 182
building associations, 13
Business and Industrial Corporation, 46, 47, 102, 151, 152, 155, 156, 224–228, 232
Business Consortium Fund, 46, 47, 55, 56, 66, 69, 75, 76, 84, 102, 109, 121, 135, 136, 137, 152, 155, 156, 224–228, 232
businesses, black, 14; access to procurement of goods and services, 27–28; accounting procedures, 56–58, 67–68, 76–77, 87–89, 112–115, 137, 152, 179, 206; advertising, 91–92, 114, 138, 167, 180–181; capital-intensive, 9, 33; centers of, 14, 19–21; Central region, 101–156; characteristics, 39–46; chemical, 102–142; computer management, 70–80; construction, 80–98; customers, 32, 58, 68, 91, 115–116, 137–138, 166–167, 180–181, 192, 206–207, 210, 212, 229–230; decisions to start, 7, 54–55, 61–62, 72–73, 81–82, 104–106, 130–132, 146–148, 160–161; default in, 27; development of, 7, 36–37, 39–42; disadvantaged, 28; diversification in, 37; East region, 51–100; emerging, 33, 101, 157, 158, 215; employees, 40, 45, 58, 68, 78, 90, 117–118, 138, 152–153, 168–169, 179–180, 193, 207, 211, 229–230; engineering systems, 158–171;

equity positions in, 27; expectations for ownership, 217; formation, 39–42; furniture, 60–70, 199–210; gender hypothesis, 233–234; geographic concentration, 42, 42*tab;* "golden era" of, 17; growth of, 39–42, 40*tab;* Heritage Paper Company, 53–60; history of, 9–24; impact on community, 7; initiation data, 7; internal and external social factors, 36–37; inventory, 56–58, 67–68, 76–77, 87–89, 112–115, 137, 152, 179, 206; longevity, 48, 233; manufacturing, 142–154; marketing, 91, 138, 167; mom-and-pop, 9, 34, 45, 157; nontraditional, 33; owner stereotyping, 8; paper, 53–60; partnerships, 39, 40; perceptions of, 8–9; plans, 6; profit margins, 66, 67; radio broadcasting, 171–183; receipts from, 39–40, 41, 45; regions, 48, 233; revenues, annual gross, 56–58, 67–68, 76–77, 87–89, 112–115, 137, 152, 165–166, 179, 191–192, 206; service-related, 17, 21, 41; shipbuilding, 184–199; size, 48; skill-intensive, 9, 33; small, 8; and social climate, 9; sole proprietorships, 39, 40, 45, 186; starting, 6, 51–100, 106–108, 132–134, 148–150, 161–162, 174, 185–189, 221–222; subchapter S corporations, 39, 40, 45, 51, 72, 104, 130; succession, 58, 78, 96, 118, 140, 208, 231–232; suppliers, 58, 77, 90–91, 115–116, 137–138, 180–181, 192, 206–207, 210; as threat to white-owned business, 14–15; time-of-entry variable, 35; traditional, 8, 17, 20, 26, 31, 33, 51, 157; traits necessary for success, 34–35; West region, 157–212
Butler, John Sibley, 9, 14, 19, 22

capital: access to, 26–28, 52, 55–56,
    64–66, 74–76, 83–87, 101–156,
    162–165, 174–178, 189–191,
    203–205, 218, 222–224, 235–236;
    accumulation, 9–10; barriers to
    acquisition of, 6; bases, 27;
    cultural, 37; debt, 34, 47; equity,
    34, 47; expansion, 156; intensive
    business, 9, 33; investments, 27,
    47, 113; leveraged, 27; operating,
    55; personal, 6, 9–10, 20, 44*tab,*
    45, 55, 222–223; pools, 121;
    privately invested, 27; risk, 27;
    sources of, 7, 20, 44*tab,* 45; start-
    up, 20, 44, 156, 218, 222; venture,
    27; working, 8
cash flow, 27
Center for Leadership Development,
    118
Characteristics of Business Owners
    (CBO), 43–46
Chase, James, 216–217
Children's Legal Defense Fund, 170,
    230, 231
Civil Rights Act (1964), 25
Civil Rights movement, 9, 24;
    educational opportunity, 9;
    impact of, 25–38; legislation in,
    37; and middle class, 31;
    violence during, 13
Civil War, 9, 15
Clay, Jesse Paul, 71, 78
cleaning establishments, 8, 10
Clinton, Bill, 239
clothing and tailoring, 10
Commission on Human Concerns,
    167, 169
community: activities, 78–79, 92–94,
    118, 138–139, 153, 169–171;
    bifurcation of, 30–34;
    development, 9, 17, 18, 22;
    economic development of, 7;
    "giving back," 211; impact of
    black business on, 7; involvement,
    58, 68–69, 77–79, 89–96, 115–118,
    137–140, 152–154, 157–212,
    229–232; organizations, 230–231

Community Reinvestment Act
    (CRA), 238
competition, 89, 114, 138, 158, 239;
    for government contracts, 28
Computer Management Services,
    Inc., 52–53, 70–80, 99
computer services, 33
construction trades, 9, 10
consultants, 5
contracts, 33, 56, 66, 163; bidding
    for, 87; for collateral, 66;
    commitments for, 6; decrease in
    awards, 29; federal, 77; financing,
    47; government, 28, 56, 72, 87,
    111, 136, 199; negotiating, 77;
    procurement, 28; public works
    projects, 28; rule of two, 239–240;
    set-aside, 56; time limited, 193
credit lines, 65, 66, 74, 83, 109, 126,
    134, 155, 163, 177
Croson decision, 28–29, 37, 94, 239
Cuffe, Paul, 10

Daly, Bettye, 124–126, 127–142, 155,
    156, 223, 225, 226, 235
debt: capital, 34, 47; financing, 135;
    installment, 31; junior, 175, 224;
    long-term, 27, 47, 109; senior,
    175, 176, 224; short-term, 47
*Declining Significance of Race, The*
    (Wilson), 31
Delta Sigma Theta, 231
DeMagnus, Albert and Sharon, 52,
    70–80, 98, 99, 100, 221, 226, 232
DeSable, John Baptiste, 10
desegregation, 159; and traditional
    business, 31
development: business, 7, 36–37,
    39–42; community, 7, 9, 17, 18,
    22; economic, 7
discrimination: eliminating, 25; in
    housing, 32, 33; impact on
    businesses, 52; past, 29; racial, 99;
    redline, 26; remedies for, 29;
    reverse, 29, 216
Diversity Lending Intervention, 238
Dole, Elizabeth, 198

Du Bois, W.E.B., 18
due process, 30

economic detour theory, 22
Economic Opportunity Act (1967), 26
Economic Opportunity Loan
    program, 26
Edelman, Marion Wright, 170
education, 221, 237; lack of, 30–31;
    levels attained, 54, 62, 71–72,
    103–104, 106, 128–130, 131,
    143–144, 159–160, 172–173,
    221; limitations in, 101;
    parental encouragement for, 52,
    81, 159
Ella's World Class Cheesecake,
    Bread, and Muffins, 169–170, 211
entrepreneurs: advice to others,
    59–60, 70, 79–80, 96–97,
    126–127, 141–142, 166, 182–183,
    194–199, 209; age levels, 43–46,
    220; business experience, 52;
    decision to start businesses,
    54–55, 61–62, 72–73, 81–82,
    104–106, 130–132, 146–148,
    160–161, 185, 199–200, 219–220;
    early years, 53–54, 61, 70–72,
    80–81, 103–104, 128–130,
    142–146, 158–160, 172–173,
    184–185; education attained, 54,
    62, 71–72, 103–104, 106,
    128–130, 131, 143–144, 159–160,
    172–173, 221; family
    background, 53–54, 70–72,
    80–81, 103–104, 128–130,
    142–144, 158–160, 172–173,
    184–185; family exposure to
    business, 43, 44; marital status,
    43–46; need for support system,
    66; role models, 58–59, 78,
    94–96, 117, 139–140, 194, 208,
    217, 218; supervisory experience,
    44, 45
entrepreneurship: gender hypothesis,
    233–234; history of, 9–24;
    longevity thesis, 233; motivation

for, 52; push-pull factors, 52, 99;
    region hypothesis, 233;
    socialization for, 218–219;
    successful, 218–228
Entrepreneurship and Self-Help
    among Black Americans (Butler),
    9
EOA. See Economic Opportunity Act
    (1967)
EOL. See Economic Opportunity
    Loan program
Equal Business Opportunity policy,
    238
equity: capital, 47; investment, 87;
    positions, 27
Erving, Julius, 117
Evanbow Construction, 53, 80–98,
    227
Evans, Levi, 81, 83, 94
Exemplar Manufacturing, Inc.,
    142–154, 155, 220, 228, 230, 236
experience, 126, 237; lack of, 6

Federal Communications
    Commission (FCC), 176
financing: access to, 26–28, 52,
    55–56, 64–66, 74–76, 83–87,
    101–156, 162–165, 174–178,
    189–191, 203–205, 218, 222–224;
    alternative, 224–228; bank, 5,
    44tab, 52; collateral for, 33, 86,
    175; contract, 47; debt, 135;
    defaults on, 26, 27; guaranteed,
    26; long-term debt, 27; mortgage,
    32; sources, 45; start-up, 6, 44tab.
    See also capital; loans
Foley, Eugene, 21
food preparation and service, 8, 10,
    12, 15, 20, 41tab, 42, 51
Ford Foundation, 47
Forster, Janee, 14
Fortune 500 corporations, 28, 47, 72,
    109, 115, 225
Frances, Almer, 10
franchises, 127
Fratoe, Frank, 36

Free Frank, 11–12, 13
free persons, 9, 10, 11, 12, 15
funeral parlors, 8, 20, 21, 51
furniture making, 11

Gardner, Ed, 116
Garrett, James, 10
Gary, Ted, 123
Gatson, Arthur, 117
gender, 48; barriers, 7; expectations
    for ownership, 217; hypothesis,
    233–234
George, U. M. and R. S., 19
Gertrude Anderson Foundation,
    170–171, 231
glass ceiling, 99, 105, 219
Godfrey, Jolene, 171
G O Furniture, 199–210, 211, 223, 230
Goldberg, Whoopi, 171
Gord, Robert, 10
Graves, Earl, 127
"Great Compromise," 15
Great Depression, 18
Green Power Foundation, 200, 203,
    204, 211, 212
grocery stores, 10, 14, 20

hair care, 8, 14, 17–18, 20, 32
*Hall v. deCuvis,* 15–16
Harlan, Robert, 10
Hayes, Rutherford B., 15
health services, 41*tab*
Henderson, Henry, 95
Heningburg, Gus, 93
Heritage Paper Company, 52, 53–60,
    236
Hester, Maria, 105
Hill, Anita, 169, 171
Hodges, Norm, 200, 203
Hoffman, Mike, 123, 124
Home Modernization and Supply
    Company, 19
homestead associations, 13

immigration, European, 18, 23
Income of Her Own, An, 171

Inner City Broadcasting Company,
    174
insurance, 9, 10, 21, 79, 126, 137,
    192, 212; refusal of, 13, 14; white-
    owned, 13
interest rates, 32, 56, 84–85, 135
Interracial Council for Business
    Opportunity, 82, 99
inventory, 26, 67–68, 76–77, 87–89,
    112–115, 152, 179, 206;
    computerized, 56–58, 137;
    loans, 47
investment, 118–124; capital, 27, 47,
    113; equity, 27, 87; loans, 47

Jackson, Jesse, 93
Jamieson, Dr. May, 171
Jim Crow laws, 19
Johnson, Anthony, 10
Johnson, Johnny, 117
Johnson, Magic, 127
Jordan, Michael, 117

Kappa Alpha Psi, 231
Ketch, John, 200–210, 211, 212
KGFJ Radio, 171–183, 224, 227
Knowles, George, 89

land: accumulation, 11; speculation,
    11–12
leadership, 4
legislation: Black Code, 13; Civil
    Rights Act (1964), 25;
    emancipation, 14; employment,
    13; Executive Order 8802, 25;
    Executive Order 11246, 25; Jim
    Crow, 19; Public Works
    Employment Act (1977), 28; for
    "set-asides," 28, 29, 37; Voting
    Rights Act (1965), 25; weapons,
    12
Leidesdorff, William Alexander, 10
Little, Wilbert, 110
Llewellyn, Bruce, 117, 127
Lloyd, David, 184–199, 210, 212,
    222, 226

loans, 26, 133, 190; business, 33; contract-financing, 47; guaranteed, 47, 83, 125; high-risk, 46; investment, 47; low-interest, 64–66; mortgage, 32; personal, 33
Lockhart, Catherine, 47, 151–152
Los Angeles Economic Development Council, 170
LYNX, 121

McCampbell, Charles, 52, 98, 99, 236
McHenry, Emmett, 78
McWorter, Frank, 11–12, 13
Mama Said, 231
manufacturing, 10, 14, 21, 26, 33, 142–154
market(s): access to, 235–236, 239–241; analysis, 58, 149; coethnic, 16, 17, 21, 22, 51; competitive, 67; constriction of, 16; housing, 32; national campaigns for, 32; open, 15–18, 22, 23, 219, 239; protected, 31, 32; reaching, 5; research, 5; saturated, 5; and segregation, 31
Martin, Harold, 3–6, 223
Match, Renee, 168
Mavade Footwear, 6
MayDay Chemical, Inc., 111, 124–142, 155, 223, 225
Mays, Bill, 102–127, 132, 133, 134, 136, 139, 155, 156, 222, 228
Mays Chemical Company, 102–127, 155, 228
mentors, 58, 78, 92, 139, 166, 170–171, 194, 231
merchandising, 10
Meridian Bank, 66
MESBIC. See Minority Enterprise Small Business Investment Company
Michel, Harriet, 28
Michigan Minority Business Development Council, 135, 139
Michigan Strategic Fund, 47
Minority Business Council, 207

Minority Business Development Agency, 36, 216
Minority Enterprise Small Business Investment Company, 27, 121, 178, 204; insolvency in, 27
Minority Executive Council, 181
Mitchell, Perrin, 164
mobility, 3, 4, 9, 15
moonlighting, 218, 219
Mortgage Company of Durham, 19
mortgages, 32
Moss, Charlie, 55
Mutual Building and Loan Association, 19
MVP Products, 5–6, 223, 229

NAACP, 93, 94, 115, 139, 230
National Association of Black Accountants, 118
National Association of Black Manufacturers, 207
National Association of Black-owned Broadcasters, 177
National Association of Broadcasters, 176, 181
National Association of Contract Agents, 91
National Association of Minority Contractors, 87, 92, 93
National Association of Negro Women, 231
National Minority Business Enterprise Legal Defense Fund, 93
National Minority Supplier Development Council, 28, 55, 56, 91, 92, 93, 109
National Negro Business League, 16
National Negro Finance Corporation, 20
National Purchasing Council, 110
New York–New Jersey Minority Purchasing Council, 55, 91
Norman, Bill, 105
North Carolina Mutual Life Insurance Company, 19

O'Connor, Justice Sandra Day, 29

Oliver, Melvin, 32
Operation PUSH, 93
Osborne, Alfred Jr., 52

partnerships, 39, 40
Payne, Andy, 109
Philadelphia Commercial Develop-
    ment Corporation (PCDC), 64–66
Pierce, Joseph, 20, 21
Pierce, Phil, 147
plans: business, 6, 63, 72, 83, 107,
    133–134, 149, 162, 166, 170, 175,
    189, 221, 222; financial, 72, 73;
    marketing, 73, 133, 221; sales,
    107–108
*Plessy v. Ferguson*, 16
post–Civil Rights era, 157, 215–241;
    duality in business development,
    33; economic rights in, 6; outlook
    for entrepreneurship, 52
pre–Civil Rights era, 21;
    discrimination in, 52; economic
    subordination in, 37
Presbyterian Economic Development
    Corporation, 83
Presley, J., 10
procurement: access to, 26;
    programs, 71
profit margins, 66, 67, 132
Public Works Employment Act
    (1977), 28

quality assurance, 193

racial: discrimination, 99; ideology,
    37; valuing of neighborhoods, 32
racism, 16, 21; institutionalized, 154,
    215, 219; permanence of, 216
Raime, Marlana, 110
Rebuild Los Angeles, 169
"Register of Trades of Colored
    People," 14
research: on entrepreneurs, 34–38;
    market, 5; time-of-entry variable,
    35
retail stores, 8, 26, 33, 41*tab*

revenues, annual gross, 56–58,
    67–68, 76–77, 87–89, 137, 152,
    165–166, 179, 191–192, 206; early
    black businesses, 10, 11, 20
Ridley-Thomas, Mark, 170
rights: circumscribed, 12; denial of,
    16, 25; economic, 3, 37, 216, 218;
    limitations in, 7; political, 15, 16;
    protection of, 25; restrictions of,
    12; social, 15, 16
risk, 147, 162; capital, 27
Robiou, Marcial, 47, 76
Royal Knights Savings and Loan
    Association, 19
rule of two, 239–240

Sanders, Ellen Ann, 52, 60–70, 99,
    228, 233–234
Sawyer, Chips, 161, 162, 166
segregation, 21, 51; caste, 16; on
    common carriers, 15–16; de facto,
    22; eliminating, 25; government-
    sponsored, 16, 22;
    institutionalized, 32; laws, 16;
    legal, 16; and protection of
    markets, 31; residential, 32;
    "separate but equal," 16
"set-asides," 28, 29, 37, 111, 136,
    226, 239
sexual harassment, 168–169
Shapiro, Thomas, 32
Shearer, William, 171–183, 210, 212,
    224, 227
Sheltered Market Programs, 136
shipbuilding, 10
shoe shops, 8, 10, 20, 21, 26, 51
Simpson, Jacob, 13
slavery, 7, 9, 11, 12, 13, 15
Small Business Administration, 26,
    33, 75, 76, 83, 86, 102, 111, 121,
    152, 155, 156, 162, 163, 164, 178,
    189, 204, 220, 224–228, 232; 7(j)
    programs, 26, 86, 164; 8(a)
    programs, 28, 55, 56, 73, 83, 85,
    86, 110, 161, 189–190, 191, 201,
    202, 203, 205, 226, 227, 240;

Small Business Administration (cont'd): loan failure rates, 26; Minority Enterprise Small Business Investment Company, 27; seminars, 72; Specialized Small Business Investment Company, 27–28, 46, 224; strategies, 26
"Small Business and Economic Development in the Negro Community" (Brimmer), 31
Smith, Freeman M., 19
Smith, Joshua, 78
Snoddy, Anthony, 142–154, 155, 220, 228, 230, 236
social: ambivalence, 30; climate, 9; goals, 47; reform, 25; resources, 36; rights, 15, 16; separateness, 16
sole proprietorships, 39, 40, 45, 186
Southern California Broadcasters, 176
Specialized Small Business Investment Company, 27–28, 46
SSBIC. See Specialized Small Business Investment Company
Stansbury, Vernon, 117
start-up companies, 6
"strict scrutiny," 29
Stuart, M. S., 22, 23
subchapter S corporations, 39, 40, 45, 51, 72, 104, 130
subcontracting, 28, 90
Sumanco, Inc., 52, 60–70, 228, 233–234
Sutton, Percy, 117, 174

teamwork, 180
technical assistance, 27, 47
technology, 4; transfer, 166–167
Thompson, W. A., 10
T. P. Parham and Associates, 19
Trotter, Eunice, 119
Truly Disadvantaged, The (Wilson), 31

unemployment, 26
Union Insurance and Realty Company, 19

United Negro College Fund, 69, 92, 118, 230
United States Constitution, 25; Fifth Amendment due process clause, 30
United States Department of Agriculture, 136
United States Department of Commerce, 202, 203, 216, 226; Minority Business Development Agency, 36
United States Department of Defense, 166, 239
United States Department of Labor, 71
United States Department of Transportation, 30, 137, 166
United States Supreme Court: Adarand v. Pena, 29–30, 239, 240; Bakke decision, 29; Croson decision, 28–29, 37, 94, 239; Hall v. deCuvis, 15–16; Plessy v. Ferguson, 16; "strict scrutiny," 29
United Way, 118, 139, 230
Urban Coalition, 93
Urban League, 69, 92, 93, 115, 177, 230

vagrancy, 13
violence, 13–14
Voting Rights Act (1965), 25

Walker, Madame C. J., 17–18
"War on Poverty," 26
Washington, Booker T., 15, 16
wholesale enterprises, 10, 21, 26, 33, 41tab
Wilcot, Samuel T., 10
Wilcox, J., 10
Williams, Ella, 158–171, 210, 211, 220, 231, 234
Williams, Willie Mae, 14
Wilson, Kenneth, 14
Wilson, William Julius, 31

# ABOUT THE AUTHOR

Michael D. Woodard is President and CEO of Woodard & Associates, a national consulting firm based in Washington, D.C., and the Atlanta, Georgia, area. The firm provides management training and project evaluation services to corporations, government agencies, universities, and foundations.

Michael Woodard earned his Doctor of Philosophy degree at the University of Chicago Department of Sociology in 1984. Dr. Woodard maintains an active research agenda on economic development among African Americans and has published many articles on this topic. He has taught at the University of Maryland, University of Missouri, and UCLA. His next book project is entitled "Bootstraps: Self-Help and Entrepreneurship among the Black Underclass." Dr. Woodard can be contacted at Woodard & Associates, 3509 Connecticut Avenue, N.W., Suite 190, Washington, D.C. 20008, (202) 483-4472, or 1009 Milstead Avenue, Suite 200, Conyers, Ga. 30207, (770) 860-0064.